Nothing
but the
Truth

Also by Adrian Plass

A Year at St Yorick's
Adrian Plass Classics
An Alien at St Wilfred's
Clearing Away the Rubbish
Colours of Survival (with Bridget Plass)
From Growing Up Pains to the Sacred Diary
Ghosts
Never Mind the Reversing Ducks
Nothing but the Truth
The Sacred Diaries of Adrian, Andromeda and Leonard
Stress Family Robinson
Stress Family Robinson 2: The Birthday Party
The Visit
Why I Follow Jesus
You Say Tomato (with Paul McCusker)

Nothing but the Truth

A Collection of
Short Stories and Parables

Adrian Plass

ZONDERVAN™

GRAND RAPIDS, MICHIGAN 49530 USA

ZONDERVAN™

Nothing but the Truth
Story titled "The Cellar" copyright © 2002 Adrian Plass

Father to the Man first published in Great Britain in 1997 by
HarperCollins*Publishers*. Copyright © 1997 by Adrian Plass

The Final Boundary first published in Great Britain in 1987
by Kingsway Publications. Copyright © 1987, 2000 by Adrian Plass

Requests for information should be addressed to:

Zondervan, *Grand Rapids, Michigan 49530*

Adrian Plass asserts the moral right to be identified as the author of this work.

ISBN 0-310-27859-7

Interior design by Nancy Wilson

Printed and bound in the United States of America

02 03 04 05 06 07 08 /❖ DC/ 10 9 8 7 6 5 4 3 2 1

This book is dedicated to my son Joe,
who understands parts of me
better than anyone else.

Contents

Preface

These stories are part of my truth. Some are light and funny, and some are dark. A small number are products of a process that feels a little like diving in deep water without breathing equipment. Far beneath the surface of Christian confession and commitment, questions and concerns circle each other endlessly in the blackness. What you have to do is swim down and down as far as you can go, grab hold of whatever your fingers touch and then race to the surface before you run out of air. Until you regain the sunshine and open your hand there is no way of knowing what has been retrieved from the depths. Discovering that these denizens of the deep are far less frightening when exposed to the most revealing light of all has been very helpful to me. I do hope you will feel the same.

Small World

They say you should never go back.

I read a short story once that began with those exact words, and broadly speaking I suppose at the time when I read them I would have agreed. You never know what's going to happen when you take the risk of going back. That's why I was so surprised to find myself on Platform Nine of Clapham Junction Railway Station at a quarter to ten one cold autumn morning, probably the coldest of the year so far, waiting for a train that would take me to Winchester for the first time for more than two decades.

With less than ten minutes to go before the train was due to arrive, part of me didn't really believe I would actually get on when it rumbled to a halt. Why in a month of Sundays, I kept asking myself, should I actively court the pain and disappointment that could easily result from such an emotionally loaded expedition? What was the point of risking some kind of inner disaster when, at a pinch, I could manage to go on living with the tightly tied knot that had been in my stomach since I was a young boy? It was my wife who had finally persuaded me to do the thing I feared so much.

'You may be able to go on living with it,' she said one day, 'but I'm not sure the rest of us can. Seriously, John, why don't you pick a day and just go. I know it won't be easy, but you'll be so glad when you've done it. I'll come with you if you want. I tell you what – I'll take you out and buy you an Indian as a reward when you get back.'

She was deliberately being flippant about something that really mattered to her, but she was right. There's something about the idea of an Indian meal that brightens just about anything up. It was the trigger. I said I'd go, but on my own.

'Winchester, Winchester, Winchester . . . ' I whispered the word neurotically over and over to myself as I paced up and down the long platform trying to keep warm. For me, the very word sagged with significance, like one of those poems that tries to make you feel too much.

I did board the 9.56 when it arrived. If I hadn't been as frozen as I was I might have dithered and changed my mind, but it was *so* wonderful to step into the heated interior of the train. Not only that, but I also found a vacant window seat by a table almost immediately.

On the other side of the table sat a young chap of about eighteen, lost in the private world of his personal stereo. Outside this little universe all that could be heard of the recorded sound was a featureless buzz. Settling back into the warmth and comfort of my new surroundings I found myself idly wondering if this was a happy person. He looked quite together and content I thought, the sort of young man who is just beginning to feel a genuine confidence in himself. He had a well-cared-for, secure look about him. Good parents probably. A mother who'd consistently done her very best for him, a father who was never intrusive but always there if he was needed when things started to fall apart. Sports. Advice. All that stuff. Yes, by the look of him that was exactly the sort of father he'd got. And would he realize just how bloody fortunate he was in that respect? Oh, no! You could bet your life he . . .

I squirmed in my seat as all the old boringly familiar feelings of helpless rage began to mount in me. How long was I going to have to put up with the past reaching out to grab me by the throat like this? What a maniac I was becoming. Pushing the hair brusquely back from my forehead with one hand, I dragged my attention away from the innocent music lover on the other side of the table, and gazed out of the window. As if in some fever dream, I rehearsed the past in my mind as I had done a thousand times, helplessly aware that ten thousand repetitions would never make any difference to the way things had been.

I never had fully understood why my parents separated. I lived with my mother, a very efficient, undemonstrative, quietly unhappy woman. The only thing she ever said about the failure of her marriage was in answer to an unusually direct question when I was about ten.

'Why did Daddy go away and leave us when I was little?'

'Your father can only cope with very small worlds.'

That was all she said and all she would say. It was typically enigmatic. What was a ten-year-old supposed to do with that? I hadn't the faintest idea what she was talking about. Perhaps if I'd thought about it a little more I might have begun to under-stand. After all, Dad had created a little world for him and me to be together in, and it hardly changed at all in the short time that I knew him.

It began a few days after my eighth birthday. Mother an-nounced quite dispassionately one morning that my father had come back to England to live. He wanted to see me that after-noon in Winchester. Did I want to go?

I knew I had a dad, but he'd left when I was little more than a baby, so I had no memory of him at all. My mother kept no photographs of her ex-husband in our house. Many times, in the course of my early years, I had lain awake at night, picturing his face just above the end of the bed in the darkness of my room, and imagined making a special trip to find him. In my fantasies he was always overjoyed to see me. We would embrace, and he would explain why it had been so difficult for us to be together, and say how much he had missed me since going away.

Here was a chance to see him in reality. I felt shy but excited. I remembered looking into my mother's face, searching for a clue to the solution of the obvious problem. Did she want me to go? But my mother's face never gave information of that sort. There were no clues.

'Yes, please,' I said, 'I'd like to go, mother.'

Later that morning my mother drove me to Winchester in our blue mini. We stopped just outside the Old Market Inn. There was a man leaning against a gatepost a few yards away. Mother didn't even get out. So much for my secretly cherished dreams of parental reunion!

'That's your father,' she said, pointing. 'You'll like him. I'll pick you up again at five o'clock.'

Suddenly, there I was, at eight years of age, standing outside a pub in a strange city with a strange man, watching the familiar shape of our little car accelerate away and disappear round the corner. Looking back, I can hardly believe what my mother did. I cannot begin to imagine doing anything so clearly irresponsible with one of my own children. For a few seconds I did experience real panic, but small children readily accept bizarre things, and, in any case, my mother had told me I would like my father, and she was the sort of woman for whom every opinion laid down was a winning card. I had never known her to be wrong before.

Nor was she wrong now. All he said in a quiet, resonant voice as I walked hesitantly in his direction, was, 'John? I'm your dad,' but his eyes smiled from far inside and there was a feeling of safeness about him. I recall being obscurely pleased that he continued to lean on the gatepost as I moved towards him. He let me do the last bit of the trip.

This first meeting was a long way from the emotional splurge of my night-time fantasies, but from the moment I encountered my father's chuckling good humour I absolutely adored him. That day we sat on the grass outside the cathedral in the sunshine, and ate our way through a picnic he'd brought. I remem-

14

ber every crumb. There were three different kinds of sandwich – ham, banana and cheese – two kinds of cake – Battenburg and cherry – two chocolate biscuits wrapped in shiny coloured paper, and an apple each. There was a bottle filled with ready-diluted lemon squash and two disposable paper cups to drink it from.

He asked me questions about myself as we ate, listening in a very still way with his head on one side as I gained confidence and chattered away about home and school and friends and football.

When he asked me which team I supported I suspended the whole of my beloved Arsenal team and said, 'Which one do you support?'

'Aston Villa,' he replied.

'So do I,' I said, and from that day forward I did.

When we'd finished eating he packed everything away in a brown and green leather shopping bag and stood up.

'Well, John,' he smiled, 'do you think we're going to be pals?'

I looked at him then and thought to myself that he was a 'hands in his pockets' sort of man. His clothes were brown and soft, so were his face and hair. He was comfortably untidy and his eyes seemed a little bit hurt as well as being smiley and kind.

'Oh, yes, Dad,' I said, relishing this word that had suddenly become so unexpectedly and wonderfully substantial, 'we'll be pals all right.'

We spent the rest of the afternoon walking slowly round the inside of the cathedral, stopping every now and then for me to ask a question, or when Dad wanted to explain something. He seemed to know an awful lot about everything without having to use a guide, and I think I sensed, even then, that he was introducing me to something he loved.

Mother picked me up at five o'clock – on the dot, of course. She didn't get out of the car this time either, or even look in the direction of my father, as far as I could see. Poor Mother. I'm sure I must have rabbited on about my new 'pal' all the way back home, but all I can remember her saying was, 'I told you you'd like him.'

'But,' I said in real puzzlement to myself in bed that night, 'how could you possibly *not* like someone so nice?'

Three or four times a year for the next four years the pattern of that first visit was repeated. There might be fruit cake instead of Battenburg, and the weather might drive us under cover to eat our picnic sometimes, but in every other way our outings stayed exactly the same, from the brown and green leather shopping bag to the paper cups. It never struck me as odd that we always met in the same way, and always did the same things. On the contrary, I loved it. I loved him. It was simply the way things were. I didn't mind in the least that I never saw where he lived, and never really learned anything about the rest of his life, because we seemed to belong to each other totally for as long as those all too infrequent afternoons lasted, and that was all that mattered to me. As time went by Winchester Cathedral and everything connected with it glowed richly in my imagination with a sparkling Christmassy brightness, a reflection of the joy I found in just being there with my father.

He died at the wrong time, you see. I was twelve. It was two days before my next visit was due. When my mother gave me the news, delivered in that same dry, disinterested way, it was like being punched in the stomach very hard when you're not expecting it. And then – well, I've never been quite sure what happened then. I think I managed to switch something off right inside me, and I felt nothing. I don't know if I was ever quite able to forgive my mother for the way she dealt with me over my father's death. I wasn't taken to any kind of service and there was no grave because his body had been cremated. The ashes were distributed somewhere or other by somebody, my mother said, with an almost non-existent emphasis on the 'somebody', and that was it. He was gone. Nothing to remind me of him, and a complete inability to grieve. I don't think I shed a single tear.

The years went by. I grew up. I got married. My mother died. I had two children. I was very nearly happy – happy but for the nagging, ever-present knowledge that one day I was going to have to deal with the little unexploded bomb that lay like a lump of cold metal in the pit of my stomach. I was never quite brave enough to face it, the mixture of grief, sorrow and heartache that might explode and tear me to pieces. I kept well away from Winchester.

Now my wife had talked me into going back. She had seen, over the years, how the pain of this emotional containment affected not just me but her and the children as well. Often it manifested itself in black moods that had no very clear link to the past, but were nevertheless closely connected with those distant days.

Sometimes, specific incidents triggered irrational bouts of anger. When Sam, aged nine, asked me why I supported a 'rubbish team' like Aston Villa, I flew into a terrible rage, demanding to know why I shouldn't and what it had got to do with him. For that brief, black period I felt as if I was eight years old and he was bullying me. Realizing what was really going on was so strange – like regaining consciousness after a particularly vivid dream. Poor, confused Sam forgave me freely.

Another time, I was walking around the local shopping precinct with my wife, when I happened to notice that a woman walking beside me was carrying a shopping bag that closely resembled the one my father used to pack our picnics in. Brown leather with inlaid green patches. The sight of it made me feel sick in my stomach. I was low for days. So many things ...

Well, I was going to tackle it now. Soon after alighting from this train I would be stepping back into the only world that my father and I had ever shared. Resting my face against the cold surface of the window I closed my eyes and dozed fitfully for the rest of the hour-long journey.

By 11.15 I was sitting in the warmth and comfort of the Old Market Inn in Winchester. The walk down from the station had set up such a screaming tension in me that my hands and teeth were tightly clenched by the time I turned into Market Street, but I was beginning to feel a little better now. I couldn't have faced going into the cathedral straight away, and the only delaying tactic that I could think of was the pub. I'm not a great drinker at the best of times, let alone on an occasion like this, so I simply ordered a hot chocolate and took it over to a seat by the window that looked out towards the cathedral. Resting my elbows on the table in front of me I cuddled the hot china mug in my hands. It felt like a mini-version of one of those old stone hotwater bottles that I could just remember having in bed with me when I stayed with my grandmother as a small child.

Through the window I could see, a hundred yards away, the west door of the cathedral, the door that my dad and I had walked through so many times. Now, on this desolately bleak October afternoon, a mere trickle of warmly dressed visitors was passing in and out of the building.

I decided to give myself a talking to.

'Now look!' I whispered into the side of my mug, 'you are an adult. You are not a child. You are allowed to choose what to do for yourself. If you decide to get up and walk back to the station and take the next train home, then that is fine. That is absolutely fine. You've lived with this fear in your gut for twenty years. You might as well put up with it for another decade or two. Why tear yourself to pieces for nothing? Give up! Go home! You don't even really know what you're looking for, and you probably won't find it here anyway. Apart from anything else, how are you going to handle a thumping great anticlimax, if that's what it turns out to be? Go on – go home. Finish your hot drink and get back to the station.'

Haranguing myself like this has always helped me to make decisions, and it did now. I stood up, buttoned my overcoat, wrapped my scarf round my neck, and left the pub. Seconds later, breathless with quivering anticipation and the icy cold, I was striding across the Close with almost robotic determination towards the west door. I was about to pay my first visit to Winchester Cathedral since the year of my twelfth birthday. As I reached the door and pushed it open I realized that it was also the only time I had ever entered it on my own.

Despite the cold I was perspiring heavily as I came through the inner door and stood motionless for a moment at the west end of the nave. The abruptly overpowering familiarity of my surroundings made me feel quite faint. Then, suddenly filled with a brittle excitement, I swung round and peered up at the strange jumble of stained-glass fragments that almost filled the top half of the west wall.

'What's that all about then, John?'

I remembered the question. I remembered my answer.

'Cromwell smashed a window, Dad, and the people saved the pieces and hid 'em and tried to put them back together later, but they couldn't get it right so they put them all over the place like a giant jigsaw puzzle so they'd still got their window, whatever old Cromwell thought he'd done. Is that right, Dad?'

It was right. It was right! Dad had told me, so it must be right.

I turned round and started to walk along the south aisle. I was in a trance. I was twelve years old. I remembered everything. There was Doctor Warton's memorial, and there, listening forever to their famous headmaster, were three of his pupils dressed in their funny old-fashioned clothes.

'Where will we find three little tiny monks, John?'

I was *so* proud.

'Over here, Dad, sitting by the bishop's feet.'

And then, a bit further up, the list of people from something called the Hampshire regiment, who had all been killed in the war.

'Listen, Dad! Listen! Listen! Listen to the names – Shadwell, Smallpiece, Smith, Spanner, Stammer, Steele, Stone. Are they real names, Dad?'

'Yes, they're real names and they really did die, son.'

On to the South Transept, and the oldest oak chairs in England.

'Are we allowed to sit on them, Dad?'

'Yes, go on. Nothing to say you can't, is there? They've put up with four hundred years of assorted English bottoms. If yours makes much difference it's probably time for them to be turned into firewood anyway.'

I always sat on both of them, enthralled by the thought of those hundreds and hundreds of different backsides perching there over the years.

Next came the grave of Isaak Walton, the fisherman, followed by the memorial to Bishop Wilberforce, son of the man who tried to free all the slaves. Over there were the Pilgrim Gates, and up to the left, in their chests on top of the wall, were the bones of the old kings. Most frightening to me as a small boy was the horrible cadaver of Bishop Fox in its tiny prison behind iron bars, put there by him to remind the world that no one lives forever.

Oh, Dad . . .

I came to a place where candles glowed and flickered on a wrought-iron stand. Taking a fresh candle I lit it from one of the others and put a coin in the nearby box. Stepping back, I stared at the little flame as it wavered and nearly died before starting to burn steadily. The candle was for my father. Its flame was alive, and he was dead. I began to perspire again. That bomb inside me was about to go off and I was terrified. Instinctively I moved away from a small group of people who were peering at something beside me, and turned quickly into the retrochoir, deserted now, but filled, like every other corner of this building, with four years of Dad and me.

'See those words under that grille, son? They're all about St Swithun, the saint of the cathedral. Do you remember what that first bit means?'

'Whatever partakes of God is safe in God. Right, Dad?'

'Right, son.'

I couldn't stand it any more. I had to get out. I set off down the north presbytery aisle, intending to head straight for the exit at the other end of the building, but a loud group of tourists forced me aside into the choir, and suddenly I knew, like a child desperate not to throw up in the wrong place, that I wasn't going to make it. I crumpled on to one of the front choir stalls at the foot of the presbytery steps, trying to look as if I was intensely interested in the tomb of Rufus, the Norman king who died mysteriously in the New Forest.

'What did they find when they opened old Rufus up, John?'

'An arrowhead, Dad. Somebody shot him!'

'Oh, Dad, oh, Dad! Why did you die?'

I slumped forward, my face in my hands, and wept. The explosion wasn't as wildly violent as I'd feared, but the sobs that passed through my body in wave after shuddering wave shook everything in me. And there was so much anger in it. Grief I'd expected, but not anger. Perhaps that was why I'd switched off after that first thudding shock all those years ago. Probably I just couldn't handle the idea of expressing intense fury to someone I had loved so much.

I certainly expressed it now.

'You left me! You left me alone! You just left me! Oh, Dad, why did you leave me?'

Sheer strength of feeling drove me to my feet. As far as I can remember there was nobody else in the choir, but I honestly don't think I'd have noticed if there had been. And it was at that moment, through the tears that had waited so long to be shed, that I found my eyes fixed on Dad's favourite thing of all, the carved figure of Christ on the cross right at the centre of the great screen above the high altar.

For one of the very few times in my life, some words of Jesus came, quite unbidden, to my mind.

'My God! My God! Why have you forsaken me?'

Whatever partakes of God is safe in God.

'Is that right, Dad?'

'That's right, son.'

A small world.

A Letter to William

Dear William,

It was really marvellous to see you up at Euston the other day. The first time we've met in five years, and we only had seven minutes before my train went. I caught it by the skin of my teeth, incidentally. Into Bangor by three o'clock, and more or less straight onto the bus near the town clock after that. We arrived at Llanberis around four o'clock, and by quarter past I was sitting in the hotel cleaning my walking boots ready for the morning. Amazing really! I love trains – just as well really, the way things are with me at the moment. Actually, that's one of the main reasons for writing to you. I realized by the look on your face the other day that you were finding one or two of the things I said rather odd, to say the least. As far as I can remember, one chunk of our conversation went roughly as follows:

YOU: How come you're looking so fit?

ME: Well, it might have something to do with the fact that I've climbed Snowdon seventy-odd times in the last six months.

YOU: *(After a convincing fish impression.)* You've what?

ME: I spend a lot of time climbing –

YOU: Yes, I heard what you said, but why on earth would you want to—

ME: *(Glancing at my watch and panicking.)* Look, I haven't time to explain now – it all started when I went to Scotland.

YOU: Scotland? Snowdon's in Wales, isn't it?

ME: Yes, of course it is, but – look, I'll write. Okay?

I haven't been able to forget that expression of puzzled concern on your face as I flapped off with my bags, so here I am, writing to put you out of your misery. Only you'll have to bear with me. It's rather a long story, and it starts more than nine months ago when I was still teaching at that prep. school in Bromley without any reason to believe that I'd ever do anything else. Then something happened.

I had a phone call one evening from that chap Dudley Nicholls. Think a bit and you'll remember him. Same course as us at FE college. Fleshy fellow with a deep voice and lots of money. Drove that big estate car of his dad's as soon as he passed his test. We used to cadge lifts off him quite a lot. He asked us once if we thought you ought to take your socks off when you make love in the back of a car, and you said no, you didn't think that would be sufficient. Derry Mimpson threw a cup of hot chocolate over him when he was sitting in the next-door lavatory once. He squealed and squealed, and you got cross with Derry. Gottim? Good!

Now, do you also remember that about two-thirds of the way through our second year, Dudley changed suddenly and unaccountably? He started smiling those funny crinkly smiles, and looking at us as though we'd missed out on the treat of the century. And he wouldn't come to the pub any more, or smoke or swear, and he started sighing when one of us told a dirty joke, and in the end you told him that if he didn't tell us what was the matter with him you'd make him eat his car keys. So he told us. We were down behind the shrubbery at the end of the college gardens – remember? He went all glassy eyed and told us he'd become a Christian, and that he'd given his life to God, and given up all his bad ways, and was going to lots of Bible studies and prayer meetings and goodness knows what else at this little church he'd found behind the wool shop in Station Road. I was all ready to take the mickey, but you were really nice to him, William, you really were. I can see you now, nodding seriously and saying what a good thing it was to find something to really believe in.

Then he said would we come to one of the services, and you said you knew about that sort of church and that, although you respected people who went, there were too many meetings and too much about what you shouldn't do and not enough about actually *doing* things, and I just sort of agreed with you, so we didn't go. We didn't see so much of him after that, did we?

Anyway, he and I kept in touch after we all left college, and later he became an assistant manager in a supermarket down near Sevenoaks, so we weren't really living that far apart. I knew he still went to church, although he didn't talk about it all that much. We used to meet for lunch once a month or so. He liked talking about the old college days mostly. Got quite wistful. Used to mention you a fair bit, William. I think he respected you a lot. (Can't think why!)

Where was I? Ah, yes – the phone call. He sounded a bit odd on the phone – puzzled and strained perhaps. He said he wanted to talk to me, ask me about something, and could he come up that Saturday on the train and spend a couple of hours at my place. I was quite intrigued, and I told him to come by all means. Told him I'd meet him at the station and all that, and asked him if he could give me some idea of what it was all about. There was silence at the other end of the line for a while, then he spoke.

'I've found an ad in the paper – well, not an ad, a sort of announcement, and I don't know what to do about it. I want to know what you think.'

That's what he said, and that was all he'd say about it on the phone, so we said goodbye and that was that until Saturday. I don't mind telling you, William, I was a trifle nervous about me in the role of advice-giver. To be honest, I think old Dudley saw me in a sort of 'Williamish' aura. If you'd been around, you're the one he'd have gone for. Still – you weren't, and he couldn't.

So, there we were on the Saturday, Dudley and I sitting opposite each other in my sitting-room. We'd gone past the 'How are you? Would you like a cup of coffee?' stage, and Dudley took this folded sheet of newspaper from his inside pocket and passed it across. I spent a couple of very bewildering minutes studying a recipe for home-made marmalade before Dudley realized I was looking at the wrong side and made me turn it over. On the other side was this ad-cum-announcement – must have been about quarter-page size – and it was, as Sherlock Holmes might have put it, very singular. I'll write it out for you now, as near as I can remember it, just as it appeared on the page:

UNITED KINGDOM CHRISTIAN RECRUITMENT CENTRE
HALSTER, SCOTLAND
WE ARE NOW THE SOLE AGENTS FOR SALVATION ET AL
IN ENGLAND, WALES, SCOTLAND
AND NORTHERN IRELAND.
VISITORS WARMLY WELCOMED.
NO APPOINTMENTS NECESSARY.
CAUTION: PREVIOUS ARRANGEMENTS
MAY NOT BE VALID.
WE WILL ADVISE WITH PLEASURE.

As you can see, there's no telephone number, and as for the address – well, whoever's heard of Halster? Now, you're going to smile when you read this next bit, and I don't blame you. It sounds ridiculous, but it's true. There was a sort of glow all around that bit of the page. I'm not kidding, there really was. I remember blinking and shaking my head to get rid of it, but it wouldn't go. It was in the page, or in the air around the page, or – something. When I looked up Dudley was nodding and smiling in an excited sort of way.

26

'You can see it too, can't you?' he said.

'The shininess, you mean?'

'Yes,' he said, and he leaned over, took the paper from my hand, and smoothed it out flat on the coffee table between us. 'Not everyone sees it, you know – most people don't. The thing is ...'

You remember what a worrier Dudley used to be. We used to say he looked just like Tony Hancock when there was something on his mind. Well, he looked just like that now, except that there was this excitement queueing up to appear on his face as well.

'The thing is,' he went on, 'that I don't know whether being able to see it means you're ... well, all right, or whether it means ... something else.'

How I wished you were there, William. I was completely flummoxed. Shiny newspapers? Sole agents for salvation? I seemed to hear the gates of the funny farm clanging shut behind me as Dudley's deep voice motored on.

'I'm going up there. I'm going to go up to Halster to find this place and ask them if I'm really ... well, ask them for some advice on ... things.'

Well, you know me, William. It costs nothing to humour someone, and nobody ever really wants advice if it doesn't agree with what they're going to do anyway, so I just nodded and shrugged a bit and said, 'Why not?' and things like that. Dudley stared down at the paper for a minute when I'd finished, and when he looked up he was biting one side of his lower lip and looking a little uneasy.

'The thing is, Ray,' he said through his chewed lip, 'I don't fancy going all the way up there on my own, so I was going to ask if you'd come with me.'

Guess who suddenly got very objective. 'What about the cost?' I asked him. 'I'm broke.'

'I'll pay,' said Dudley.

A free trip to Scotland. My objectivity took a bit of a nose dive, but I felt I ought to keep trotting out the arguments against – for Dudley's sake.

'I can't just up and leave the school,' I pointed out. 'It's my job. I won't get time off during the term.'

Dudley nodded – he'd thought of that. 'It's only a fortnight or so until the Easter holidays,' he said, 'and I can get a week off then, no problem. What do you say? Go on, say you'll come.'

Well, the only objection left was the obvious one, wasn't it?'

'Look, Dudley,' I said, as gently as I could, 'I'm sure I'd enjoy a trip up to Scotland very much, and it's very generous of you to offer to stand the expenses, but have you thought about how you're going to feel when you get up to this God-fors ... this place, and find that there is no Christian recruitment centre or whatever they call themselves?'

'I don't mind taking the risk,' Dudley replied earnestly, 'and anyway, what about the glow – the shininess? You can't explain that away, can you?'

I picked up the piece of paper again and peered closely at it. The glow was still there, a faint, whitish light that seemed quite separate from the substance of the paper itself. I turned it over and stared at the marmalade recipe again. No glow there, nothing at all. I held the sheet up flat and level with my eyes, the announcement uppermost, but out of my vision. To my surprise there was no sign of the mysterious light rising above the surface of the paper. Very strange indeed.

'Tell you what, Dudley,' I said at last, 'you let me take this paper to a friend of mine who's a chemist, and if he says it's just ordinary paper with nothing in it to account for the light effect, then I'll come with you. Agreed?'

'Agreed!' said Dudley.

So off I went after school on the Monday to a chap called David Stolle (you wouldn't know him) who runs the chemistry department at one of the polys in town. Too harassed to breathe as usual, he passed me on to one of his research assistants who promised to do the business and post the results – and the paper – back to me before the end of the week. I suppose I was quite excited when the envelope arrived on Friday. I know I tore it open as soon as it plopped onto the mat that morning. Couldn't make sense of it at first, William. You know how thick I can be with printed stuff. Eventually, though, I gathered that the list of compounds that the chemist fellow had typed out were all perfectly normal ones, and as for anything that could produce the kind of glowing effect I'd described – well, there was nothing. Not only that, but the fellow had added in a rather terse note at the bottom that he hadn't been able to see any kind of glow on the paper anyway, so perhaps I had been mistaken in my original observations. Bit shirty, I guessed.

Then, rather gingerly, I took the folded piece of newspaper out of the envelope and opened it up slowly and carefully. Had I been dreaming last Saturday? No, I hadn't. You'll just have to take my word for it, William. That announcement shone just like it had before, and I had to accept that there was no way of explaining it. Later that day I rang Dudley and told him the trip was on.

Believe it or not, William, but as the days went by I began to get quite excited about our safari into deepest Scotland. And when I say *deepest* Scotland, that's exactly what I mean. I found a big map of Scotland at school and brought it home with me. Imagine how I felt on discovering that Halster was a tiny village way up on the west coast, just about as far away as anywhere could be without crossing the sea to some remote island.

'How come,' I said to Dudley on the phone that evening, 'the sole agents for salvation are tucked away in the back of beyond where no one can get at them?'

'How come,' replied Dudley with unaccustomed alacrity (good phrase that, eh, William?), 'that Jesus was born in a stable?'

I gave him that one.

School finished on Friday. Dudley came up after work that evening and stayed the night so that we could set off sharp in the morning. I woke up at some absurd hour and had an 'I must be a loony' attack. But it passed, and by the time we were out on the road the next day, enjoying one of those deliciously crisp early spring mornings, I was just glad to be going somewhere. You know how it is when you set out on these really long journeys. Mild ecstasy for the first hour, then a period of quiet horror when you realize just how far you've still got to go, and then you sort of settle down and sleep or chat or listen to the radio and accept that you'll probably never do anything but sit in a car for the rest of your life. Mind you, I couldn't complain about lack of comfort. Dudley had one of those great big foreign cars that pumps itself up before starting. Huge inside. Not bad on an assistant supermarket manager's salary, eh? Something told me Mum and Dad were still footing one or two of their little Dudley's bills, not that I said anything, of course. Good for him, I thought.

We did pretty well that first day, ending up in some town a little to the south of Carlisle. We spent the night in a grotty little hotel beside a main road. Poor old Dudley was so bushed by then that we'd decided to stop at the next place we came to, and 'The Lay-By' was it. (I still don't drive by the way, and, no, I still don't know why not, William. Okay?) Dudley had something to eat and then dragged himself off to bed, and I decided to watch a bit of television in the 'Lounge'. The 'Lounge' turned out to be a large cupboard full of armchairs with a portable, black-and-white television on a shelf in the corner. The only other occupant of the room was a large elderly lady who introduced herself as Mrs Jones. She said she'd been staying at 'The Lay-By' for some years, and thought she'd probably die there because she had no family left and didn't get about much now because her hip was so bad. She was a nice old thing. I ended up telling her about our trip, and what started it off, and she said could she see the advert. Well, I hadn't actually mentioned the 'glow', but after she'd unfolded the sheet of paper, found her glasses in her bag, and peered at the printed words for a minute or so, she said, 'Ooh! Look at that! It's all shiny!' So then we talked about that, and I told her about Dave Stolle's report – his assistant's report I mean – and she made me copy the words from the announcement onto a page in a tiny little notebook that she fished out of her bag. And when she looked at the words I'd written, she said,

'It shines in my little book too.' Blow me down if she wasn't absolutely right! There was a sort of scaled-down glow on that little sheet of paper, just like on the big one. I shivered all the way down my back when I saw that. Anyway, I went off to bed soon after that. Mrs Jones wasn't up by the time we left early in the morning, but I mention that little chat I had with her for a special reason which I'll tell you about later.

I can't remember if you've ever been to Scotland, William. I hadn't. It's just plain breathtaking. By the time we'd passed Loch Lomond and driven between these two mountains standing like giant gate-posts at the south end of Glencoe, I felt just about gorged with beautiful scenery. Then there was a car ferry to get across to the peninsula where Halster was situated, and last of all we had to take a long, narrow, winding road through countryside that was all heather and cragginess, until we quite suddenly found ourselves in a little sloping village that, by our calculations, had to be Halster. It really was small, William. A single street lined with little dark grey cottages – sorry – crofts, and down at the far end, a wedge-shaped deep blue area. That was the sea. There were two shops, one of them more of a trading post than anything else, and a church, grey like the crofts, but bigger. Then there was one pub with a sign saying that bed and breakfast was available, and that was about it really.

We parked the car in a space next to the church and walked slowly along the street feeling a bit down. We'd come an awful long way and I suppose I'd expected somehow that this place, this recruitment centre, would be a golden palace-like building, impossible to miss. It was a bit of an anticlimax to actually be in Halster and find only the two rows of crofts, mostly single storey, with their tiny weather-proof windows and low front doors. We decided to try one of the shops. Shopkeepers knew most things, we reckoned. We were right. A long, thin, very Scottish gentleman in the little general store was as helpful as we could have wished. Obviously, we were by no means the first travellers to ask about our particular destination.

Back to the car we went, quite enlivened again now, and a couple of minutes later we turned up a narrow, north-pointing dirt track near the top end of the village. Ten minutes later we were there. It still wasn't very impressive, but at least we knew we were in the right place. On a tattered wooden notice-board set at the entrance to what looked like a farmyard were the words 'Christian Recruitment Centre' painted in big yellow letters. We left the car next to a big Land-Rover-type vehicle beside one of the outhouses and walked across to the biggest building, the farmhouse we supposed, and knocked on the door. It was late afternoon by then, William. There was a viciously cold wind blowing through that farmyard, and the countryside around was just a dark frowning mass. For two pins I'd have run for the car at that moment and cleared off back to anywhere where there was lots of noise and light and ordinariness. Then the door opened.

When I say that the door was opened by an elderly man with lots of white hair and what I always think of as a sailor's beard and twinkling eyes and a pipe clenched between his teeth, and that suddenly I didn't want to clear off after all, that doesn't really tell you a hundredth of what I thought and felt. When I was a kid, I used to have a particular dream sometimes. In this dream I'd arrived at the place where I needed to be. Don't ask me where it was. It was just – right. There was lovely music and this soft weepy feeling in my stomach. My parents were there and we were all smiling. I think there were coloured lights too, and a sort of deep bubbling excitement about what was going to happen next. Someone was coming, I think.

Anyway, that was a bit how I felt when the door opened and this genial old character ushered us into what was clearly the farmhouse kitchen, and sat us down at the big old table in the centre of the room. I felt so warm and light and – sorry, I'm rabbiting on again. I'll get on with it. When we were all settled with a mug of hot cocoa – delicious stuff – our host leaned back in his chair and smiled at us through his pipe smoke.

'Right,' he said in his rumbly voice, 'my name's Angerage – Bill Angerage. Who are you two fine chaps?'

We introduced ourselves.

'And what can I do for you?' he asked.

'I want to be a Christian,' blurted out old Dudley, 'or rather I ...'

He didn't get any further. Our new friend's face lit up like a beacon. He jumped to his feet, came round the table, and smacked Dudley heartily on the back as though he'd just heard the most wonderful news in the world.

'Marvellous! Marvellous!' he kept saying. 'That's really marvellous! You've really made my day, young man!'

He would have hugged Dudley if he could I think, but the 'young' man who'd made his day was curled back in his chair, a bit overwhelmed. Very pleased though, I could tell. Then he turned to me, his eyes all alight and hopeful.

'You too, Ray? Do you want to join us as well?'

I was very confused inside, William. That's why my answer was so pathetic.

'I only came along to keep Dudley company,' I said, my voice all high-pitched and strangled.

'Ah, well,' said Bill, staring at me for a moment, 'you're here, you're here. Now, down to business.'

He went back and sat down again on the other side of the table.

'Now, as you'll have realized from our little ad in the paper, things have changed a lot – radically I might say. The whole business of prayer, Bible study, church services, et cetera, has been scrapped. Direct order from HQ. All that sort of stuff goes out the window. No need any more for discussions about salvation by faith, or about who's in and who's out. The whole thing's been completely redesigned. You can still get total forgiveness, eternal life, love, joy and peace, the whole package as before, but the terms are different – very different.'

Dudley's brow was furrowed with puzzlement and worry.

'But, Mr Angerage ...'

'Call me Bill, Dudley, there's a good chap.'

'Bill, er ... all those things you said don't matter any more. If we don't have those – I mean, what's left? What do we have to do?'

'Aah!' said Bill richly, pulling on his briar with deep relish. 'Now we come to it. What indeed?' He chuckled to himself for a moment, then folded his arms on the table and leaned towards Dudley, his pipe jutting out at an angle from the side of his mouth. 'All you have to do, my friend, is climb Snowdon three times every week.'

Some silences are very loud, aren't they? This one was. Eventually, all the things that had rushed around in the quietness flowed down and were condensed into the single tiny word that Dudley said after a long pause.

'Why?'

Bill raised a hand so that he could wag his finger.

'Ours not to reason why, mate. If HQ says that's the way it's to be done, then that's the way it's to be done. Faith – that's what you need. The instructions are very simple. Snowdon – three times a week.'

'And there's no other way to get forgiveness and – all the rest?'

Bill shook his head. 'No other way, my friend,' he said slowly. 'Worth it though, isn't it?' he queried, his eyes twinkling even more than before.

'Oh, yes – yes, of course,' answered Dudley, but I could see his mind was working hard on this new idea.

'But what happens about my job, Bill? I mean, I wouldn't be able to carry on with what I'm doing now, would I? Good heavens ...' Dudley's eyes opened wide as the implications of the thing became clearer. 'It must take a day to climb right up Snowdon and back again, so that means three days plus travelling. I'd hardly have time to do anything, let alone get a decent job of any kind. I wouldn't have any money. I wouldn't ...'

'What about your parents, Dudley?' I interrupted. 'Isn't there a chance that they'd ...'

Dudley flushed. 'No,' he said dismally. 'They'll give me just about anything I want if I go on living nearby, but they've made it clear ever since I left college that if I ever move right away from them, then that's it. I'm on my own. I don't think whizzing home from Wales for flying visits a couple of times a week would count as living nearby. Besides,' he added rather pathetically, 'I don't really like travelling all that much.'

'Don't you think,' said Bill gently, 'that the travelling or even living in Wales itself, might be worth it if you get eternal life and happiness in return? After all, you travelled all the way up here, didn't you? That's our first screening process after you're attracted by the light. Well, here you are. You've got this far.'

Dudley was tracing the shape of a stain on the table top with his finger. He spoke without looking up.

'Do some people come all the way up here and then decide not to ... go ahead then?'

'The vast majority,' said Bill, his eyes sad for the first time since we'd met him. 'Some try to compromise despite the fact that I always make it quite clear that the three climbs are an absolute base-line minimum.'

'How do they compromise then?'

'Well, there's one church down in the South for instance. The minister came up here – he'd seen the ad just like you – said he agreed with everything I said, went off happily back home and wrote me a letter a few weeks later to say that he'd discussed the whole thing with the church council and they'd come up with an "inspired idea". They hired a carpenter to construct a four-foot-high model of Snowdon with two steps going up one side and two going down the other. Every Sunday, each member of the congregation has to go up one side and down the other. They've built it into the service. It comes just between the third hymn and the sermon.'

'And that doesn't count?' said Dudley, obviously hoping that it might.

'It's not climbing Snowdon three times a week,' said Bill.

Silence reigned for another minute or two. Dudley took a biro and a piece of paper from his inside pocket and started to write something. His brow was puckered and there were many crossings out. Bill just sat puffing his pipe and watching patiently. At last, Dudley looked up.

'Bill, listen!' he said earnestly. 'I've just been thinking. There must be other jobs that need doing, besides the actual climbing. Supposing I adapted all the choruses we sing in our church at the moment so that they fitted the new way of things?' Another and even greater inspiration seized him. 'We could call it *The Snowdon Songbook*.'

Bill was slowly shaking his head, but Dudley seemed quite carried away by the idea.

'Look, I've just been trying one or two out. Err . . . this one for instance: "Hallelujah, I'm a Christian." You know the one I mean. This is what it sounds like when it's changed. Listen – listen!'

Dudley held his piece of paper in one hand and began to sing the words he had written in a feverishly joyful voice:

> 'Hallelujah, I'm a climber,
> I climb all day,
>   I climb up Snowdon,
> climb all the way.
>   Hallelujah, I'm a climber,
> I climb all day.'

I looked away in embarrassment. Bill started to speak. 'Dudley, I don't think . . .'

But there was no stopping old Dudley.

'Just a minute, just a minute!' he said. 'What d'you think about this one? Used to be "Marching to Zion". Listen!'

The awful voice started once more in some strange alien key:

> 'We're marching to Snowdon.
> Beautiful, beautiful Snowdon,
> we're marching upward to Snowdon,
> the beautiful mountain of God.

'And what about this one:

'What a friend we have in Snowdon,
all our -'

'No, Dudley!' Bill's voice was no louder than before, but it contained a note of authority now that cut Dudley off in mid-warble. 'It's no good simply singing about it. You've got to do it. You've got to climb Snowdon three times every week.'

He swung a hand out in the vague direction of the rest of Scotland.

'Why, I could take you to a place only a few miles from here where they've set up Snowdon counselling services, Snowdon discussion groups, and courses in "The real meaning of climbing". But none of them actually do it. One of our chaps who comes from that same town, and pops up from Wales very occasionally, isn't allowed into any of those groups because he's "in error" with his simplistic approach to Snowdon. No, Dudley, if you want to write some songs to keep you going while you're on the slopes, then that's fine – good idea in fact! But not instead of. Won't wash with HQ, you see.'

Dudley was really chewing at that old lip now, William. And his eyeballs were dancing about all over the place as he tried to think of a way to get what he wanted and keep what he'd got.

'What about friends?' he said feebly. 'How do I keep up with all my friends? I'll never see them. They'll think I'm mad. They'll think . . .'

Dudley's voice trailed away. You could see he was answering his own questions in his head. Hadn't quite given up yet, though. He banged the table with the flat of his hand suddenly and sat bolt upright. Obviously thought he'd hit on a winner.

'I'm not fit! I won't get up there – not even once. It's not fair! What about that?'

Bill nodded patiently. He'd heard it all before, I expect.

'You turn up and climb as far as you can, and we'll make sure you get to the top from there, even if you have to be carried to the nearest mountain railway stop. Don't worry! Young chap like you, you'll be fit as a fiddle in no time. Wouldn't surprise me if you were nearly running up inside a fortnight.'

Well, that was about it really, William. Dudley didn't have anything else to say, and this Bill Angerage didn't say much more either. He told Dudley to go home and think about it, and if he decided to go ahead to drop him a line and he'd fix it all up and arrange some help with the practical side of things. He looked at me when he said that as well.

I've never known anything as cold and dark as that farmyard after Bill closed the front door of the house behind us. We stayed at the pub that night in Halster, and started driving back the next morning, talking all the way about the things we wished we'd asked but didn't.

As soon as I got home, I sat down and wrote two letters. One was to the headmaster of my school, giving a term's notice. The other was to Bill Angerage at the Christian Recruitment Centre, saying that I wanted to do the Snowdon thing. And that, William, together with bits of part-time work, is what I've been doing for the last six months or so. It's very tough, but I have got very fit. And there are other things ... but I'll tell you about them when we meet again. Do me a favour will you, William. Find the bit where I copied out the advert for you and have another look at it. If you can see a sort of shininess around it, well ... give it some thought anyway.

Dudley? Well, he's still chewing it all over, and I'm still working on him when I can. I think he'll make the right decision in the end.

Oh, and Mrs Jones – the old lady in the hotel, remember? I met her down in Llanberis a couple of weeks ago. She was in a wheelchair, and just about to do the two or three yards she can manage at the foot of the first slope, before going down to get the train. She was in terrific spirits. Said she'd never been so happy in her life. Great, eh?

One more thing, William. I said Dudley didn't say anything else to Bill Angerage after his 'I'm not fit enough' speech, but there was one thing. It was when we got to the door. Dudley stopped in the doorway and, as far as I can remember, this is what he said:

'I don't see what was so wrong with the old way anyway. The people in my church never did anyone any harm. Why do you want to go and make it all so much harder?'

'You really don't understand, do you?' said Bill. 'We haven't made it harder, we've made it much easier.'

See you on the slopes one day?

Yours,

Ray.

Nearly Cranfield

Nanna is dead. Nanna is dead. Nanna is dead.

This so-called fact beat like a pulse in his brain all through the day and far into the night. They were only words, but they were frighteningly insistent, drumming and drumming and drumming away at the part of him that believed things, until he was almost too weary to resist. He'd known there was something wrong yesterday, on the Friday. Standing in the hall he'd overheard his mother talking in a low, troubled voice to his brother, Simon, on the stairs. He couldn't hear everything she said, but one whole phrase had floated clearly over the banisters: 'We all have to be very brave.'

He knew what that meant – something dark and horrible had happened. He didn't want to know what it was until his turn came round. There was a special order for being told about things in his family. After his mother and father had talked about whatever it was, it would be Betty's turn to hear next because she was twelve and the oldest child, then Simon, who was nine, and later, assuming that the subject was a suitable one for seven-year-old ears, he would be the last one to know.

He slept as well as ever on the Friday night. Nothing had even remotely happened until he actually knew about it, and he carefully banned guessing – indefinitely.

The air in the house was like thick grey porridge when he got up on Saturday morning. His mother had onion eyes and was too bright. Betty didn't tease him. Simon didn't speak. Dad looked as if he was trying to work out in his mind how to do some job he'd never done before. Dangerous, dangerous feelings rose up from inside him and stopped just before they got to the top. He made them stop. It was like putting off actually being sick till you got to the lavatory. He was good at that. They always said he was a good boy and better than Simon, because Simon just stood in the middle of the room and let it go all over the place and people did extra large sighs because they were sorry for him *and* they'd have to come back in a minute and clear it all up as well. Being sick was funny. He'd always thought it was really your stomach suddenly losing its temper with the last meal you had because it had said something rude, and ordering it out the way it came in with a loud roar. Sometimes . . .

'Christopher, can we go upstairs for a moment? I want to have a little talk with you. Don't bother to put your things in the sink, darling, just come along with me.'

Upstairs – that meant it was a very big thing. You only went all the way upstairs for a little talk when it was a *very* big thing. Like when he'd done murals on the new wallpaper for Daddy, and Mummy wouldn't let Daddy talk to him till she had. But this wasn't going to be a telling off, he knew that. It was going to be something sad.

'Can I just go to the toilet first, Mum?' he said at the top of the stairs. 'I'll only be a moment.'

''Course you can, sweetheart. I'll be in our room.'

He turned the key carefully behind him in the lavatory door. There! He was locked in. If he stayed here for ever and didn't unlock the door again, he'd never hear about the sad thing and then it would never have happened. He sat on the edge of the lavatory and waited.

'Christopher, darling. Hurry up, there's a love.'

Mum was calling. He'd have to go. He stood irresolutely for a moment thinking that he'd been in the toilet too long to just do number one and not quite long enough to have done number two. He waited for a few more seconds then rattled the toilet-roll holder loudly and rustled the hanging length of pink tissue between the fingers and thumb of his right hand. Flushing the toilet had always been something he enjoyed. He would do it two or three times every visit if he was allowed. He just did it once now, then unlocked the door and turned to the left towards the bathroom, away from where his mother was waiting in the big bedroom.

'Just washing my hands, Mum,' he called.

'Good boy,' she responded automatically. 'Hurry up though.'

He washed his hands as well as he could. If he really had just done number two there would be trillions of germs rushing down the plughole now, choking and gasping on the microscopic mouthfuls of soap that were like poison to them. Remembering to turn the taps off, he gave the inside of the basin a perfunctory wipe and pulled the big yellow towel from the radiator. He dried each hand four times. Four was his special number, and five was first reserve, but was hardly ever used because it got so sulky about having that spiky extra one hanging off at the corner. Four was nice. Settled and square. He loved four.

'My, oh my, nice and dry,' he chanted. That was what Nanna always said ...

Dropping the towel on the floor in a big yellow heap, he shot out of the bathroom and ran along the landing until he was just outside the big bedroom. Shoving his hands into his jeans pockets, he tried to feel ordinary and not unhappy, ready for when his mum had talked to him and it turned out to be nothing very much after all.

When he got into the bedroom his mother was sitting on the far side of the big bed with her back to him, looking out of the window. He stood by the door waggling one leg and hoping that she wouldn't pat the bed and ask him to come and sit beside her.

That would be it if she did. That would really be it. He knew it would. Everything would go like a huge soft black quicksand, and he'd sink and sink until he cried.

'What, Mum?'

She laid a hand flat on the eiderdown beside her and smiled over her shoulder at him.

'Come and sit here, love. I want to tell you something.'

He jiggered over to her and plonked down on the bed, his hands still stuck in his pockets. He knew he'd got to sit there, but he didn't have to *be* there.

'Can I go an' buy a valve to blow up my football today, Mum? It's been soft for ages.'

With a little stab of helpless sympathy, he saw the hurt in his mother's eyes. She thought he cared more about a valve than about her needing him to be her little loving boy. No, Mum! No! I care, I care! I'm here inside and I care!

'Sweetheart, there's something very sad I have to tell you. I've told the others and we're all being as brave as we can.'

Not Nanna. Not Nanna. Please, Mummy, don't tell me Nanna's dead. Don't tell me . . .

'I'm afraid Nanna passed away in her sleep last night.'

Passed away? Did that mean she'd died?

'What's "passed away", Mum?'

His mother's eyes were all wet now, and she was shaking her head as if she'd run out of words. He'd done it all wrong. He'd known he was going to do it all wrong. She should have told him while he was standing by the door, then he could have worked up to being nice on his way over to her.

'Does it mean dead, Mum?'

She was crying properly now. She couldn't speak. She just nodded. Then Dad's voice came from the doorway.

'Pop off downstairs now, Chris. Mum's a bit upset. I'll be down in a minute.'

'Can I play with the Lego in my room, Dad?'

'Yes, good idea. Off you go.'

He listened outside the door for a moment. There was just murmuring at first, then he heard his mother's voice. It sounded hurt and puzzled.

'He didn't seem to react at all. Why didn't he cry or look upset? I don't understand it. He loved her so much.'

Back in his bedroom he pulled the big red plastic box from under his bed, and started to build a Lego house. He had loads and loads of Lego, given to him for birthdays and Christmas, or for no reason at all, which was usually best because it was a surprise. He decided to make a massive house that no one could break up, using every single tiny little piece of Lego in the box. He would put all the little Lego spacemen and ambulance drivers and firemen and petrol-pump attendants onto the base, and build up the walls around them, then make a roof out of sloping blue pieces so that no one could get out at the top.

He thought about Nanna.

Nanna lived a very exciting half-hour bus journey away in Cranfield. From the top of the bus you could sometimes spot deer in the forest a while before you got to the first houses, and there was a fire station after that, which, if you were lucky, had its big doors open so that you could see the bright red engines inside like two huge toys. Then the bus stopped outside the baker's, but you didn't get off. You waited until you were nearly at the top of the hill that led out of the High Street, then you pressed the red button that rang the bell to tell the driver you wanted the request stop, and the bus stopped right at the top of the hill like a tired old monster, and you got off and you were there. You would feel as if you were crackling like a happy fire as you pulled your mum up the drive towards Nanna's green front door. Then a voice would call out through the letterbox, and it nearly always said the same thing.

'Who's this coming up my front path? Who's this coming to see me?'

Nanna was a bright light with grey hair and a green cardigan, and a spinning top that was old but still hummed, and a box full of wonderful things to make things with, and a drawer full of blown eggs, and a garden with pear trees, and lots of time to read stories, and stone hot-water bottles, and a Bible like a pirate's treasure-chest, and plans for being nice to people that you could help with, and she was the only other person in the whole world, apart from your mum and dad, who you'd take your clothes off in front of, and she was still there living in Cranfield right now, whatever anyone said, and tomorrow he would go there and see her and no one could stop him.

'All right, Chris?'

His dad was standing at the door looking worried.

'Yeah ... D'you like my house I've made, Dad? I'm going to Cranfield tomorrow.'

'I like it very much, Chris – it's really great. Better than I can do. There's no point in going to Cranfield, son. You heard what Mum said, didn't you?'

''Bout Nanna being dead, you mean?'

'Well ... yes – you do know what that means, don't you?'

'Yep.'

'What do you think it means?'

'Like Sammy.'

His dad squatted down beside him, pleased.

'That's right, Chris, and you loved Sammy very much didn't you? Do you remember what we did when Sammy died?'

'Had a fureneral in the garden.'

'Funeral,' corrected his dad. 'That's right, and that's what'll happen with Nanna as well. Nanna's gone to be with Jesus, so she won't be needing her old body any more. Jesus will give her a new one. Do you understand?'

'Yes.'

'But that doesn't mean we don't feel sad about Nanna dying, does it? Because we loved her and we shall miss her very much.'

'Can we go to Cranfield tomorrow?'

He could tell his dad didn't want to get angry.

'Chris, have you listened to anything I've said? We're not

going anywhere tomorrow, and we all have to be very kind and thoughtful to Mummy because she's very upset.'

There was a little pause. He wriggled inside. His dad spoke again.

'You're very upset about Nanna too, aren't you, Chris?'

'Mmmm . . .'

He knew it wasn't enough. His dad wouldn't be able to help being a bit angry now. He was standing up and scratching his head and taking deep breaths.

'I just don't understand, Chris. I would have thought – well anyway, do your best to be a good boy and not make things difficult for everybody. Okay?'

'All right, Dad. I *am* going to Cranfield tomorrow, Dad.'

That was it.

'All right, Chris. You stay there and talk nonsense to yourself, but I've got too much to do to join in with you, I'm afraid. Just don't get in people's way!'

He'd let Dad make it all okay later on. It wasn't Dad's fault – he just didn't understand.

Saturday went on. Great aunts and rare aunts appeared. They moved heavily from room to room like big brown wardrobes on squeaky castors. He spent much of the day on the stairs. He was only allowed to sit on the even-numbered steps. If he sat on the odd ones he would be taken to a Japanese prisoner-of-war camp and tortured. The fourth one down was the safest. All the steps in Nanna's house were safe. The little squirrel in his stomach was very still whenever he went to Nanna's house. He was going there tomorrow. He was going to Cranfield tomorrow. He was going to see Nanna.

Nanna is dead.

Lying alone in the dark he fought those three words until long after the time when he usually went to sleep. Then, when he did slip into unconsciousness, he had one of the really bad dreams.

This time he was laying a big table for dinner. In his left hand was a basket containing knives, forks and pudding spoons. He was enjoying himself at first, walking slowly round the table putting a set of cutlery carefully at each place. He took a special pride in making sure that every knife and fork was absolutely straight, and that every dessert spoon pointed the same way. At last, his task complete, he took a step backwards to admire his handiwork. In the process, he happened to glance at the basket still hanging from his left hand. Then the horror began. There was a knife left in the basket. He had left one place without a knife. Terrible, nameless dread seized him as he rushed round the table at crazy, panic-stricken speed, desperately searching for the empty space so that he could put the mistake right before some hideous punishment was inflicted on him. Suddenly he saw the space, and with a little sob of joy, reached into the basket with his hand, only to find that the knife was gone. Then a door smashed open behind him and someone came in ...

No one went to church next morning. Dad did the breakfast. Betty took Mum's up on a tray. Simon went off with a friend to play. The air was warm and quiet. A radio was on in the distance. Cars hummed round the corner by their house from time to time. A white dog tapped past on the smooth brick pavement at exactly nine fifty-three. It tapped back again at one minute past ten. He watched everything from the window on the stairs and timed it on his watch with real hands. He'd asked specially for a watch with real hands. He hadn't wanted the other sort. Nanna had said, 'Digital, figital, fiddle-dee-dee!' He hadn't been able to say it. They'd laughed ...

'I'm off now, Dad.'

Dad was looking at the paper, his eyes were dark and tired. He looked up and frowned.

'Off? Off to where? What do you mean?'

'Cranfield. I'm going to Cranfield like I said, Dad.'

Dad leaned his head back on his chair and closed his eyes. He spoke in the weak, slow voice that meant he wasn't going to say anything else after he'd finished.

'Chris, you can go to Timbuctoo if you wish, for all I care just at the moment. If you want to go and play in the field, then for goodness' sake go! Make sure you're not late for lunch. Be careful. Goodbye.'

He could go to Timbuctoo if he wished. Timbuctoo was in Africa, in the Sahara desert. It was a lot further away than Cranfield. He decided to believe it was permission. He set off at ten-fifteen, with ten pence in his pocket and his very light blue anorak tied round his waist, to walk to Cranfield.

He knew the first bit very well because it was one of the walks they often did as a family. Turn right at the end of the village, walk straight across the common until he found himself on the black tarmac path, then follow the path until he came up to the very busy main road which had to be crossed if he wanted to get any further. If in doubt wait until you can't see or hear any traffic at all, then go straight over. He waited for a long time to make absolutely sure, then hurried across. Down the leafy track between the tall green trees, over the big flat car park where the fair came sometimes, down a little hill, and there he was at the place where he and Mummy caught the bus to Nanna's when Daddy didn't come. The next bit was easy too. Round the sharp corner by the sundial church and you were at the bottom of the long steep hill where you first started to get really excited about going to Nanna's. Cranfield was not till you got to the very top of this hill. It might even be a bit further than that. All you had to do was decide you were going to walk and walk and walk until you got there, and you had to *really* mean it, then it would happen.

He stopped at a little shop halfway up the hill to get some provisions for the rest of the journey. Sweets seemed a good idea because you could get enough with ten pence to make it look like a lot. He pulled one of the little white paper bags from the string where they hung, and filled it with the smallest, cheapest sweets he could find, then took it to the lady at the counter and waited while she added it all up.

'Ten pence, dear, please.'

The lady was old and nice. He gave her his ten-pence piece.

'Bye then.'

'Bye.'

He felt good now that he had a full bag of sweets. Full things had a special, fat, rich feel. He decided that he wouldn't have a sweet until he'd walked another five hundred steps. By then he should be nearly at the top of the hill. If he wasn't, he would wait until he actually touched with his foot the first bit of pavement that was flat. That would make him carry on.

There was a cosy tingle in his stomach as he made these tough plans. He always enjoyed really meaning something.

Five hundred steps later, he wasn't even in sight of the top of the hill. He fixed his eyes on the ground and decided not to look up until he got there.

When he reached the top at last he stopped and lifted his head. The road swept down and away from him, curved up on the opposite side of the valley, and disappeared between fir trees in the far distance. No sign of Cranfield – not yet. It must be a lot further than he'd thought. Never mind. It was probably just past those trees on top of that other hill in front of him. He'd have one strawberry chew now, and nothing else until he got past those trees and could see what happened on the other side. All you had to do was walk and walk until you got there.

It wasn't just past the trees, and it wasn't on the other side of the big roundabout, and it wasn't at the crossroads after the reservoir (though he did remember seeing that from the bus), and it wasn't at the end of a great long stretch of flat road between fields planted with something unbelievably, startlingly yellow, and it wasn't through a black, echoing railway arch, and it wasn't even just after the forest where, today, there were no deer.

He was running out of sweets. Just walk and walk.

Nanna bought him sweets sometimes.

'Let's put our coats on,' she'd say, 'and let's tiptoe down to the shops and buy ourselves a little treat.'

Sweets or a doughnut. She always let him choose. Then she'd do her real shopping. Shop to shop to shop they'd go, making each different place shine because they were in it being happy. Cranfield sparkled and shone like a Christmas tree because of Nanna. The butcher's shone. The butcher's meat shone. The post office twinkled. The kerb was made of precious grey stone. The houses glowed sweetly. The air had springs in it. Why should Jesus have Nanna all to himself?

He had one small gob-stopper left, and he was nearly there. He knew he was nearly there because he had come to the place where the bus turned right, away from the mainroad, and Mummy always said, 'Get your things together, Chris. We're nearly there.'

He turned to the right, took a few steps along the quiet tree-lined avenue, then stopped and sat down on a low wall that bordered a graveyard beside a little dumpy grey church. Opposite him, right on the corner, was a signpost. It told him that Cranfield was only half a mile away. In a very short time he could be walking up Nanna's drive and waiting excitedly for the green door to open and the thin, familiar figure to put her arms out for one of their special cuddles.

The walk home was much worse than going. His legs were beginning to feel like jelly, and his stomach was rumbling and aching with hunger. The gob-stopper hadn't lasted very long, and it wasn't the sort of thing he wanted now anyway. As he trudged doggedly along the way he had come, he dreamed of thick jam sandwiches, meat and potatoes, apple pie and custard, sponge pudding with treacle poured over it, and big blocks of red and white ice-cream. It was Sunday, so they would've all had a jolly good dinner while he was away. Chicken probably. He wondered without much feeling whether Dad would smack him when he got back or just shout. Betty would be all big sister, and Simon would be extra nice and good, enjoying Chris being the naughty one. Mum would say, 'How could you, Christopher?' and let him

51

off quite soon. He supposed he'd go to school tomorrow as usual. He didn't mind that. He liked school. Especially he liked his teacher, Miss Burrows. Her eyes lit up when he made a particular kind of joke, as though she'd peeped inside his head and knew what was going on in there. Nanna had been like that. Now that Nanna was dead, there was only Miss Burrows (and sometimes Dad when no one else was around) who really knew that funny bit of him.

Funny that he hadn't gone to Cranfield after all, despite being so close. Sitting on that wall he'd suddenly felt cold and scared at the idea of seeing Nanna's house with its eyes shut and all the sparkle gone. He wouldn't have been able to lift the horse's head knocker and drop it again if he'd thought that the hollow, clonking noise had to travel through a sad, empty hall into a sad, empty kitchen where there was no one with flour over her hands who would drop whatever she was doing to come and let him in. He'd always wanted to be allowed to play with lots and lots of flour. He'd like to push his hands into its smooth crumbliness, and move them around underneath the surface, then walk around making white handprints on things and people. What would Mum and Dad say if he said he wanted a barrel of flour for his next birthday? Three guesses!

Just walk and walk and walk.

How long was it till his birthday? One – no, two months. That was about eight weeks, which was a long time until you suddenly got there and it was now. Dad had promised him a bike. He really, really hoped it wasn't going to be a good-as-new bike. He wanted a brand-new, shiny, perfect bike like the one Simon got last year, only better. There'd been talk of him having Simon's, but he didn't want Simon's. He wanted . . .

He stumbled suddenly as a huge yawn seemed to take all the strength out of his body. He felt so tired now, but he hadn't got the energy to stop. All he could do was walk and walk like a walking robot until he came up against the longest brick wall in the world, or home or something. He noticed in a misty, dreamy sort of way that he was back at the edge of that busy main road that he'd crossed years and years ago this morning. Lots of cars and things roaring to and fro, but somehow he just didn't seem able to stop . . .

'Chris! Christopher! Stop – don't move!'

He stood still, blinking at the frantically gesturing figure on the far side of the road. It was Dad. Dad had come to meet him. Good old Dad. Dad was coming over now. He was bending down and picking him up. It was very nice to be picked up, and Dad didn't seem angry at all. He seemed all soft and quiet and gentle, like someone who's had a big surprise that's made them feel shaky.

'Chrissy – Chris, where on earth have you been? I've been out looking for you for hours and hours. We've all been worried sick.'

The jogging motion of being carried was a very sleepy one.

'Been to nearly Cranfield, Dad. Told you I was, didn't I?'

'You told me? Chris, you never . . .'

He could feel his dad remembering.

'You've walked to Cranfield and back, son?'

'Nearly, Dad. Can I have a jam sandwich when we get home, Dad?'

'Sixteen miles, Chris? We never thought . . . we told the police you'd gone to the field. Sixteen miles . . .'

'Can I, Dad?'

'You can have the whole larder, Chrissy. Mum's still got your dinner on a plate for you. Why did you go?'

'Jus' wanted to – dunno.'

They were home. Dad knocked on the back door with his foot. Mum opened it and gave a little cry when she saw who it was. She held her arms out and suddenly he was being held by Mum instead of Dad. She wasn't angry either. She had a big smile on her face and tears were swimming around in her eyes. He'd never noticed how much Mummy looked like Nanna before. She was Nanna's daughter, so it wasn't surprising really. Dad was standing close beside her still. They were both looking down at him.

53

'He's been to Cranfield,' said his dad softly.

'Mum?'

'Yes, my darling?'

'Nanna's dead, isn't she?'

'Yes, sweetheart, she is.'

Then he started to cry.

Stanley Morgan's Minor Misdemeanour

It was the woman's eyes that changed everything. She had such beautiful eyes, warm and liquid, with a greenish tinge. He wanted to dive into them in slow motion, just slide quietly into their depths and swim lazily around. Every now and then he dreamed that he was doing exactly that. Sometimes his dreams had nothing to do with swimming. He doubted that those dreams would ever come true, because, if they did, it would mean that he had committed a sin, and Stanley Morgan had never been very good at sin.

Even before becoming a Christian in his early twenties, Stanley's life had been a strikingly mild affair. Fear of the wild, unknown country that must surely await those who strayed from the path of rectitude had always been stronger than the occasional desire to step out and explore things that his mother and father had taught him to regard as unequivocally wrong.

Only once, just after his sixteenth birthday, had he attempted a wholehearted submission to temptation, and even that had gone ridiculously awry.

Transported by lust and the local bus service, Stanley had travelled to a market town several miles away from the one where he lived, with the sole intention of buying and secretly reading a copy of *Penthouse Magazine*. At the end of the bumpy half-hour

55

journey this desire to feast his eyes on photographs of naked female flesh was still burning just sufficiently to propel him into the newsagent's shop next to the railway station, but it was a struggle from that point onwards. He spent a ludicrous amount of time gazing earnestly at items of stationery, racks of greetings cards and boxes of chocolates.

Eventually, face flaming, he laid a pad of writing paper, two Biros, one Mars Bar, a copy of the *Daily Telegraph* and *the* magazine down on the counter at the far end of the shop. He clutched at a pathetically optimistic hope that the attractive, modestly dressed young lady who was about to take his money would say to herself, 'Ah, here we have the sort of respectable person who reads the *Daily Telegraph*. He's probably going to use this pad and these Biros to do some kind of objective research on the contents of this vile magazine that he couldn't possibly have bought for any other purpose.'

Certainly, the girl did throw a curious glance at the youth with the beetroot-red face, and eyes that would not meet hers, but it was only much later in life that Stanley was able to reflect ruefully on the fact that she probably connected such palpable embarrassment with his choice of newspaper, rather than his purchase of the magazine.

Escaping from the shop, Stanley swallowed hard, mopped his brow, rolled his *Penthouse* up in his *Telegraph,* and stepped out in a manner which he hoped might be construed as non-lustful purposefulness by anyone who might care to watch him, away from the shops and houses, up the tree-lined hill behind the coach station, and along a narrow footpath that curled its way across the bracken-covered common behind the town. After following the path for two or three hundred yards, he glanced swiftly around, then changed direction suddenly, walking straight into the middle of the waist-high green fronds, and ducking out of sight with an abruptness that would have surprised and alarmed anyone who happened to witness his dramatic descent.

Down in the unexpectedly cosy, green-lit chamber, shaped and formed by the weight of his own body, Stanley shivered deliciously with sheer pleasure at the thought of the warm wickedness to come.

Now!

Extracting the Mars Bar from his jacket pocket, he peeled its wrapper back and bit half an inch off one end, then, shifting to a more comfortable position, he unrolled his paper, feverishly anticipating a feast of photographs displaying all the female curves and crevices he had so often imagined but never actually seen in real life.

The magazine was not there.

No matter how much he shook his newspaper and pulled its pages apart, that magazine, the focus of his one excursion into deliberate, organized evil, just wasn't there. He must have dropped it somewhere between the shop and the point where he'd turned off the path. It must have just slid out and fallen to the ground without him noticing as he walked along. Were there to be no female curves and crevices? No nothing? Oh – rats!

Stanley's self-image, far from buoyant at the best of times, sank to an even lower level. Here he was, after much careful plotting and planning, concealed among thick bracken in a deserted place, with nothing more lascivious than a partly eaten Mars Bar and the _Daily Telegraph_. What a fool! About to stand up, he paused, wondering what passers-by would think if they spotted him rising from the undergrowth with a newspaper clutched in his hand. They'd think – goodness knows what they'd think!

When he did finally get to his feet, there was only one person in sight. An elderly, barrel-shaped, waddling little man, closely accompanied by an elderly, barrel-shaped, waddling little dog, seemed so deeply engrossed in some kind of reading matter as he strolled slowly along that he noticed neither Stanley's tentative ascent to the outside world, nor his breathless, panic-stricken series of hopping strides to the theoretical respectability of the footpath.

So relieved was Stanley to escape unobserved from his hiding place that it wasn't until a minute or so after passing the stroller and his dog that he realized what the absorbing reading matter in the man's hands must be. He had caught the merest glimpse of something flesh-coloured and pneumatic without registering what it was. It was – surely it had to be – his missing magazine. Stopping dead on the path and turning on his heel, Stanley tried to picture himself catching the man up and demanding the return of his *Penthouse,* but his nerve failed him. He couldn't do it. He simply could not face the idea of laying claim to that garish symbol of wrongdoing.

The bus journey home was not a happy one. Every bump was a penance.

The rest of the Mars Bar turned to ashes in his mouth. The *Telegraph* was boring.

Years passed, but the memory of that day haunted Stanley. It had been the one occasion in his life when he had committed (or attempted to commit) a carefully considered act of rebellion. He regretted it for four reasons. Three of these he was able to admit to himself, and one he wasn't.

First, he felt guilty about doing it at all. The very thought of his neat, confident, morally organized mother or his small, broad, fiercely trouser-braced father finding out what he had tried to do, sent a shiver of horror right through his body.

Secondly, he felt guilty about the barrel-shaped, waddling man who had found his magazine on the path that day. Suppose, he asked himself worriedly, that man had been a nice, clean, uncorrupted sort of person before encountering the sea of curves and crevices that were undoubtedly depicted on the pages that he had been studying with such concentration? Might Stanley have been inadvertently but nevertheless culpably responsible for an innocent man's moral downfall?

Thirdly, he was deeply troubled by the revelation of potential evil within himself. If it had been possible for temptation to lead him from the narrow path (literally and figuratively) for that short distance on that one occasion, was it not likely that, down on some dark and desperate level of his personality, there lurked hidden impulses to attempt even more extravagant excursions, or perhaps even to abandon the path altogether? Stanley decided to work hard at developing the habit of keeping tight reins on his thoughts and feelings in order to obviate such an unwelcome possibility.

The fourth regret, one that Stanley found it quite impossible to look at clearly, was actually a species of mourning for something quite indefinable that he might, or perhaps even should, have discovered, but didn't, on the common that day. In a misty, confused sort of way he remembered the short, unsatisfactory space of time in which he had been buried in his Stanley-shaped, dark green, brackeny world, as an encounter with a woman, someone soft and sweet who had dissolved in his arms at the moment when that unrolled newspaper had revealed his loss. There were times, in unguarded moments, when this strange and powerful non-memory would invade his peace so forcefully that he felt like crying, but the experience always confused and disoriented him. How could something so cheap and sordid and downright silly from the past produce feelings of such sad beauty in the present? The answer was, of course, that it couldn't. Stanley pushed these feelings back down into himself whenever they appeared, but on a deeper level still, he yearned to meet that 'woman' again.

Becoming a Christian at the age of twenty-three felt to Stanley like a solution to his most pressing problems. The recent death of his parents, within less than six months of each other, had naturally distressed him greatly, but it had also left him with a little knot of panic in his chest that seemed to never quite become untied. Silly questions flashed into his mind and had to be dismissed because they didn't make any sense.

Who would be his mother and father now?

Who was sure enough about what you do and what you don't do to keep him on the right track?

Getting involved with a fellowship that met on Sunday mornings at one of the local junior schools not far from his home was exactly what he needed. The person in charge was very strong and supportive, and most of the people who went were enthusiastic and easy to get along with. Everyone seemed to want to be clean, and free from sin, just as Stanley did. Being part of such a body gave him a good, safe feeling, especially after he joined the house-group that gathered just before eight o'clock every Wednesday evening at Brian and Madge Ford's house. Brian and Madge were the leaders of the group. They took a close, pastoral interest in each fellowship member entrusted to them by the eldership of the church, and their attitude to Stanley was no exception. Both of them were very warm and caring indeed towards him and he liked and respected them greatly.

On the occasion of his fifth attendance at the Wednesday meeting, Stanley made an announcement to the other group members as everybody sat, as usual, around the edge of the Fords' conveniently large sitting-room, on bean-bags, dining-room chairs and a big comfortable three-piece suite, drinking coffee, tea or squash after the Bible-study and time of prayer. He had reached a decision about his life in general and his spiritual life in particular, he told them. He wanted to make a personal commitment to Christ. There was much rejoicing as a result. In fact, he could not have hoped for a more gratifying response. It turned out that Stanley's conversion was the answer to a great deal of prayer on the part of just about everyone present. After Brian had helped him to say his own prayer of commitment, and several other folk had thanked God for working so effectively in Stanley's heart, Madge disappeared into the kitchen, returning a few moments later with a newly-opened bottle of wine and some glasses so that the house-group could celebrate the beginning of their new brother's walk with the Lord.

It was the first time that Stanley had relaxed inside for a very long while. He could almost feel that knot in his chest untying itself – or perhaps he should say – *being* untied. It was such a relief.

There was one worry. Stanley wanted everything in his new life to be as right and as clean as it could possibly be. He arranged to see Brian privately, indicating that there was something serious in his past that needed to be dealt with and forgiven. When the two men met, Brian quietly assured Stanley that there was no sin so terrible that it could not be confessed to God and forgiven by the power of the resurrection of Christ. They faced each other in silence across Brian's kitchen table for at least two minutes after that, but finally Stanley summoned up the courage to describe what had happened on the common all those years ago. It was a hard thing to do, but the feeling of relief afterwards was so wonderful that he found himself shedding a tear or two.

At first, Brian had seemed just a little taken aback by the exact nature of Stanley's 'serious' sin, but, clearly sensing how important the memory was to the nervous young man sitting at the other side of the table, he had responded with entirely appropriate gravity, quietly asking one or two relevant questions and nodding solemnly at the answers.

Encouraged by his house-group leader, who was a firm believer in practical spirituality, Stanley prayed out loud for forgiveness, and thanked God that the magazine, the vehicle of temptation, had slipped from his grasp during that walk across the common. They both prayed for the barrel-shaped waddling man, asking that he also should be forgiven for any sin arising from his exposure to those potentially corrupting images, and pleading that, if he was still alive, he should find Jesus for himself and inherit the eternal life promised to all those who are hidden in Christ.

Finally, Stanley asked if it would be all right to make an apology to his parents posthumously, as it were. Brian carefully explained that the Bible tends to frown on actual attempts to communicate with the dead, but went on to say that, in his opinion, it would be perfectly all right for Stanley to tell God how much he regretted doing something that would have hurt his mother and father if they'd known about it. That would be almost the same as apologizing directly to them, he suggested. It was.

All in all, it was a most satisfactory experience for Stanley. He was not metaphorically inclined, generally speaking, but he told Brian that it was as if he had just pulled out some heavy piece of furniture that hadn't been shifted for years, and finally faced the task of cleaning away the muck that had been allowed to accumulate behind it. Brian congratulated him on the aptness of the metaphor, and gently pointed out that light cleaning on a daily basis would mean that he'd probably never need to move any heavy pieces of furniture again. Stanley liked this idea very much, and made it the basis of his prayer life from that day onwards. Whenever daily devotions were discussed in the house-group, Stanley's contribution was always the same. A little light dusting, he would tell them – that was what he did every morning – a little light dusting. Then he would smile at Brian, and Brian would smile back. It was something special between them. It gave Stanley a warm, secure feeling. He belonged, and his feet were safely on the path. No more excursions for him.

More years passed, and that other memory, the one that wasn't really a memory, the one that quite erroneously placed an aura of sweetness and loss around an event that was actually an experience of sin and temptation, was buried so deeply inside Stanley, that, if he had been asked, and if he had understood the question, he would have replied that it had gone altogether. He had never mentioned those strange, meaningless yearnings to Brian, partly because he would have been unable to put them into words, but mainly because it was the only genuine pearl he had, and, although he didn't know it, giving it away would have left little or no reason for hanging on to the field in which it was hidden.

Very occasionally, a shadow did pass unexpectedly across the bright regularity of his life, but Stanley was gradually acquiring techniques for dealing with such problems. One Sunday, for instance, a visiting speaker at the fellowship had instructed everybody in what to do when the devil knocked at the door of their lives, trying to peddle his deception and lies.

Send Jesus to answer the door – that was his recommendation.

Stanley found this piece of advice particularly helpful, and employed the speaker's suggestion whenever his equilibrium was threatened by seductive shadows or temptation or inappropriate stimulation. He became very good at it. In fact, so much of a habit did it become to send Jesus to the door that he more or less abandoned the idea of ever answering it himself. Why take the risk?

Life was peaceful and good.

From the time of his conversion, Stanley had prayed consistently, if not passionately, that he might one day be married and have children of his own. Having a family, he felt, would see him comfortably through to that important point where he would need to take just the one necessary stride from the end of his earthly path on to the streets of heaven. The girl – or woman, he should say nowadays, of course – would have to be a Christian, naturally, that went without saying, and he was a little troubled about how the sex thing would work itself out – you couldn't have a family without that happening. If they were both Christians, though, he told himself, there would be few problems that could not be solved through prayer and patience.

He was absolutely right. Three days after his twenty-seventh birthday a new person called Alison joined the house-group (still run by Brian and Madge, though some of the old members had left and been replaced by others), and from the moment Stanley saw her he somehow knew that this newcomer was one day to be his wife. Later, after they had become engaged, Alison told Stanley that she had felt exactly the same when she first saw him. They treasured the knowledge of this coincidence that, of course, wasn't a coincidence at all, welcoming it as confirmation of the rightness of their plans to be united as man and wife.

The avoidance of sex before getting married was more of a problem for Alison than Stanley, but she also enjoyed the fact that he was being so strongly principled in that area. Stanley rather enjoyed the feeling that he was being strongly principled as well, and actually did almost believe that he was.

The wedding itself was a marvellous occasion. Most of the fellowship turned up to witness the ceremony, and Stanley invited one or two colleagues from the Land Registry in Cambridge where he worked, not just because they were friends, but also because it was a good opportunity for them to hear the Gospel in an indirect but nevertheless very effective way. They could hardly have failed to be impressed. The singing was loud and enthusiastic, and the fellowship leader's talk was wise but humorous. Alison's widowed mother, who had found Stanley highly satisfactory from the moment she first met him, later described the service as 'deeply moving'.

The reception was a bright, happy occasion. It made Stanley feel very special and important, but, as Brian had pointed out the night before, there was nothing wrong with being the star at your own wedding, as long as you remembered who was the real star in the rest of your life. Every now and then, during the eating and the speeches and the cutting of the cake, Stanley felt a stab of worry about his forthcoming initiation into the physical side of marriage, but there were too many immediate distractions for such concerns to seriously affect the happiness of the afternoon.

The wedding night itself turned out to be rather tentative and incomplete, but Stanley and Alison had read some good books and received a lot of excellent advice on matters relating to sex. They knew that these things took time, and would be that much better in the long run if qualities of patience and mutual sensitivity were faithfully applied to their ongoing development as sexual partners. Certainly, as the years passed, they did achieve a quiet compatibility, punctuated infrequently with moments when something more vital seemed to happen.

Once, only half waking in the middle of the night, Stanley had made love to Alison in the sleepily mistaken belief that she was a completely different person altogether. That encounter had been suffused with such passion, drama and midnight music in the velvety darkness, that both of them lay quite stunned and motionless afterwards, staring up in the direction of the ceiling, unable to find any clue in their experience of each other to solve the mystery of what had just happened. In the morning Alison's eyes shone, and she sang in the shower, but Stanley felt guilty and frightened. He resolved that such a thing would never be allowed to happen again. Dreams and real life had no business overlapping.

Mark was born, much to the delight of Stanley and Alison and Alison's mother and Brian and Madge (who had promised to take on god-parent roles in the child's life), on the anniversary of his parents' wedding. Brian joked with Stanley about the expense and hard work that would be involved on that day each year. Mark was a robust, contented baby, whose favourite thing was to stare with bright, curious, gently flicking eyes at a butterfly mobile bought for him by his Nanna. Every now and then he would break into a gurgling chuckle and wave his chubby fists at the gently moving coloured shapes. Stanley sat and stared at Mark for hours sometimes, hardly able to believe his good fortune, and wondering where on earth or heaven his little son had come from.

Two years later, Ruth, a sister for Mark, was born early one beautiful morning in springtime. She was small with a great pile of fine, dark hair and impossibly miniature, almost transparent hands and feet. Later, looking at the tiny figure lying naked in his arms, Stanley realized two things: that love does not become thinner because it is spread further, and that he knew nothing at all about women.

By the time Stanley reached his late thirties the Morgans had been able to move into a larger house with a back garden more suitable for young children. Money was not plentiful, but it was more than adequate, and the family was beginning to establish its own traditions and routines, a development that particularly pleased Stanley because he did like to know just where he was with everything. Quite often, when he was absolutely sure there was no one else about, he would sit on one of the wooden bar stools in his kitchen at home and run through a check-list of the important things in his life, naming them out loud, and reassuring himself as he went along, that each element was safe and functioning healthily.

Wife, son, daughter, God, church, house, job and physical health – these were the components of Stanley's existence that had to be oiled and serviced regularly, as it were. He was painstakingly conscientious in his attention to each one of them, and grateful to God for helping to make his life run so easily. He secretly played with the idea that there was an element of reward in his good fortune. After all, he had hardly put a foot wrong since the incident on the common all that time ago. Having said that, he knew – of course he did – through the teaching he'd received over the last few years, that it was impossible for anyone to actually earn his or her way into good favour with God. Of course he knew that. Of course he did. Still – everything was working out extremely well.

Then something happened.

One of the very sensible decisions that Stanley and Alison had made together was about walking the children to school in the morning. Stanley was able to work a flexisystem as far as his hours of employment were concerned, but because the Land Registry was quite a long way away, he had to choose whether to leave later in the morning and see the children before setting off, or go to work very early and see them at the other end of the day before they went to bed. After considerable prayer and discussion it was agreed that Stanley would, for the time being at any rate, begin work at ten o'clock, thus allowing time for him to walk Mark and Ruth the three-quarters of a mile from home to school each morning. Stanley, in particular, felt strongly that this daily half-hour of contact would prove to be very important in developing the right kind of relationship between himself and his children, and Alison was pleased because it gave her a head-start with 'getting on', the phrase she used to describe her housework.

For some time Stanley had no cause to regret the decision that he and Alison had made. Ruth was a bright, incessantly chattering little girl, who trotted happily along with her small hand in his big one as she communicated her views on life, school and the world in general, never seeming to doubt that her father was paying close attention to every word she said. Mark, a serious child, but no less contented by nature now than he had been as a baby, walked on his other side, speaking infrequently, but usually asking deep and thoughtful questions that resulted from a great deal of preliminary pondering, on those occasions when he did have something to say. Sometimes the two children would speak to him at exactly the same time, each appearing to regard the conversation of the other as background noise which could be reasonably and cheerfully ignored. Stanley became rather good at punctuating his carefully considered replies to Mark with enthusiastic nods and appreciative noises in the direction of his daughter, who needed little else in the way of response to maintain her small but freely-flowing stream of consciousness.

After only a few days Stanley found himself really looking forward to his regular morning walk. He basked in the sunshine of his children's affection and closeness, experiencing a quiet (but surely innocent) pride in the picture of happy Christian family life that the three of them must undoubtedly be presenting to passers-by.

It wasn't until this pleasant morning ritual had been going on for several weeks that two disturbing patterns began to emerge.

There were bound to be patterns, of course. Mornings had to be timed properly. Stanley and the children set off each day at exactly eight-thirty, arriving at the gates of Park View Junior School just after ten to nine, in order to leave nice time for Mark and Ruth to relax for a few minutes, greet classmates, and say goodbye to their father before two loud blasts on a whistle signalled the time to line up and go in.

On every single week-day morning between eight-thirty and ten to nine, Stanley and Mark and Ruth passed children and parents walking in the opposite direction on their way to Whitefields, another junior school (definitely an inferior one in Alison's estimation) situated only a few hundred yards from the road where the Morgans lived. After a few weeks Stanley was able to predict with consistent accuracy the time and place at which he and his own children would encounter quite a selection of these Whitefields parents and pupils, none of whom was known to him by name, as they happened to be neither friends nor members of his church. After waving goodbye to Mark and Ruth and setting off for home, he would, at equally predictable intervals, meet most of the same people during the walk back. It was the pattern of daily encounters with two of these fellow parents that began to disturb his life.

The first was more of an irritant than anything else, but, as the days and weeks went by, it increasingly spoiled Stanley's enjoyment of the whole of the first half of his walk to school with the children. This early part of the journey involved a long, dead-straight section of pavement running along the side of a main road which, at this time of the morning, was frantically busy (Stanley had insisted from the beginning that the children should hold his hands particularly tightly as they negotiated this potential hazard). It so happened that, almost every morning, as the Morgans rounded the corner opposite the garage (Mark and Ruth tightening hands automatically as they embarked on this three-hundred-yard stretch) another little family group of two very small boys and their father would come into view at the other end of the footpath. At first, passing each other and their charges with difficulty on the narrow pavement, there had been no more than an exchange of politely rueful smiles between the two fathers, a silent acknowledgement that they were colleagues in mild adversity. So frequently did they encounter each other, however, that the nature and quality of these regular exchanges grew by infinitesimal degrees each day, until, eventually, the two men were greeting each other with the familiarity and warmth of old friends.

Stanley hated it. He hated turning the corner each morning, only to see the tall, skinny figure with the prematurely greying hair appear at the other end of the road, with the two robin-shaped children toddling along on either side. What were you supposed to do with your hands and your face and your body when there was a one-hundred-and-fifty-yard walk between you and the point where you would meet the person you were walking towards, and you were visible to each other for the whole of that expanse? At what point did you begin the greeting process? If you began to smile too soon it would look as if you believed the relationship had a significance that it didn't actually have at all. But how could you avoid catching someone's eye too early in the course of a long, straight, uninterrupted walk like that? You couldn't. Not unless you gazed with inexplicable interest at the path, or your feet, or the traffic, or the brick wall that ran beside the pavement for almost the whole, eternal distance.

Stanley found himself building up an extensive collection of activities to fill the void. Looking at his watch was one, suddenly taking a deeply concentrated interest in what one of the children said was another. Occasionally, he even stooped (literally as well as metaphorically) to unnecessarily untying and retying one of Ruth's shoelaces, to the little girl's slight bewilderment. This was a good one, as it could be stretched to last very nearly half a minute, quite a chunk out of the endless eye-catching time that had to be filled somehow.

Stanley's misery was only increased by a growing realization that the other father was finding the whole thing just as excruciatingly difficult as he was. He observed covertly that the tall grey man had developed ploys of his own. On more than one occasion, for instance, he had plucked some very ordinary-looking leaf from the bushes that grew over the top of the wall and studied it with frowning concentration for fifty yards or so, and then, as if submitting to clamorous requests, he had bent down to show it to his patently uninterested sons, tapping and pointing and explaining, seemingly so engrossed in the joy of imparting knowledge that he completely failed to notice the impending Morgans. Once, he had taken a comb from his pocket, and, before applying it to his sons' immaculately tidy hair, spent some moments moving it carefully around in his hands, as though the imbecilically simple task of checking that the teeth were pointing outwards rather than inwards required a great deal of serious thought.

At the point on the path when the two families actually met, Stanley and the grey-haired man would, with apparent suddenness, become aware of each other for the first time that morning, exchanging chappy pleasantries with a relaxed geniality that was certainly in direct disproportion to the way that Stanley, and probably the other man as well, actually felt. The return journey was blessedly free of a similar encounter, as the grey-haired man, much to Stanley's relief, must have gone on to whatever work he did after dropping his children at school.

One Saturday, in the local supermarket, whilst doing the weekly shop with Alison and Mark and Ruth, Stanley, to his horror, found that they were directly behind the grey-haired man, his children and a lady dressed in a tracksuit who was presumably his wife, in the check-out queue. When their eyes met both men displayed bright and instant pleasure at meeting so unexpectedly, but neither of them attempted to introduce the other to their respective wives, and the grey-haired man hurried his family away as quickly as possible after paying their bill.

When Alison asked who the man was Stanley didn't quite know what to say. His problems with those morning encounters happened on a level of consciousness that he would have had the greatest difficulty in communicating to himself, let alone his wife. He frowned and smiled as if a little puzzled and apologized for not effecting introductions. He said that he knew he'd met the man somewhere, but couldn't remember where. Later, as they had their after-shopping drink and doughnut in the cafeteria, little Mark announced solemnly, after a great deal of cogitation, that he thought the man in the queue might be someone they met on the way to school sometimes, and Stanley said, oh, yes, now he came to think of it, that was probably right, and he was surprised he hadn't realized it before. Well done, Mark!

After returning from church on the following day, Stanley sat on his usual chair at the kitchen table drinking coffee while Alison prepared Sunday lunch at the other end of the room. Feeling that her husband was unusually quiet, Alison asked if anything was wrong. Stanley said, no, there was nothing wrong, but he'd been thinking about the mornings and walking the children to school, and had more or less decided that the time had come to change his work hours so that Alison could spend that special half-hour with Mark and Ruth each day. In fact, he continued, he had sensed during the service just now that he was being directly led into such a decision. Stanley believed what he was saying even though he knew it to be quite untrue.

Alison was extremely surprised to hear this suggestion for such a radical change of routine in their lives. She pointed out mildly that they had always prayed together in the past before making big decisions, and asked what was different about this time. Stanley became quite irritable for the first time since their marriage, spluttering incoherently about Ephesians and husbands and wives. Alison cried a little into the potatoes, and, then, with a sudden flash of intuition, asked if all this had something to do with the grey-haired man they'd met in the supermarket yesterday. At this, something short-circuited in Stanley's system. He banged his fist angrily on the table, rushed out of the kitchen and ran upstairs to his bedroom where he lay on his back staring up at the ceiling, hardly breathing as he tried to understand what was going on. There was something happening deep inside him, right under the surface, something to do with the morning walk and the grey-haired man, and yet nothing at all to do with him, and yet, something about the feelings inside him – was he in love with the grey-haired man? Panic-stricken, Stanley rolled across the bed, physically removing himself from the place that had been occupied by such a preposterous notion.

Of course it was a preposterous idea, but he *was* in love with someone – something. Hugging his knees to his chest and closing his eyes tight he found himself sinking into a green darkness filled with sweet, tearful sadness. There was a face just visible in the shadows. Beautiful, seductive eyes – eyes that looked at him for just an instant before turning away. Where had he seen those eyes, not just once, but often – almost every day? Suddenly he knew.

Stanley got off the bed, washed his face in the bathroom, dried it and his hands on his favourite big, blue fluffy towel, took a few deep breaths and went downstairs. He explained to a very worried Alison that he had been feeling a little tired and things had got a bit out of proportion. He was really sorry that he had upset her so much, and he hadn't meant it about the morning walks. They should have lunch as usual and forget what had just happened. Alison was very pleased that things were back to normal, but the incident had frightened her. Later, she asked if Stanley felt that he might like to go round and visit Brian and Madge that afternoon. Perhaps they could pray together that whoever or whatever had attacked their happy lives before lunch would stay away in future. Knowing that he wouldn't, Stanley said that he might well do that, and the rest of Sunday was peaceful.

That night Stanley lay awake for hours, full of worry and guilt and excitement, thinking about the thing that had really been disturbing him about his morning walk to school with the children. Until today he had somehow managed to pretend that nothing was happening at all, but now, there it was, right in front of his mind. It had been invisible, but now he couldn't make it go away even if he tried, and he didn't know what to do about it. He tried to think clearly, hoping that if he teased the thing out into its component parts it might look insubstantial and silly, and perhaps just go away.

It was a woman. It was a woman who was not Alison. It was a woman whose identity was as much of a mystery to him as that of the grey-haired man. Stanley had never spoken to her. She had never spoken to him – not with words, anyway. It was a woman who walked her daughter to Whitefields School each morning, just as the grey-haired man walked his sons. He knew she must start out later than the grey-haired man, though, because she didn't pass Stanley and the children until they reached the line of fir trees at the top of the school lane, just after turning right by the roundabout. Stanley tried to picture exactly what the woman looked like, but apart from a vague impression of colourful clothes, dark, glossy, shoulder-length hair and very shiny black shoes, he found it very difficult. He realized that he had never quite dared to look directly at the woman.

Her eyes were the only part of her that he was absolutely sure about. As he thought about them a trembling ripple seemed to pass through the entire length of his body. Those eyes were – well, they were so large and long-lashed and inviting, so full of something he had always ached to have, without knowing what it was or even whether it really existed. Stanley knew, as he lay there in the dark, that he had thought about nothing but the woman's eyes for weeks and weeks.

It had begun in such a small way. The woman happened to glance up at him as they passed on the pavement one morning, that was all, but, even at that ridiculously early stage, he had, with a sudden inward little gasp of wonder, seemed, just for an instant, to see in her eyes the possibility of finding his way through or down into a different kind of world, a warm, dreamy place that he had given up all hope of ever visiting, let alone inhabiting. It happened again the next morning, and the next. It happened on every school-day morning.

As the days went by that little flick of a glance had seemed to increase in duration, until now, every morning, the woman's eyes held his for what must surely be a fraction of a second longer than was appropriate for two strangers passing on a footpath. Then, on the way back, he would pass her again, but this time she would be walking much more quickly, and her eyes would be very deliberately averted, almost as if, he told himself, she realized the danger of making any sort of contact when their respective children were not there to act as a buffer of respectable restraint. She might well be lying in the dark herself at this very moment, perhaps thinking about Stanley and wishing, as he wished, that – that what? Stanley closed his eyes and rolled his head from side to side in a reluctant attempt to dispel the wrongness from his mind.

How on earth had he managed to convince himself that it was the business of the grey-haired man that had disturbed him so much? Was he going mad? Was he possessed by some evil force or spirit that was twisting his mind and trying to turn him into a different kind of person? A light perspiration broke out on his face and forehead as he considered this possibility. Turning his pillow over he rested his cheek on the coolness of the other side. What should he do? Time to send Jesus to the door? But even as he asked himself the question he guessed that this particular matchstick model had no chance of surviving tonight. He was right. It was smashed and swept away by the flood of what he was feeling and wanting. And the confusing thing, the really confusing thing, was that right in the centre of this overwhelming torrent of dark and sinful feelings, Stanley could have sworn that he detected a small, shining wave of absolute rightness. How could that possibly be? He must be mistaken. He must be!

All of this night-long worrying and thinking and teasing-out resulted in one thought only. Stanley knew what he wanted now. The desire of his heart was entirely visible for the first time. He couldn't wait for the morning to come. He couldn't wait to see those eyes again.

Next morning the encounter with the grey-haired man was a different matter altogether. From the moment the single tall figure and two small ones appeared in the distance Stanley kept his eyes firmly fixed on the other man's face, determined that he would not flinch for any one of the following one hundred and fifty yards. He succeeded, and greatly enjoyed seeing his fellow parent thrown into a state of mild panic as he was forced to employ an even greater variety of avoidance strategies than usual. At the point where they actually passed, Stanley produced one small, utterly self-contained smile, and was rewarded by an expression of puzzled embarrassment on the face of the other man, who had automatically launched into the over-familiar greeting mode that both of them usually used.

Now it was nearly time for _her_. In not much more than one minute's time he would see the woman who was making his whole being buzz with excitement and anticipation. Unconsciously, he took his hand from Ruth's and passed it across his hair. He pictured himself cleaning his teeth earlier that morning and was glad that he had. He drew himself to his full height as he walked, instead of allowing the top half of his body to incline towards the children and their conversation as he normally did. Mark and Ruth were both chattering happily away now, although he had absolutely no idea what either of them was talking about. It was very nearly time. Just a few more yards and there she would be.

Perhaps, this morning, he would let some very small indication of his feelings show in the glance that he threw her when they met, just the merest hint of an acknowledgement that he knew what was going on between them, and that he wanted something – whatever that something turned out to be – to happen.

Suddenly, as they turned the corner, there she was, hurrying along past the fir trees towards the roundabout with her daughter. She was there! Stanley tingled with yearning and a sudden nervousness. How was it going to be possible to convey all that he wanted to communicate in one small glance? If he attempted to inject a new significance into the look he gave her was it not possible that he might accidentally transmit aggression or annoyance, thereby repelling rather than attracting her? Stanley quivered with frustration. He had such scant experience of dealing with the opposite sex. Studying the toes of his well-shined shoes as he walked, he tried out a variety of expressions in the hope that he might hit on one that seemed exactly right.

They had started to walk round the curve of the roundabout now, and, by a rough estimate, were likely to encounter the woman and her daughter at a point thirty yards down from the top of the road that eventually led to the school. If he timed it correctly, Stanley reckoned, he should be able to lift his head and look into her face just as he and the children passed the first of the fir trees that stood on their left after they had turned away from the roundabout. Taking a deep breath, he checked the distance quickly out of the corner of his eye. Yes, a few more yards – say, ten of the reduced strides he had to do on the way to school because of the children's shorter legs – and then it would be the ideal moment.

It was as Stanley actually began to count down from ten to nought, that young Mark decided he really did want an answer to the important question that he had asked three or four times already without getting any response at all from his distracted parent. Raising his voice as he asked the question yet again, the little boy began to tug rhythmically at the sleeve of Stanley's jacket, hoping to wake his daddy up from the dream that he appeared to be in as he strode along making faces at the pavement.

Stanley was furious. Only seconds to go before the most important thing in the world happened, and this irritation had been set up just to deprive him of one little moment of happiness. He felt a savage anger towards its perpetrator, but for now he ignored his son, gritted his teeth, and continued to count down towards nought. At 'three' Ruth compounded her brother's offence by pointing out in her high and infuriatingly clear 'helpful' voice, that Mark was trying to ask him a question.

Postponing a reaction to either of his children, Stanley reached 'nought' in his counting before raising his head. And yes. Yes! Oh, yes! There it was. There they were. There were the eyes. There was the only question that truly interested him. There was the promise, the invitation, the possibility of being soaked and absorbed at the same time; the prospect of sinking through deep, warm waters, where closing one's eyes and drowning would be nothing but a pleasure. There, too, was a slight curve of the soft, full lips, a coquettish smile that was as good as an extended hand. He didn't remember ever seeing the smile before. Now, he would look forward each morning to the smile as well as the eyes. As for all his practised expressions, he had used none of them, but he was quite sure that his soul had been in his eyes. She knew. She must know.

After passing the woman and her daughter, and when he was sure they were out of earshot, Stanley turned on his children with a fury that frightened both of them and made Ruth cry. It was the first time they had seen him lose his temper, let alone get so _very_ angry. He said that he didn't think it was too much to ask that he should be allowed a little peace in the mornings when he walked them to school, and that he would answer questions when he wanted to, not at a time when it just happened to suit Mark. As for Ruth, the whole thing was nothing to do with her and she should mind her own business and not shout in the street. He added that if Mark ever pulled his jacket around like that again when he was busy thinking about something important, he would most likely give him a smack. Did they understand? Mark and Ruth nodded miserably, not understanding at all. The rest of the walk to school was conducted in virtual silence. Stanley was too excited to feel guilty yet.

After depositing the children, Stanley set off on the journey back to his house with a light step and a rapidly beating heart. In less than five minutes he would see her again and – well, who could say what might happen? Anything was possible. In fact, when he did pass the woman as they negotiated the path by the roundabout in opposite directions, she hurried past him as she had always done when they met on the return trip, except that, this time, although she hardly glanced at him at all, that small curve of a smile appeared on her face once more, and Stanley knew with a further little lift of his spirit that it could only be intended for him.

From that morning, and for the following two weeks, the Morgan household seemed to Alison like a ship that has run into perilously stormy weather, and is in serious danger of sinking without trace or being wrecked against jagged rocks. She really was at her wits' end. Over coffee with Madge while Stanley was at work one day, she tearfully asked how anyone could change so much and so suddenly. Since nearly two weeks ago, everything she said and did seemed to infuriate him beyond measure. It was almost as if, she explained, her very existence annoyed him. He acted as though she ought to be feeling guilty about bothering him by being in his life at all. She had wondered if something was going wrong at work, but when she very gently mentioned that possibility, he had told her so witheringly that she was being about as stupid as it was possible for a human being to be, that she'd burst into tears, and that had irritated him even more. He couldn't stand her crying at the moment, which made things especially difficult because that was what she felt like doing most of the time.

Madge gently asked Alison what she had done to try to improve the situation. Alison described how she had determined to be patient, knowing that Stanley must be going through some sort of dreadful crisis, and that it couldn't really be anything connected with her. She'd tried things like preparing his favourite meals at suppertime, but apart from perfunctory thanks he hardly seemed to notice the effort that she made. She'd tried hard to look attractive and be more interested and interesting in the evenings, thinking that perhaps Stanley was beginning to find the unvarying sameness of people and places each day weigh heavily on him, but all her attempts to start conversations and show that she cared what was happening to him provoked the same tone of weary exasperation in his voice. She was beginning to dread that tone. In fact, she told Madge, every single attempt she'd made to improve the situation had failed before it was given a chance to begin working, and she was running out of ideas.

Madge wanted to know how Stanley had been with the children. Not as bad, Alison told her, but even though he was making more of an effort with them (he still seemed keen to walk them down to school each morning, for instance) he was much snappier and more quick-tempered than he'd ever been in the past.

In addition to all these things, Alison said, Stanley was tending to come to bed much later than he ever had before, and when he did eventually arrive he would turn his back on her in such a pointed way that she had stopped trying to make any contact with him at night for fear of his anger and rejection. All in all, the situation was just horrible, and she was getting so worn down with it that she didn't know how much longer she could carry on.

Madge asked if it was likely that Stanley would agree to see Brian for a chat and maybe some prayer? Alison explained that Stanley was 'off' everyone in the church at the moment, but she decided not to tell Madge how, as well as speaking in a very negative way about the church in general, Stanley had made some very sarcastic comments about Brian in particular, describing Madge's untidily dressed husband as the 'Shambolic Shepherd', and declaring that he was planning to take an indefinite holiday from everything to do with church.

The two women prayed together for a little while, then Madge departed, leaving Alison alone, lonely, and desperately wishing that everything could hurry up and go back to the way it used to be.

Stanley, meanwhile, was plunging wildly from invigorating sensations of being fully alive for the first time, to intolerable extremes of guilt when he dared to think about the unhappiness that would be caused to others if the dreams that filled his head at the moment were ever to come true. But he was trapped inside what he wanted. He wanted the woman with the beautiful eyes. He knew that. It was like a fever in him. She somehow represented the fulfilment of a promise that had been made to him by – by whom? He didn't know. He just knew that he had a right to something connected with her, even if it turned out not to be the woman herself. He had a right.

On the second Saturday following the Monday when he had established his dominance over the grey-haired man, Stanley drove the twenty miles into Cambridge to buy a new carpet-sweeper. Alison had asked if she and the children might come with him so that they could all go to the pictures and have something to eat out, but he had clicked his tongue and sighed and looked so put out by the suggestion that she had given in straight away and said it didn't matter.

All the way to Cambridge Stanley thought about the woman with the beautiful eyes. The weekends were such a waste of time. He never saw her at any other time but weekdays. All he wanted was for Monday to come so that he could meet her on the way to school and on the way back, and see the little smile that he now felt was specially his. Nothing else had happened. Perhaps nothing else ever would happen, despite the variety of passionately hopeful scenarios that he rehearsed continually in his mind. But it might. Roll on Monday.

He bought the carpet-sweeper in a large electrical store next to a garage and a supermarket and a cinema on the edge of town. It was as he was about to go out of the shop, carrying the new sweeper in a big cardboard box, that he met the woman with the beautiful eyes just as she was coming in. She was not alone. Behind her, shepherding the little girl he was used to seeing with the woman on every week-day morning, and followed by a dark-haired boy of about fourteen who was the image of his mother, came a tall, friendly-looking man who could only have been her husband.

The woman stopped when she saw Stanley, and gave a little amused laugh before she spoke.

'Good morning. Isn't it funny how you don't think people exist outside the times when you're used to seeing them? Darling, this is a man whose name I haven't got the faintest idea of, whom I meet every single day of the week on the way to school with Suzie. Man-I-meet-every-day-of-the-week-without-knowing-your-name, this is my husband, David, and these are Thomas and Suzie.' She glanced at his purchase. 'And we all hope you'll be very happy with your new Hoover.'

After he had introduced himself and a few more pleasantries had been exchanged, Stanley said polite goodbyes to each member of the family and returned to his car, carefully stowing the new carpet-sweeper along the back seat. After closing the rear door he stood quite still for a moment, staring across the tops of the other cars.

The woman with the beautiful eyes had been bright and witty, probably not a Christian, but certainly the sort of person one could very easily like. The rest of her family seemed to be the same. Pleasant people. Perhaps he and Alison could get to know them. Maybe they could come to dinner one evening when Brian and Madge were there as well. That would be really nice.

He locked the car and set off in search of a public phone. There was a whole row of them just outside the supermarket. One was free. He inserted a twenty-pence coin, punched in his own number and waited, listening to the ringing tone. At last, Alison's voice, laden with trouble, said, 'Hello, Alison Morgan here.'

'Hello, Ali,' said Stanley, 'it's only me.'

'Stanley! Where are you?'

'Cambridge, of course. I've just bought a Hoover.'

'Oh, right! Good. So, what did you . . . ?'

'It wouldn't be too late to bring the children up on the train, would it? If you came now. I could meet you at the station.'

'Well, yes, I could, but I thought . . . '

'Let's take them to the pictures and then have a cream tea. What do you think?' Silence. 'What's the matter?'

'Nothing – sorry, I was just so pleased that you wanted us to . . . '

'Don't be sorry, Ali. Listen, get a move on now and come up, and then when we get back, and the children are safely in bed, let's light a fire in the sitting-room and lock the front door and bring that thick rug down from our room and make love on it in front of the fire.'

'On the rug in front of . . . ? Stanley Morgan!' She sounded far more pleased than shocked.

'Yes, on the rug – the one I chose – the green one.'

Marl Pit

I've always rather resisted the idea that one should go grubbing about in the past hoping to find something that will help to explain the present. Perhaps I don't think enough about things like that. I don't know. My life has always seemed quite happy enough without all this close examination of one's own entrails that seems to happen so much these days. My wife laughs at me and says I'm plain vanilla to everyone else's raspberry ripple, and I wouldn't know a complex if one batted me round the ear. She's probably right. I'm an uncomplicated sort of character. Fond of the family, keen on work, love my pipe – that sort of thing.

I've never seen any sense in the suggestion that none of us are anything like we appear to be. You know the sort of thing: 'He's so noisy and confident. I'm sure he must be a very shy man ...' Load of rubbish if you ask me, but that's how a lot of people go on. If you can prove he was in love with his teddy bear when he was two, they say, that will explain why he can't bring himself to play shove-halfpenny with left-handed Welshmen now that he's forty. That sort of thing's not for me and never has been. Why, I can't remember much about last week, let alone things that happened when I was a child. Sufficient unto the whatsit is the thingummybob thereof, I've always said. My son's the same – sleeps like a baby (he's sixteen), gets up with a smile, strolls through the day doing this and that, yawns a bit when it gets late, goes to bed, head on the pillow, fast asleep in seconds. Just like me.

Now, the reason I say all this is to show just how unusual it was for me to suddenly remember every detail of that one particular day twenty-seven years ago, when I was about nine and a daily attender at the little junior school up on the other side of the common near our village. It was my wife who triggered the memories off at breakfast one morning. She looked up from the paper and said, 'You lived in Natcham when you were a kid, didn't you?'

'Yes,' I said, 'we were there until I was about eleven. Why – what about it?'

She looked down at the paper again and tapped one of the columns with her finger. 'There's a bit here about a court case, and one of the men – the defendants – comes from Natcham. Might be more than one Natcham, I s'pose. Here, you have a look. I'll start clearing up.'

I wasn't wildly interested, but I read the article with time-consuming care to give my wife and son plenty of opportunity to clear the breakfast things and wash them up without my valuable assistance.

The piece in the paper was about a criminal trial involving four men who were accused of brutally assaulting an elderly night watchman in the course of a major robbery. It appeared that the injuries inflicted on the old man were way out of proportion to what would have been needed to keep him quiet. The prosecution described the attack as 'vicious and bestial'. It was a horrible story, and I wasn't very anxious to dwell on it, nor was the name of the Natcham dweller very significant at first. His name was Duncan Tapman, age thirty-six, the same as me. It wasn't until I'd laid the newspaper aside after much over-elaborate straightening and refolding, that the whole thing hit me. Duncan Tapman! Of *course* I remembered Duncan Tapman, although I hadn't thought about him for years and years. And with the return of that memory came a whole set of other memories, all connected with a wet Friday in late autumn when I was a not very confident junior, and Duncan Tapman was . . .

'Well?' My wife suspended sink duties for a moment. 'Ring any bells?'

I was feeling a bit shocked. I knew that I needed to take this flow of memories that had fountained up from nowhere into my mind, and carry them carefully, like the contents of a brimming beaker, to a quiet place where I could safely examine them. There was nothing to say to anyone else about it until I'd done that.

'Mmm . . . maybe. I'm not sure.'

Later that morning I set out to drive up the motorway to visit a friend in hospital in Northampton. It was ideal. Time and space to find out why the recognition of that name earlier on had been accompanied by such a sharp stab of guilt. Something to do with that Friday. An almost unbearably pungent flow of emotions passed through me as faces and scenes from the past appeared with extraordinary clarity in my mind. Who was our teacher at the time? I could see her perfectly, but her name escaped me for the moment. She'd been very thin with a scraggy neck and black hair caught up somehow at the back. Impossible to say how old she was. All adults were 'about fifty' when I was a junior. But I didn't like her. There was no doubt about that. I didn't like her at all. I remembered how powerful she had seemed. Grim and powerful, glaring down from a desk at the front that seemed to my childlike eyes a good ten feet higher than the regimented rows of sloping desks at which we sat. I remembered wondering in a private, embarrassed sort of way, whether Miss Duncannon might be a variety of witch. Duncannon! Of course! She was called Miss Duncannon, and her fingernails were so long that she could reach out and poke a boy sitting right at the back of the class without even getting up from her desk at the front. I laughed aloud at the absurdity of this non-memory, a sort of impressionist memory I supposed. Because she was like that. She could control and punish and disturb any boy in the class without effort. She was an expert.

Pulling out to overtake one of those drivers who seem to need a slow slow lane, I remembered that the Friday in question had started with one of those demonstrations of total control. A boy called Roger Burn had swung his satchel carelessly as he came in that morning, and accidentally torn a section of the new 'frieze', a wall decoration that the whole class had been working on every day for the past week. There had been loud cries of 'Oh, Roger!' followed by the much more ominous 'You wait till Miss Duncannon sees that!'

We all waited with considerable relish to see what Miss Duncannon would say when she saw 'that'. She never disappointed the more bloodthirsty element in the class. This morning was no exception. I was reading my brother's copy of *The Eagle* when she swept in and took up her customary stance behind the teacher's desk, her beak of a nose impaling our spirits to her will as it travelled slowly through a one hundred and eighty degree arc. We were all on our feet by then, of course, including the wretched Roger whose cheeks had turned to the colour of raw pastry as he awaited his fate.

'Good morning, class.'

Her voice was resonant, unmarried, business-like.

'Good morning, Miss Duncannon.'

We performed the usual chanted greeting with mechanical rectitude.

'Sit!'

We sat.

'Answer your names as I call them – Ablett, Arnold, Atwood, Avingdon, Bance, Benson, Burn, Crowhurst . . .'

Roger's 'Present, miss' had been an unintelligible, strangled bleat.

'Volume, Roger!'

We knew that this meant 'say it again, but louder'.

'Present, miss.'

An intelligible bleat this time. The register proceeded.

Anyone who could have overheard me as I motored up the M1 that morning would have been bound to conclude that I had mislaid my marbles with a vengeance. I went through that twenty-seven-year-old register two or three times at the top of my voice, filling in gaps each time, until I was fairly sure that I had total recall of the list of names. It fascinated me that all that information had been pigeonholed somewhere in the back of my mind for all those years. I shook my head slowly in wonder as I drove.

'Does anyone have anything they would like to tell us?'

That had been Miss Duncannon's next question. She always asked it. We were allowed five minutes each morning to broadcast information about ourselves to the rest of the class. Naturally, we did this in the only really meaningful way at play-time and on the way home from school when there were no grown-ups about, but Miss Duncannon insisted on the daily formal exchange and woe betide us as a class if one or two of us didn't squeeze out a sick grandmother or a new bike. Perhaps we would rather do sums or copy out from the board, Miss Duncannon would suggest, if no one was concerned enough about others to let them know what was happening in our lives. Very recently deceased relatives were especially popular with all of us, including Miss Duncannon, and, if I remember rightly, the bereaved class member as well in most cases. Miss Duncannon would deliver a soberly dramatic little lecture on how John or Michael or Frankie would be feeling sad and upset today, and how we must be specially thoughtful and careful with them between now and going-home time. John or Michael or Frankie would then move through the day in a sort of physical and verbal slow motion, exhibiting the fragility that was expected of them and postponing any real grief until they had enjoyed their suddenly acquired celebrity status.

There had been no dead relatives on that Friday, but there had been a torn frieze which, as headline news, was easily on a par with a death in the family.

'Please, miss . . .'

It was Richard Arnold, the class sneak. He was very useful to us. We could hate him for telling tales and hiss imprecations at him afterwards, but we needed him to trigger the X-rated scenes of pedagogic vengeance and chastisement that were so awesome and so enjoyable.

'Yes, Richard?' said Miss Duncannon, melting infinitesimally. 'What do you want to tell us?'

Roger Burn sat two desks away from me. His mouth was drooping open and he was blinking very hard every few seconds. All I remember thinking was what a wonderful stroke of luck it was to not be Roger Burn.

'Please, miss, Roger tore our frieze that we done. He tore it with his satchel when he came in this mornin'.'

Everyone sat up a little straighter, folded arms a little tighter. You could have cut the silence with a guillotine. Miss Duncannon studied the place on the wall near the back of the classroom where part of the frieze hung limply, its jagged edge indicating the scene of the crime. Then she looked at Roger, her eyes like little black bullets.

'Well, Roger Burn, I think there's something we ought to say!'

If ever anyone needed a script in a hurry it was Roger Burn that morning. I could see his mouth twitching suddenly as he desperately sought a form of words that would spring this hideous trap that he found himself in. I knew exactly what he was thinking. He was thinking that whatever he said would turn out to be evidence of his callous indifference to others. If he just said he was sorry, Miss Duncannon would reply that sorry doesn't get friezes mended. If he said it was just an accident, Miss Duncannon would say that she might just have to smack his hand accidentally with a ruler for being so thoughtless. If by some miracle he was able to convey coherently that he was very sorry about accidentally damaging the frieze that everyone had worked so hard on, and that he would repair it at his own expense and in his own time as carefully as he possibly could, then Miss Duncannon would say that that was all very well, but wouldn't it have been much better if it hadn't happened in the first place. Roger was in a no-win situation, and he knew it.

'We're all waiting, Roger! What are we waiting for you to say?'

'Don't know, miss.'

A delighted, shock-filled, air-trembling silence.

'You've just damaged a piece of work that has taken us all week to finish, and you don't know what to say? Is that possible? I'm very sorry to find that you have no feelings at all about what you've done.'

No one looking at Roger at that moment, pale and quivering with confusion and dread, could possibly have seriously claimed that he had no feelings at all about what he'd done, but his internal mechanism was stuck on 'don't know', and none of us were about to argue the point with the teacher.

'I'm still waiting, Roger Burn, and I do not intend to wait much longer! Now, what do you say?'

Roger reminded me of a baby bird I'd once seen, cornered by a cat, its heart hammering frantically against its chest, quite unable to move or make any sound other than a terrified little chirp.

'Don't know, miss.'

'Well, little master don't know ...'

We giggled obediently.

'I'm going to give you one more chance to find out that you do know! Everyone else knows, don't you, class?'

One or two hands shot up towards the ceiling, but Miss Duncannon wasn't interested in hearing from anyone else. She quelled them with a tiny gesture.

'What am I waiting to hear you say, Roger Burn? And this is the last chance you get!'

Roger's life seemed to have escaped through his open mouth. All that was left were those three hoarsely spoken words.

'Don't know, miss.'

I found myself jabbing the accelerator of my car in anger at the memory of what happened next.

Miss Duncannon went icy cold and just stared at Roger for a few seconds, then she spoke in a dry, deceptively casual voice.

'Come out to the front, Roger, and face the class.'

He stumbled his way to the front and stood facing us. He looked like the sort of suet pudding that you have to throw away in the end. I thought how sad my mother would be if it was me out there, and she could see me. I hated Miss Duncannon and I wished it wasn't all so exciting.

'Well now, class. Here's a boy who doesn't know. Whatever you ask him, all he can say is that he doesn't know. But why doesn't he know? The answer must be that he doesn't know because he's a fool. So what you see standing in front of you here is a fool whose name is Roger. Are you a fool, Roger?'

Roger's face wasn't white any more. It was deep crimson.

'No, miss.'

Miss Duncannon left her desk and walked forward until she was standing beside her helpless victim. She bent forward from the waist and spoke right into the side of Roger's face.

'So you've discovered something you do know, have you? Well, I don't agree with you. I think you are a fool, and I'm going to prove it. Do you think I can prove it?'

'N-yes ... don't know, miss.'

'Go and bang your head against that wall, Roger – over there by the door.'

Hesitantly, Roger, still bright red in the face, walked stiffly over to the yellow-painted wall and stood for a moment with his forehead resting against the plaster.

'That's it,' coaxed Miss Duncannon as though humouring a lunatic, 'bang it against there a few times. Off you go.'

Like some sick-at-heart animal performing a foolish trick, Roger banged his head against the wall three times, then looked back at his teacher.

'Roger,' she said quietly.

'Yes, miss?'

'Only a fool would go and bang his head against the wall when he's told to. Go and sit down.'

Quite a lot of children laughed of course, as she knew they

would. She really was an expert. Some smiled, *I* smiled, mostly out of fear. I didn't want to be next.

Duncan Tapman didn't laugh or smile. His place was the one between mine and Roger's, and I noticed that as Miss Duncannon returned to her desk, his face was set and angry and his left hand, the one nearest me, was clenched so tightly that the knuckles looked bloodless. It frightened me a little.

Duncan Tapman ...

As I moved out of my lane onto the approach road to the Newport Pagnell services in search of coffee, I thought about Duncan Tapman. By the time I was seated with my drink in the midst of the bustling cafeteria, it had all come back to me.

Duncan Tapman's face had been closed up in a way that, as a child, I never really understood. It was as though there were bruises right inside his head, so tender that if he relaxed his face the pain would be unbearable. There was a pronounced puffiness around his eyes as well, although actually his face (like the rest of him) was bony and tough looking. I knew him, at that time, simply as one of the two roughest boys in the school. He lived in a rough road, he did rough things, and he used rough words, not, as we did, with deliciously conscious wickedness, but naturally and casually. He never came to tea at our houses and we didn't ask him to play with us. He was outside. He didn't belong. He wasn't like us. He had a strange solitary independence which we didn't understand, like one of those grim-faced gunfighters on the films who won't hurt you as long as you don't get in their way. We were rather scared of him, I suppose.

I wasn't the only one who had noticed Duncan's clenched fist. Miss Duncannon missed nothing. Her eagle eyes were fixed on that left hand of his as it rested, quite still, on the desk in front of him.

'What have you got in your hand, Duncan?'

'I 'aven't got ...'

I was close enough to Duncan to see what happened next, although for a while I wasn't sure what it meant. He had obviously been about to unclench his fist and show Miss Duncannon that there was nothing in it, when a strange little light appeared in his narrow eyes and the whole of him seemed to relax slightly. Instead of opening his hand, he just loosened his fist a little so that it looked as if he could be holding something about the size of a ping-pong ball. He spoke again, quite politely.

'I 'aven't got nothing in my 'and, miss.'

I'm sure Miss Duncannon realized that this boy was never going to bang his head against a wall just because someone told him to, but she was quite capable of varying her methods to suit individual cases.

'I can put up with a great many things, Duncan, but I cannot stand a liar. I shall ask you once more. What are you holding in your hand?'

The atmosphere was electric. No one had been expecting a second feature, least of all one involving the enigmatic Duncan.

'I'm not 'olding anything in my 'and, and I'm not a liar, miss.'

Duncan drew his closed hand towards his chest as though guarding its contents from attack. Miss Duncannon nodded twice, slowly, her thin lips compressed with anger. But she must have felt she was on very solid ground. Why had the boy not simply opened his fist if he had nothing to hide? She drew herself up very straight. In an old book about the First World War at home, I'd got a picture of a judge putting on the black cap before sentencing Sir Roger Casement to death for treason. If Miss Duncannon had had a black cap available now, I was sure she would have put it on.

'What is the punishment for lying in this class, Duncan?'

'Cane, miss.'

'Correct! So if you persist in telling me untruths, you know what your punishment will be.'

Her voice rose into terrifying gear.

'Perhaps you think that one fool in this room is not sufficient. I think you must believe that I am as great a fool as Roger. Is that what you believe?'

'I 'aven't got nothing in my 'and, and I'm not lying, miss.'

Duncan covered his fist protectively with the other hand.

Miss Duncannon was really angry now, but still well in control. She took her cane from its two supporting hooks on the wall, her eyes never leaving Duncan in case he dropped 'it' while her back was turned. Laying the length of bamboo with cruel delicacy on the front of her desk, she sat down and beckoned with one skinny forefinger.

'Come up to my desk, Duncan. That's it – now stand beside me here so that everyone can see you. Now, you say that there's nothing in your hand?'

Duncan paused for the barest fraction of a second, as though debating inwardly whether to own up or not, then, still cradling his fist to his chest, answered as politely as before.

'Yes, miss. There's nothing in my 'and, and I'm not tellin' lies.'

'Very well!'

Miss Duncannon shot a hand out and grabbed Duncan's left wrist, pulling it towards her and twisting it so that when his hand opened, everyone would be able to see what was inside.

'Now, class,' she said, 'I'm going to make Duncan open his hand in front of you all. If there's something in there, then he's a liar and I shall cane him, but if there is nothing in there' – she spoke with dry, totally assured irony – 'then I am a fool and Duncan had better take over as teacher.'

Reaching round with her other arm, she prised Duncan's fingers open to reveal a completely empty hand.

For Miss Duncannon it must have been as if the sun had set in the east. She remained quite motionless for a few seconds, while her face seemed to turn a yellowish colour. You could see her going over in her mind the words she had just said. A ripple – largely of unease – passed through the class. We may not have been very keen on Miss Duncannon, but there was something uncomfortably off-centre about what had just happened.

'Can I go and sit down again please miss?' asked Duncan quietly.

Miss Duncannon seemed to come to with a start. She looked with narrow speculation at Duncan for a moment, then spoke with dismissive briskness as she released his wrist.

'Yes, Duncan, go and sit down. We've wasted quite enough time already this morning. Sit up straight, class! Let's see how well we know our seven times table.'

It was a fine retrieving performance, and most of the class hardly realized what had happened. I knew, though, and Roger Burn knew judging by the little smile on his face, and I'm quite sure Miss Duncannon knew what had really occurred.

Duncan had punished her for what she had done to Roger.

I glanced at my watch. Lost in the intensity of my memories I hadn't noticed that time was passing. Swallowing the cold remains of my coffee with a grimace, I hurried out to the car and was soon 'burning rubber' as my son puts it. I didn't allow my thoughts to return to Duncan Tapman and the other significant event of that Friday until much later in the day after I had visited Jeanette. My visit followed the usual pattern. A long, chatty walk through the beautiful grounds of the mental hospital, lunch at the restaurant that catered for patients and their friends, and the usual tearful farewell at the door of Jeanette's unit. She was an old friend of ours – very sick – and we were all she had really. I promised we would all come up for a day in the spring.

Motoring back that afternoon I found that my thoughts about Jeanette and her situation drove me back almost irresistibly to my memories of earlier in the day and the event which must have had a lot to do with the moment of guilt I'd experienced on first recognizing Duncan's name in the newspaper.

The rest of that Friday had been fairly uneventful as far as school was concerned. It was too wet for us to play out after dinner and at play-times, so we were all pretty lively by the time we escaped Miss Duncannon's care and popped out of school like a succession of little corks from a bottle. I set off to walk home over the common with Roger Burn, who had fully recovered from his ordeal of the morning, and my other best friend,

Michael Atwood, who sat directly behind me in class and lived two roads down from me in the village. These friends of mine were deeply, vitally important to me. In fact, at that time, they were probably *the* most important thing in my life. Being alive was about having friends, doing things with friends, working out ways to keep friends, and, sometimes, learning how to cope with being hurt by friends. That didn't happen very often, and it was probably unintentional and meaningless when it did happen, but it always knocked the bottom out of my world for a short time, and revealed a soft, emotional part of me that was occasionally responsible for slightly bizarre emotional outbursts. One of them happened on this damp, chilly, autumn afternoon, and it was all because of what these friends of mine did to my school cap.

We all wore caps – green and yellow ones – at our school. As far as I could remember they were always either too big, or too small, or if you did find that yours fitted, it probably didn't belong to you anyway. It was as much a part of life as Dan Dare and six-of-chips that, every now and then, your cap would be snatched from your head by a friend or foe and carried gleefully to a safe jeering distance. That left you with the choice of employing 'chase and kill' tactics, which was exactly what the snatcher hoped you would do, or trying to give the impression (not easy for your average healthy junior) that the whole thing left you too bored for words. Either way you usually got your cap back in the end, or if not your cap, a cap. My mother never seemed to mind too much if I ended up with headgear that wasn't strictly my own, as long as it was in as good or better condition than the one I started off with. In my time I'd both suffered and inflicted this traditional schoolboy insult many times, but on this particular afternoon I felt it had got rather out of hand.

As we reached the village end of the common, Roger, who was rather hysterically high-spirited after quitting the scene of his earlier ignominy, grabbed my cap from the back of my head and ran off holding it high in the air, making Red Indian noises by wobbling his finger in his mouth as he went. This didn't trouble me too much, but when we rounded the next bend in the path, he was waiting by the edge of the dank and reedy pond that everyone called the Marl Pit. Goodness knows what it had been originally, but over the years it had been used by local people for dumping all their unwanted rubbish, and now it was a foul smelling expanse of black water with the legendary bottomless centre so beloved of schoolboys and tourists everywhere.

Roger waited until I was inches away, then, with a shrill whoop, he drew his arm back and flung the cap as far as he could towards the centre of the pond. Michael laughed, of course – so did I. It was more than your life was worth to look upset. But already my mind was racing with dismal questions. How on earth would I get the silly thing back? What would my mother say if I went home with no cap at all? I wasn't supposed to go anywhere near the Marl Pit anyway. If I waded in and somehow avoided drowning, then went home soaked to the skin, my mum would kill me. If I didn't wade in and went home capless, she'd kill me even more.

My friends had started to shy stones and mud at the green and yellow target as it lay flat on the surface, supported by reeds or rubbish just under the water. They made noises like artillery shells as they lobbed their ammunition. They were having a great time.

For me it had become one of the coldest and most miserable afternoons I had ever known. Retribution awaited me at home whatever happened, and here were these so-called friends of mine setting out with great relish and enthusiasm to make things as bad as they could by sinking my headwear. As a large clod of grass and earth plunketed heavily into the target area, to the accompaniment of loud cheers from Roger and Michael, I started to cry deep down in my stomach. It was a technique I'd learned early on in junior school to avoid the humiliation of crying real, wet, visible tears. There was no acceptable nine-year-old vocabulary for the feelings I wanted to express at that moment, but I could feel, rising up from inside me, the tear-laden, retardedly deep voice of that other hurt child who seemed to inhabit me at times like this: 'You're supposed to be my friends.' They loved this, of course, and the target practice continued with even greater vigour and much delighted laughter at my expense.

Several other boys, heading homeward, were passing our noisy group by the pond. One of them, taller and thinner than the rest, had left the path and come over to see what all the fuss was about. It was Duncan Tapman.

Duncan had heard my ludicrous appeal for mercy. He didn't laugh. He stood, hands in his pockets, quite still except for his eyes, looking with growing awareness from me to my friends, to my cap, and back to me. Then our eyes met. It was a moment of genuine identification. I suppose that for once, and on a level that was quite indefinable, we were equals in suffering. All of a sudden he raced off in the direction of his house, calling out that he'd be back in a minute. Five minutes later he galloped back wearing an enormous pair of rubber boots. Without saying anything he waded out towards the centre of the evil smelling pond and, reaching forwards as far as he could, retrieved the soggy lump of cloth that my cap had become. Splashing his way doggedly back to the bank, he threw it carelessly at my feet.

The peculiar desolation that always crept over the common at the end of those chill, dripping days in late autumn, was beginning to spread through the atmosphere as I bent and picked up the cap. Duncan, apparently quite unconcerned about my response to his good deed, had picked up a long whippy stick and was tapping it rhythmically against his leg as he stared out over the dark stretch of water, whistling softly to himself. My friends, unwilling to risk a challenge to this cool customer, had already forgotten the entertainment of the last half hour and were turning towards where the village lights burned richly in the dusk on the edge of the common, only minutes away.

But I had to get things sorted out before I got home that evening. I needed some definite sign or symbol that my friends were still my friends. I was a rather old-fashioned child in a way, I suppose. As

Michael and Roger started to move away from the pond I barred
their way and extended my hand stiffly and formally.

'Shake hands? No hard feelings?'

This odd, unnecessary gesture embarrassed and amused them,
but they did shake hands. Perhaps, for a second, they realized
how important it was to me.

So everything was all right.

I glowed happily between the bobbing, boy-shaped silhouettes
of my two friends as we picked our way through the tufts and
troughs of coarse common grass, laughing and jostling each
other, looking forward to tea and television.

I looked back once over my shoulder. I could just make out
the solitary figure of Duncan, still standing at the edge of the
Marl Pit, still flicking his stick against his over-sized wellingtons,
gazing up at the last livid streaks of day in an angry black sky. I
don't think Roger looked back even once.

By the time I arrived home from my Northampton trip, I was
in an unusually foul mood. My wife is wise. She waited, and
eventually, when I'd eaten and got my pipe going, she asked me
what was wrong.

'It's about this Duncan Tapman character, isn't it?' she said.

'Well, yes,' I replied, 'you see, I've always rather resisted the
idea that one should go grubbing about in the past hoping to find
something that will help explain the present. Perhaps I don't
think enough about things like that . . .'

Nothing but the Truth

Dying was a doddle. It really was. I'd just come out of Boots after buying a new toothbrush and some cream for my – well, for something that didn't really matter once I was dead (a complete waste of money in that sense, of course) – and I stepped into the road without so much as a glance to right or left. A dark-ish green, number thirty-four, double-decker bus got me. There was no pain nor discomfort, not even any awareness of nasty squelching or crunching noises, just a sort of 'POP!' in my consciousness, and suddenly, there I was – dead.

What was going through my mind when that bus hit me? Well, I can tell you the exact answer to that question, embarrassing and absurdly trivial though it is. Dogs – that's what I was thinking about. Specifically, I was having a really good ponder about those new leads that people use nowadays. You know the ones I'm on about, don't you? The ones that mean you meet the dog first on one end of its lead, and then the owner about a quarter of a mile further on holding the other end. The ones where the plastic thing in the owner's hand looks like one of those spring-loaded metal ruler things. Presumably, I was thinking, when they press a button on it the dog comes whizzing back at eighty miles an hour and goes splat! against the handle. And I was wondering why anyone would want to have their dog on a lead that's two streets long, it being more like flying a kite than walking a dog. It won't be long, I thought, before someone patents a special two-handed lead so that you can set your dog spinning round and round in the far distance by pulling harder on one side than the other. Believe it or not, my mind was filled with this ridiculous vision of the future at the precise instant when the bus struck me, and the image remained in my imagination, virtually unaffected, for thirty seconds or so after I'd passed from life to death.

I was more than a bit worried at the time. Into my mind came a vague memory that Hamlet hadn't wanted to murder his uncle while he was in the middle of a prayer because people who died when they were praying were popularly supposed to go straight to heaven. So where would a head full of dogs get me? Perhaps I'd end up with Elvis Presley's Old Shep in some canine paradise. That was my first half-witted thought after realizing that I was dead.

The second thought was about being conscious at all. I was *so* relieved! You're going to think this sounds completely mad, but I was always more frightened of oblivion than hell – this without any first-hand experience of the infernal regions, mind you. But in the previous decade or so there had been quite a bit of discussion about whether God really could allow an eternity of suffering if he was as loving as he was supposed to be. One or two eminent scholars had arrived at the conclusion that hell was actually a sort of switching off for ever. According to them, you just ceased to exist. That was your punishment. This idea scared me to death. I couldn't handle the idea that everything would stop with my last breath. All that thinking and feeling and loving and worrying and trying and succeeding and failing just snuffed out like the stub of a candle. I couldn't bear the thought of that. What was the point of anything if it all ended in nothing? But it hadn't. I was still there, feeling just the same, but presumably invisible, having retreated a step or two on to the pavement just outside Boots.

I stood and watched for a while as passers-by gathered around the end of the bus, going pale and making breathy gasping noises, and looking up and down the street the way people do when they're waiting for someone else to come and be in charge. I wanted to tell them that they didn't have to worry because I was all right, but I knew without even thinking about it that they'd never be able to hear a dead person, so I didn't try.

An ambulance drew up noisily at last, closely followed by the police and a woman who looked as if she was probably a doctor. I cannot begin to tell you how strange it is to witness the after-effects of your own sudden extinction. Inside my head, you see, I seemed to be more or less the same as when I was still alive, but I couldn't help feeling a little confused. Here I was, standing transparently in the High Street of my home town, watching what was left of my visible self being dealt with very efficiently by the two-man ambulance crew and all the others, and although, as I've already said, I was extremely happy to be existing at all, I was also conscious of a feeling of anti-climax. I'd spent a fair proportion of my life worrying myself sick about death and the hereafter. Images of Grim Reapers and lakes of fire and the Seven Horsemen of the Thingamabob, all mixed up with nightmares and bits of epic films that I'd seen over the years, seemed to have no connection at all with the sheer ordinariness of what I was experiencing now.

After a few minutes I couldn't take any more. I just had to turn and walk slowly away from the scene of my fatal accident. Having absolutely no input into such a significant event in my own history was disconcerting and rather coldly alienating. Apart from anything else, I suddenly became terribly sad thinking of how my family and friends would react when they heard what had happened to me. I wished there was some way of communicating with them, some means of passing on the fact that I was still alive in some way even though I was dead. Being hit by a double-decker bus is such crushingly bad news.

Perhaps I ought to go home and try to make contact with my wife. But how would I get there? Would I walk? I never had been able to drive. Were dead people able to use public transport like everyone else? Could I think myself there by an effort of the will? Perhaps I'd be able to float. I tried a little experiment. Closing my eyes tight shut I willed myself to leave the ground and fly, as I had done on quite a number of occasions in my dreams whilst I was still alive. Sometimes, on waking from such dreams, I had been filled with an indescribably thrilling certainty that I actually had located the specific muscle which would make flight possible. Invariably disappointed, of course, I had often expressed to my wife the hope that I would be allocated wings of some sort when I got to wherever I was going once my three score years and ten came to an end. On opening my eyes now, however, I found myself still firmly rooted to the pavement, totally ignored by all the living people around me, and feeling faintly resentful that, even after having had more than a third of my statutory allowance of years chopped off so abruptly, I was still unable to take to the air.

In fact, the whole thing began to feel increasingly annoying and odd. Although it was clear that I couldn't be seen, I wasn't able to walk through solid walls, which might have been quite fun. I tried it, making, in the process, the uncomfortable and rather unexpected discovery that it was still possible to experience pain. Nor did passers-by walk through me, or I through them as in all the best ghost stories. There seemed to be a natural path-clearing process designed to ensure that I could never make physical contact with any of these distracted folk, busily going about their warm and visible lives. I decided I wouldn't bother trying to get home. The idea of being there, seeing people I loved, and not being able to get through to them, was just too dismally awful for words.

Disconsolately, I strolled to the end of the High Street and, following the road where most of the restaurants were located, headed in the direction of the seafront. Crossing the main road by the fish-and-chip shop (would I be needing food now that I was dead?) I took two flights of steps to the lower promenade and stomped along in the wind for a while with my hands buried deep in my pockets. Eventually I came to a place where the pathway narrowed a little as it curved behind an old Victorian bandstand. The wind was very high and gusty today, sweeping the tide in as far as it would go, and crashing it with tireless, rhythmic insistence against the massively thick wall that supported the promenade. I stopped and leaned over the safety railing, closing my eyes and recalling suddenly, as the flying spray soaked my dead face and hair, all those times when my wife and I had driven the eight or nine miles from where we lived down to the coast on days like this, simply because the weather was wonderfully wild. Our favourite thing of all had been watching the great clouds of white spray thrown up by the waves as they made thunderous contact with the blocks of stone beneath our feet. Those huge lumps of granite had dumbly and successfully resisted such attacks for more than a hundred years.

I started to feel very miserable indeed. Being dead hadn't been much fun so far. Nor, come to think of it, had it been very spiritual or theological, as far as I could see. Where were the angels? Where was the Eternal City whose streets were supposed to be paved with gold? Where was my heavenly mansion, specially prepared for me by – you know? If it came to that, where was *he*, for goodness' sake? At the very least, where was the long dark tunnel with a light shining in the distance and the conversation at the far end with an impressively authoritative person in which I got to be offered a choice about whether I wanted to come back or not? I remembered hearing about lots of people who hadn't actually died, or had died then been revived, who had reported something along those lines. Where was *my* tunnel, and where were the other countless billions of other dead people, and what was going to happen to me? I was on my own and unhappy and wet and dead.

So deeply did I begin to sink into this sludge of self-pity, that it was some moments before, with my eyes still closed, I registered the fact that something had changed. All the sounds and sensations of wind, sea and spray had completely ceased, and out of the silence came a woman's voice.

'Mister Porter, my name is Miss Jordan. Would you be kind enough to follow me?'

I nearly overbalanced and fell into the sea with the shock, but it wouldn't have mattered, because when I did stand up and open my eyes, the sea and the railing and the weather had disappeared, together with every other trace of my original surroundings. Instead, I found myself standing in a very plain, grey-painted corridor (not exactly a tunnel, but close enough, I reckoned), confronted by a brisk-looking, cardiganed lady in her mid-thirties, with kind eyes, who was obviously waiting for a reply. She didn't look any more dead than I felt. I decided to check one or two things before following her anywhere, no matter how kind her eyes might be. I made a feeble attempt to tidy my hair, wondering vaguely as I did so why it wasn't wet any more.

'Err, could I ask you a question? Would that be all right?'

'Two questions if you wish,' she replied, all firmness and niceness. I stared at her.

'Two?'

'Two.'

'Right – well, here's the first one.' I took a deep breath. 'Am I dead?'

'That's a nice easy one,' she said, smiling. 'Yes, Mister Porter, I am able to state quite unequivocally that you *are* dead. A large bus terminated your earthly existence just outside Boots the Chemist less than an hour ago. Do you remember the Parrot Sketch?'

'Yes, of course, it was one of the Monty ... '

'Well, you are an ex-person, and indeed, all the other things that the famous parrot was, Mister Porter. And your second question?'

I wasn't sure how to put it. 'Well, you know. Am I ... ? Will I be ... ?'

'You'd like to know what will happen in the next stage of your existence?'

'Err, yes, I would.'

'Are you worried, Mister Porter?'

A funny thing happened at that moment. I never had been very good at admitting weakness, especially to women for some reason. Anything like tender loving care coming in my direction made me shrink inside and panic as if I was afraid the carer was trying to steal power from me. I opened my mouth to say that I wasn't really worried, just a little bit apprehensive, and that she surely must see how perfectly understandable that was, given the circumstances, but the words just didn't – or wouldn't – come out. Instead, I heard, with profound consternation, my own voice telling something that sounded horribly like the truth.

'Yes! Yes, actually, I feel very, very confused and frightened. I was alive a few minutes ago, and then I wasn't, and then I walked up to the bandstand, and then I was suddenly not at the bandstand because I was here, and I was wet, and I was suddenly dry, and – and now I don't know what's going to happen and I don't know who you are and, yes, I *am* worried, and I *do* want to know what's going to happen next.' Something important occurred to me. 'Oh, yes, and I don't know if you're the person to tell, but I've changed my mind about preferring hell to oblivion ...'

This ragged, emotional speech disturbed me a great deal, but it made little or no impact on the efficient-looking Miss Jordan, other than to cause a slight raising of her eyebrows.

'You are in the outer reception area of the Allocations Department, Mister Porter. If you would care to follow me, I shall take you along to the Waiting Room and you will be seen very soon by a member of our assessment team.' She started to turn away, then stopped and cocked her head on one side. 'As far as hell is concerned, I seem to recall that the Anglican Church – you were a regular attender at an Anglican Church, were you not, Mister Porter?'

'Mmm, that's right,' I mumbled, adding hastily and rather pathetically, 'it was a *renewed* Anglican church.'

'I seem to recall,' she went on, 'that the Anglican Church more or less abolished hell in the mid-nineties, so perhaps we should assume that heaven and oblivion are the only remaining options?'

I looked at her in silence for a moment. For all I knew this could be God in disguise (or, as anything seemed possible now that I was dead, God *not* in disguise!) testing my sense of humour or something. I decided I'd better find out.

'Was that a joke?'

'Yes,' she said, 'it was a joke – we do have them here – but your decision to plump for oblivion after all is a very wise one, if I may say so.'

Panic!

'You don't mean that I . . . ?'

But she had turned abruptly and was setting off at such a pace that I only just managed to catch her up as she reached a place where the passage turned sharply to the left. After that our progress to the Waiting Room (whatever that might turn out to mean) seemed to take for ever and ever. The journey was an eternity of grey-painted corridor, dimly lit by an invisible light source and unrelieved by pictures, windows or decorations of any kind, involving maze-like turnings to the left and right, interspersed with long, straight sections. All there was in the world – or in this world where I found myself now that I was definitely dead – was Miss Jordan's bobbing back, the rhythmic clacking of her heels on the lino-covered floor, and the dream-like, grey sameness of my surroundings.

Perhaps this *is* hell, I thought. Perhaps, for me, it has turned out to be a woman's back, an uncomfortably hurried walk that will never end, and acres of unrelieved, grey gloom. If so, it wasn't *too* bad. Well – not as bad as it might have been, anyway. Perhaps some delicate little refinements were to be introduced as time went by. Supposing I found that I desperately needed to go to the toilet? Maybe that would be it. There didn't appear to be doors of any kind in the walls, let alone ones that were surmounted by little stick-figures indicating facilities for GENTS or LADIES. What a hell that would be, to find yourself in a perpetual state of urgently needing to empty your bladder, but never being able to find anywhere to do it.

It made me feel better, thinking silly things like that as I stumbled along behind my guide. And they were silly thoughts, of course. After all, if there were to be no marriages in heaven, toilets were bound to be unisex, if they were needed at all. I knew what I was really doing. I was trying to distract myself from worrying about that awful phrase that Miss Jordan had used in such an emotionless way just now. She had said that I was in the 'Allocations Department'. Obviously, it was me that was going to have some destination or fate allocated to me, presumably by a member of the equally terrifyingly-entitled 'Assessment Team', somebody who, even now, was crouched slaveringly at the other end of the corridor, waiting to assess me before savagely consigning my soul to one choice torment or another.

Miss Jordan seemed to be increasing her pace, and I had to raise my own performance a gear or two to keep up with her. As I did so, there flashed quite abruptly into my mind, memories of the nineteen-sixties, when, as young Christians, my friends and I had been introduced to a series of little postcard-sized comic-books. Produced in America, they depicted in dark, petrifyingly vivid images the fate that would undoubtedly befall those who were foolish enough to die having failed to 'get their hearts right with God'.

I recalled a particularly unpleasant example, in which one such foolish fellow (I don't think any women were condemned in these publications) arrived at the place of judgement to discover that he was obliged to sit before a large screen in order to witness a film record, not just of his sins, but also of the moment when an opportunity to repent and turn to Jesus had actually been offered to him. Full of anguish now that it was too late, he watched himself contemptuously rejecting this offer, airily expressing a preference for being immersed in worldly, sinful things, and thereby missing out on the chance for his soul to be saved. In the final, nightmarish scenes, this wretched individual, still rather plaintively dressed in his expensive, worldly suit, was shown being prodded by grinning devils with pitchforks towards a lake of fire, screaming out and begging in vain as he fell, for 'one more chance' to put things right.

The last picture of all in this warmly encouraging little tract was a whole double-page spread given over to a panoramic view of hell, showing countless numbers of similarly tormented souls bobbing about in a sort of vast barbecue, crying out in agony of body and spirit, knowing that they were forever damned to endure, without relief, the pain of being burned alive.

These 'evangelistic tools', as I remembered them being described, were supposed to be left lying around by us keen members of the youth group, in places where unsaved young people might happen upon them by chance, and thus be terrified into understanding the love of God. I suppose they were a form of spiritual anti-holiday brochure. In later years I had laughed heartily with Christian friends about those little books. We had wondered how we could possibly have taken such dangerous rubbish seriously. Now, as I pursued the ever-accelerating figure in front of me in the direction of my 'assessment', and mentally surveyed a succession of those hideously gothic images, I was unable to raise the faintest glimmer of a smile. I felt sick with fear. Miss Jordan was right. Oblivion suddenly looked very sweet.

But what of free will? As the ever-increasing speed of our journey forced me to break into a slow, awkward trot, I found myself wondering if the right to make decisions about my own movements had been taken away when that bus finished me off earlier. After all, a lot of other things seemed to be working in the way that they had always done. I was thinking and feeling and seeing and hearing, just as I had when I was alive. And Miss Jordan had *asked* me to follow her just now. There had been no sense of being forced to go anywhere or do anything. I asked myself what would happen if I simply stopped. Why shouldn't I stop? Would I be told off if I did? Would Miss Jordan tell me off? Would she fail to notice that I was no longer behind her and wonder where I'd got to when she arrived at the mysterious 'Waiting Room'?

The pace had gradually continued to increase, to such an extent that I was now literally running to keep up. Miss Jordan, on the other hand, seemed to be moving with a smooth gliding motion, as though she was on castors or rails instead of two human feet. Panic took away what little breath I had left as my mind filled with the ludicrous notion that I might have become a helpless Mario-like character in someone else's giant video game. Sweat began to drip from my forehead into my eyes, blurring all but the outline of that fast-moving shape in front of me. I decided that I would stop. Why shouldn't I stop? I was going to stop.

I stopped.

Relief! Sinking down on to the floor, I sat back on my heels, allowed my head to hang down on my chest, and closed my eyes. All that mattered for a moment or two was the urgent need to fill my lungs with oxygen. Eventually, as my breathing returned to normal, I became uneasily aware that something had changed in the very air around me. The sweat had become clammy on my face and body, and my arms and legs had begun to shiver with cold. Opening my eyes I found that I was in freezing, noiseless, total darkness. Raising myself on to one knee, I stretched my arms out to locate the walls of the corridor, but there were no walls. I stood up and began to move tentatively, exploring more of the space around me, but still my questing fingertips met no resistance from anything at all. There was nothing but the cold and the utter darkness.

That absolute absence of light was like nothing I had ever known during my life on earth, and yet, oddly enough, it immediately triggered clear memories of a childhood experience that had not surfaced for years.

As a small boy, waking in the early hours of the morning, I had sometimes been driven by fear or loneliness to make my way along the landing to my parents' room, always the place of ultimate security for me, as I suppose it is for most small children. Once or twice, though, it had been so pitch-black on the landing outside my bedroom that I had become paralysed with fear at about the midpoint in my journey. I would remain rooted to this spot half-way along the landing for quite a long time, unable to go forward or back for fear of the night creatures that would certainly attack me as soon as they detected the slightest movement. Three or four fairly short steps in front of me, as I knew perfectly well, was the door to my parents' room. If I could just get to that door and open it everything would be fine. A streetlamp burned all night on the pavement outside their window, so that, even when the curtains were drawn, there was always enough soft yellow light to send the hungry darkness hunting elsewhere. Three short steps to safety, and yet sometimes they were far too difficult, and three too many.

Now, in this even deeper blackness, an additional memory struck me, one I had never been aware of before. Somewhere, hidden right in the centre of that awful, rigid, darkness-ridden fear, a tiny seed of cosy excitement had been at least a small part of the reason for not hurrying to where the light was. Part of me, I now saw, had actually enjoyed being tucked into my black envelope of nothingness, and as I thought and wondered about that strange piece of truth I began dimly to perceive why.

It had to do with the fact that my very earliest recollections of being alive were heavy with an aching dread of vague, shadowy enemies who offered a constant, lowering threat, even though they were invisible and impossible to identify. And the greatest terror of all, played out over and over again in my imagination, was that these ever-watchful demons were going to pounce in an unguarded moment and make me die purely from the explosive shock of their attack. That was why doing ordinary, safe things was so dangerous. You forgot about the demons. You gave them chances to get you. Standing on the landing in the dark as a small child brought me as near as I would ever dare go to a place right outside the entrance to the cave where those monsters lived. They might still kill me, but they wouldn't be able to surprise me, and that was the most important thing of all. Out there on the landing – I was in charge.

I shivered again with cold and unhappiness. Why was I thinking things I'd never thought before, in a place where I'd never
been before and wanted to leave behind as soon as I possibly
could? Why did those distant memories suddenly seem so important? This wasn't the landing, nor was this darkness anything like
the darkness of the landing. This was a place where something
more than light was missing.

'I can't see the hope in front of my face.'

The whispering of my own voice frightened me, but it was the
truth. I was in a place that was cold with the complete absence
of possibility. I knew that if I walked or ran or staggered through
this eternity of darkness for a billion years it and I would never
become warmer, and my fingertips would never touch or be
touched by anything or anybody at all.

'I'm dead.'

Sounds comic, doesn't it? But it is true that, for a while, the
fact that I'd been recently demolished by a bus had slipped my
mind. I was dead, and I was in the hopeless dark. I should have
followed Miss Jordan to the Waiting Room. I shouldn't have
stopped. I should have taken my chance with the assessment
thingy. I should never have walked into the road so carelessly
after coming out of Boots. I should have looked after my life
properly. I should have paid real attention to priorities. I should
never have insisted on taking charge of my own . . .

My miserable musings were cut short at this point by the sudden, heart-lifting realization that my right hand had accidentally
made contact with something coldly metallic and oddly familiar.
Reaching out to the left with my other hand I encountered the
smooth surface of what felt like an emulsioned wall. At the same
time the darkness began to seem less intense. A very pale light
was filtering through diamond-shaped panes of glass in a window over to my right. Diamond-shaped panes of glass? It must
be – it could only be . . .

I was back at home, in the house where I grew up. It was
night-time and I was on the landing, stuck half-way between my

own room and the one at the front where my parents slept. With my right hand I was clinging on to the top of the old-fashioned radiator, just as I had always done when I was little, and with my left I was trying to anchor myself to the opposite wall. It was just as it had always been, except that I wasn't little – I was big, and there were important issues at stake, if I could only work out what they were.

'Go for the light. Go on, go for it now!'

That was what I told myself to do, and that was what I obediently did. I took three steps forward, turned the handle of my parents' bedroom door, and walked in. For one strange, tearfully joy-filled moment I saw my long-dead mother and father, sitting up in bed reading contentedly, just as I had always pictured them. Turning their faces to me as I entered the room, they smiled with great warmth and no apparent surprise at all, but as I moved towards them the scene disappeared abruptly and I found myself stepping into a comfortably furnished office through a door which was being politely held open for me by Miss Jordan, looking as calm, cool and efficient as ever.

'Please take a seat, Mister Porter, one of our assessors will be with you directly. Would you care for coffee?'

Coffee? After death? Surely not.

'I'd love a coffee, thanks. Err, black with one sugar please. By the way, Miss Jordan, I'm really sorry I didn't keep up with you. Didn't you say that I had to – well, shouldn't I have gone to the Waiting Room before coming here?'

She smiled faintly. 'You have just come from the Waiting Room, Mister Porter. I'll get your coffee, shall I? Black, with one sugar, wasn't it? And a biscuit?'

'Yes. Yes, thank you.'

Biscuits as well!

I was beginning to feel like Alice in Wonderland. Curiouser and curiouser. As Miss Jordan closed the door behind her I glanced around the office. Apart from the fact that, as in the grey corridor, there were no windows, nothing distinguished it or its contents from any other office I'd ever seen during my lifetime. There was a large leather-topped desk with a rather old-fashioned-looking telephone on it and, somewhat puzzlingly in the circumstances, a free-standing clock of the old chiming variety, three comfortable, upright chairs matching the one I was sitting on, and a number of very pleasing pictures on the walls, including a couple of large, richly painted landscapes and a very fine portrait in oils of a youngish man. In the corner stood a grey filing cabinet with five drawers and, on top of it, a pot containing a plant with a knobbly stalk and big, green, shiny leaves. Despite the extraordinary succession of events since my death I was even more surprised by the filing cabinet than I had been by the clock. It seemed strange that such a very solid means of information storage should be needed or necessary in the ethereal realms. And what about computers? Were there no computers in heaven? How could the names and records of all the countless billions of people who had existed throughout history be contained in five drawers? Mind you, nothing was turning out as I would have expected anyway. What was a mere filing cabinet compared to the brief encounter with my deceased parents that I had just experienced and which was still making my head spin? I wondered if I would be allowed to see them again. Surely . . .

What was that on the desk?

I leaned forward. What was that lying on the desk beside the telephone? What was that flattish, cardboard thing? It was an orange-coloured file. There was a file on the desk. Craning my neck I saw that a name was printed on the front.

MARTIN JOHN PORTER

My file was lying there, not much more than an arm's length away. MY FILE, presumably a no-holds-barred account of both my public and private lives, was sitting on that desk waiting to be opened and looked at and used to decide whether I would be convicted and despatched to the barbecue, or allowed to go to the place where I was sure my parents had gone. It suddenly occurred to me that those sixties 'evangelistic tools' of ours never got round to depicting heaven, other than in illustrations of mild, modestly dressed, happy American people, queuing on rather improbably dramatic, twisting mountain pathways as they waited with admirable Christian patience for it to be their turn to pass through the Pearly Gates. Now I came to think about it, people in the various churches I'd belonged to had always been much clearer about hell than they were about heaven.

I was just toying with the idea of reaching across to helpfully square up the corner of the file with the corner of the desk, when the door opened and Miss Jordan reappeared with my coffee and biscuit on a tray. She was closely followed by a tall, pleasantly ordinary-looking man in a smart dark suit. He must have been about thirty-five, with neatly combed, wavy fair hair and a relaxed, genial, non-threatening manner. He extended an arm to shake my hand. When he spoke, the friendliness of his tone and the sincerity of the smile that accompanied his words were all most reassuring.

'Mister Porter, how nice to meet you. My name is Philip Hammond – please call me Philip. I'm a member of the assessment team, and we shall be spending about half an hour together.'

'Oh, not eternity, then,' I joked feebly and nervously.

He laughed politely, but didn't actually respond to what I'd said. Pulling out a chair and sitting down on the other side of the desk, he leaned back and continued to smile at me, drumming lightly on the edge of the desk with his fingertips as he did so. I waited. I stirred my coffee. After a while the silence drove me into speaking again.

'I was thinking just now, err, Philip – it is Philip, isn't it?'

'Philip, yes, that's right, please call me Philip.' He nodded encouragingly.

'Well, just now when I was following – when I was on my way here, I was thinking about some really silly books we used to look at when I first became a Christian. Little – err, little sort of books, they were. Postcardish sort of size. They had awful pictures in them of what hell was going to be like, all flames and devils and people screaming in a great sort of pit. Really frightening stuff. We were terrified for a bit that it was really going to be like that. We realized how silly it was later on, of course. I mean, it's just – it's just not . . . is it?'

I had allowed a little light laugh to lift my voice as I spoke these words, my dearest wish being that the man sitting opposite would echo my ripple of amusement. We would enjoy a jolly good chuckle together about the absurdity of ever imagining that human beings might end up in such an appalling state. But there was no such reassuring echo. He just went on smiling at me. I wanted to die. But I couldn't. I already had. He leaned forward, resting his folded arms on the desk.

'Mister Porter – may I call you Martin?'

'Yes, yes, of course. I'd rather you did.'

Surely, I thought, you don't deliberately get on to Christian name terms with a man just before arranging for him to be dropped into a fiery pit for the rest of eternity, do you? Surely . . .

'Martin, am I right in thinking that you're a little puzzled about' – he spread his hands out and looked from one side of the office to the other – 'all this?'

'It is a bit surprising,' I said, taking my first sip of as good a cup of coffee as I'd ever tasted. 'I suppose if I'm honest I was expecting something a tad more – well, epic, I suppose. A bit more like Revelation.'

'The book of Revelation, you mean?'

'Yes,' I warmed a little to my theme, 'you know the sort of thing I mean – vast cataclysmic scenes with horsemen, and thousands of martyrs, and trumpets, and fire falling from heaven, and giant candlesticks and err, well, scrolls being eaten,' I finished rather lamely.

'Scrolls being eaten?'

'Well, perhaps . . . '

'That's what you expected?'

'I didn't expect biscuits.' I took a bite. The biscuit was heaven. I spoke through a mouthful of crumbs. 'The thing that's so strange is that it's such a mixture. Being in that cold, dark place just now was really weird and scary, and then I was suddenly back in my house and I saw my parents, and that was even weirder, and now I'm sitting in this office with you eating biscuits and drinking coffee, and it's as ordinary as . . . as . . . ' I searched around in my experience for the epitome of ordinariness. 'It's as ordinary as Luton.'

'Luton?'

'Luton, yes.'

'Are you glad that it's ordinary – this bit, I mean?'

'Well, I'm not sure.' I brushed biscuit crumbs from my pullover. 'It's quite sort of comforting, but it all depends what happens next. I mean, if I'm on my way to the sort of thing they had in those books I was talking about, it doesn't really make any difference how ordinary it all feels now, does it?'

Another opportunity for Philip Assessment-Person Hammond to dispel my most immediate fear. But he didn't. He sat back and smiled again.

I've never been any good at silences.

'That's my file, isn't it?' I said, pointing at the orange folder on the desk. 'Are we going to go through that together, or do you already know what's in it – or what? I suppose,' I went on, recalling an aspect of the situation that, incredibly, had hardly crossed my mind since dying, 'you have to decide whether I'm saved or not. Do you call it being saved up here?'

He shrugged good-humouredly. 'We do call it that sometimes, yes. Do you think you're saved, Martin?'

What to say? Would it be adjudged pride or humility if I assumed that I was a definite candidate for Paradise? A bold assertion that, yes, I was indeed saved would, at the very least, suggest the kind of strong faith that had always been considered so valuable in the church circles I had belonged to. Or perhaps it would be better to express a more low-key, quietly humble hope that, despite my many sins and failings, I might be redeemed, and invited to partake in eternal life. I could feel all the familiar church language coming back into my mind. Maybe that would be useful when I got going in a minute, but perhaps I should begin by throwing out a few solid, qualifying facts.

'Well, I was baptized by immersion when I was thirty-six.'

Listening to my own voice, I was all too aware that I must be coming over like an eighteen-year-old informing a prospective employer that I had a B grade in A-level Biology.

'Ah, now that's interesting,' replied Philip Hammond. He pulled the orange file towards him and opened it, flicking through the pages inside until he came to the entry he was looking for. 'Yes,' he said, running his finger down the sheet and stopping about half-way, 'that's most interesting. Tell me, Martin, *why* did you get baptized?'

Earlier on, when Miss Jordan had asked me if I was worried, I had tried to give her one answer and ended up giving her another. It had been a very bad attack of involuntary truth telling. The same thing happened now. In my mind I prepared an answer that was quite solidly orthodox – something about wanting to obey the command of Our Lord that all men should be baptized by water and by the Spirit, this being the water bit, of course. But that reply just wouldn't come out, however hard I tried. For a moment or two I sat in tongue-tied silence, quite incapable of using my mouth to frame the words that I had composed in my head.

'Well, I decided to do all the things that I might discover I'd need to have done when it came to – well, to this sort of situation, I suppose. I thought if I had the whole set it would be a good insurance. I'd be well prepared.'

I was horrified by the words that were coming out of my mouth, but I didn't seem to have any choice. Or rather, I had a choice of saying nothing at all or telling the truth. Unfortunately, I was not at all confident that the truth was going to do me any good.

'The whole set?' Philip Hammond closed my file and, resting both elbows on the desk and his chin on his interlinked fingers, regarded me quizzically. 'What do you mean by the whole set?'

'You know – baptism, repentance, asking Jesus into your life. What else? Oh, yes – acknowledging the redemptive power of his death and resurrection, confessing your faith before men, all those things – the whole set. I've got them all. I was scared that I might get left behind or go to hell so I made a list of all the things I needed to do to get saved, and then I ticked them off one by one as I went along. I've done all those things. They should be in the file. Are they?'

'Hold on – we'll talk about your file again in a minute. Just going back to your baptism for a moment, the first one in the err, set. Tell me, did you give something called a testimony before going into the water?'

'Yes. Yes, I did do that, just a few words about why I was doing it – why I wanted to be baptized, that's all it was. Everyone at our church did that when they were dunked – baptized, I mean.'

'What did you say in that testimony?'

I cleared my throat. Sadly, I seemed to have total recall.

'Err, I believe I started by saying that I'd recently heard the Lord speaking very clearly about the fact that baptism was his will for me, and that I was simply being obedient to his command.'

'And was that true?'

Oh, dear.

'Do you have an equivalent up here to the fifth amendment?'

He sat back and laughed. 'You mean the thing about not having to say anything that might incriminate you? Well, we don't, but if we had you'd be very ill-advised to take advantage of it. Are you saying that you were not entirely honest in your testimony?'

I squirmed and wriggled, but there was no help for it. Out came the truth.

'Well, I certainly never actually heard God speaking directly to me about being baptized, but I sort of persuaded myself that I had a ... a feeling that he was putting the idea into my mind. I really wanted to be able to say that I had been clearly called, so I just ... well, tidied up the truth until it looked a bit more convincing. In any case, that was how you talked about that sort of thing at our church. I don't remember anyone ever getting up at their baptism and saying that they had a vague feeling that God could possibly be telling them to get baptized, and it was worth doing anyway, because it would be good spiritual insurance. You just didn't talk like that at our church.'

'All the ideas were in ready-made packets?'

I nodded. 'Yes, in a way, I suppose they were.'

'And what about the "simply being obedient to his command" bit?'

'Well, like I said, a lot of it was fear. Everyone seemed so *sure* – do you know what I mean?'

'Yes, I think so.'

'It was quite frightening when I looked inside myself to find just how *not* sure I was, if you know what I mean. I suppose I thought – well, if they've got it all sussed out it must make sense to go along with whatever they said you had to do. So I did.' I was silent for a moment. 'I did talk to God about it though, you know. It was the night before. I suddenly got all embarrassed about the idea of looking a twit in front of loads of people in my soaking wet nightgown. I remember it clearly because I was watching the end of "Question Time" on the television, one of my favourite programmes, so it must have been a Thursday evening. I felt so bad that I turned the TV off.'

Philip Hammond registered mock amazement. 'You actually turned it off!'

'Well, you're right, that was rather unusual. Anyway, I did turn it off and tried to ... to be with God. Told him how nervous I was and asked him to help me get through it. And I said how much I wanted to have a real experience of him, right there in the sitting-room.'

'And did you?'

I wondered if I might have picked up some kind of throat complaint in that cold, dark place just now. I had the greatest difficulty in serving up the next portion of ungarnished truth.

'Hmm, I may well have been about to have a real experience of him, but just at that moment I noticed the clock and realized the snooker was coming on at any moment, so I turned the television back on and – well, kept one eye on that while I was waiting for my err . . . experience of God to happen.'

He tilted his head to one side and frowned at the desk for a moment. 'So, you were waiting for God to speak to you in roughly the same way that you might have kept half an eye open for the bus while you were watching the telly in a shop window just up the road from the bus-stop. Does that sum it up?'

'Well, yes, I'm afraid it does.'

'When you said at your baptism . . . ' he studied the file for a moment, 'when you said that the Lord had "spoken clearly to you" the night before, you actually meant that he might have been going to, but you were so engrossed in the fact that Willie Thorne was heading for a possible clearance that you couldn't be absolutely sure.'

'Well . . . '

Philip Hammond suddenly threw back his head and laughed like a drain.

All very well, I thought, watching him, but where does all this leave me? When he's finished laughing his head off, is he going to put on some sort of divine black cap and shovel me off into the hands of those grinning devils with their pitchforks? If so, the merriment seemed more than a little inappropriate. He finished laughing at last and, wiping his eyes with the knuckle of one hand, spoke apologetically.

'Please forgive me, Martin, I really shouldn't have laughed like that. I suppose it's just that I never cease to be amazed and amused by the gap between the public face of what's known as Christianity, and the way things actually are for people who call themselves Christians. Seek the Lord with all your heart in the short gap between "Question Time" and the "World Snooker Championship". Marvellous!'

He shook his head as if to clear it, then bent over the file again, moving papers slowly from one side of the desk to the other. At last he picked one page up and studied it for a few moments. When he spoke again his voice was very soft.

'There was a time when you were much more sure, wasn't there, Martin? What happened?'

Oh, dear. Into the shadows.

'My father died.'

'Fairly recently?'

'Yes, a while before my baptism.'

'Your mother died when you were much younger, didn't she?'

'I was at boarding school. She got suddenly ill and died. Then Dad said I could stop being at boarding school because she was the only one who wanted me to go, and I was so pleased it was like being wrapped in cotton-wool. Mum dying was awful, but I was at home and Dad was there. Everything was soon all right.'

'But your father's death was different?'

I felt sick suddenly. 'Have I really got to go through all this?'

Philip Hammond didn't say a word. He just sat back in his chair quite calmly with his arms folded, waiting for me to get on with whatever I decided to do. I buried my face in my hands for a moment, fearful of the truth that I already knew so well. Oh, well, in for a penny . . .

Raising my head I said, 'I was feeling pretty sure about God and heaven and all that in the time leading up to when he died. Heaven especially. I really thought I'd got it all in perspective. Jesus would be waiting for us, and all the most beautiful things on earth – well, the essence of all those things would be there because – because the person who made them was going to be there.'

'What sort of things?'

'*All* sorts of things. One great long Mary Poppins list, only with different things in it – different things for each person, I mean.'

'Like a 147 snooker clearance, for instance?'

'Well, yes, I'd like to think that could be arranged for me – that would be wonderful.' I sighed ecstatically. 'But, no, seriously, I was really confident most of the time about, you know, going to be with Jesus and salvation and all the rest of it. It's true that every now and then I'd have a sudden attack of total disbelief and wonder why I wasn't out doing as many enjoyably evil things as I could before I shuffled off my mortal coil, but most of the time I felt good about it all, and I even used to tell other people what I believed. Some of them got quite interested – well, more than interested. We started a little group ... '

'What happened when your father died?'

I took a deep breath, feeling all the pain of that day and so many of the days that had followed, as though some sort of emotional photograph had been taken at the moment of his death and had remained on view ever after to my inner eye.

'I was at the hospital – had been on and off for more than a fortnight. We'd been through the same pattern over and over again. Dad would seem to go right down and look as if he couldn't possibly come through, and then he'd suddenly pick up and be talking and chatting as though hardly anything was wrong at all. Two or three times I said goodnight to him before going home to get some sleep, thinking that I was really saying goodbye. And then, in the morning, there he'd be, sitting up in bed telling the nurses off because he hadn't been given any breakfast. It all got very wearing in the end – I don't mean that I wasn't pleased he pulled through each time – course I was. It was just that, in a way, you see, I was experiencing all the pain of losing him every few days, followed by all the relief of still having him afterwards, and I was getting plain exhausted by this weird rollercoaster ride. And then, quite suddenly, he went. He just stopped breathing when he was asleep one morning and went.'

'You took it hard?'

'I took it in all sorts of ways. I was struck straightaway by the big gap between knowing someone's going to die, and knowing they have died. People say you can prepare yourself. I thought I had. But I hadn't really. It was a huge shock. A bit like being indoors and suddenly the whole house except for the floor you're sitting on flies up into the air and disappears into the far distance in a split second.'

Philip Hammond nodded gently but said nothing.

I remembered something.

'In the town near where I live there used to be a big super-market about fifty yards back from the main road in the centre of town, with a Chinese restaurant over the top. So every time you walked along the High Street it was there ... part of the scenery, even if you didn't actually really register it. Then, one night, there was a fire and the whole thing burned down. Nearly caught the other buildings but the firemen did a great job, appar-ently. Well, I read about it in the papers the next morning, and everyone was talking about it, of course, but, as it happened, I didn't have any reason to go into town for two or three days after that, and when I did I was so absorbed by whatever I was doing or looking for that I completely forgot about the fire. I'd walked about half-way up the High Street when I suddenly realized that something was all wrong.'

'There was a gap?'

'Yes, the very shape of that part of the world had changed, and because I'd forgotten about the fire I couldn't understand it. I felt as if I'd wandered into some kind of parallel universe or something. Then I remembered, of course, and felt stupid. Dad's death was a bit like that. One huge piece of my personal scenery had gone, and I felt lost and disoriented. The world was the wrong shape. All those decades of personality and life and significance and – I dunno – sheer existence, just extinguished in an instant. Such a *big* thing to happen, and such a ... a profound silence afterwards.

'The only thing was – I do remember that for two or three days after his death, we had the most amazing skies in our part of the country. Great big, extravagant brush-strokes of gold and grey and silver, with the sun pouring white light through the gaps as if the budget for special effects had been doubled. And I remember thinking that there must be some kind of celebration going on in heaven, and hoping that it might be because dad had arrived there. Made me feel quite good for a while, but only a while.'

'Were you sure he was in heaven?'

There are some questions that cannot produce anything as simple as a reply that is truthful or untruthful. I suppose I mean the kind of questions where you don't really know what you think yourself, and even if you do, there may be another reply just under the surface of what you are thinking and saying that is more true than the answer in the front of your mind. This question from Philip Hammond was like that, and I was interested, in view of my newly acquired truth-telling mechanism, to discover what kind of response I would offer him. I found myself looking into the past and seeing my father's dead face on the pillow as I had seen it only minutes after his death.

'The thing is . . . ' This was difficult. 'The thing is that he was *so dead*. He was so dead.' I felt a sob rising in my throat. 'He was as dead as it's possible to be. He'd dropped out or gone away from that thing lying on the hospital bed, and it was as if a giant full-stop had gone splat! on the end of his life. Of course, all my Christian mechanism creaked into gear – he'd gone to heaven, we would meet again – all that. But . . . '

'But what?'

The truth.

'There was a little fear in me, a . . . a little dark bud of panic.'

'A fear of what?'

'A fear of nothing. A fear that there was nothing. A fear that my dad had just stopped existing. A fear that all my talking and thinking about Jesus and God and heaven amounted, in the end, to . . . nothing.'

'And did that feeling last?'

'Not like that, no. Not in that form. I got pretty warmed up to it all again, I had to or I'd have gone mad, but from the day he died until right now the gap has been just too wide.'

'Ah!' said Philip Hammond. 'Tell me about the gap.'

'You're going to think I'm very silly.'

'On the contrary, Martin, you appear quite sane to me, and I can assure you that I do know the difference. I meet some extraordinarily deluded people in the course of my work. And they are the saddest ones, those who have worked so hard on believing the lies they tell, that lies have become the only truth they know. So sad.'

I felt ridiculously pleased by this faint praise, but I couldn't see that it would help particularly. Sanity was not likely to be a primary qualification for heaven, was it?

'Tell me about the gap,' said Philip Hammond again.

'When I was a boy ... ' I began. I stopped as it suddenly occurred to me to wonder why that orange file of mine on the desk was so thin. Bit worrying. I'd ask in a minute. 'When I was a boy my brother and I spent a lot of time playing in the farmer's field just down the lane from where we lived. There was this wooded area at the bottom of the field, and in the middle of it there was a stream with steep banks sloping down to it on both sides. We used to pretend we were cowboys, and the idea was that we'd gallop our imaginary horses down the side of what we always called "the Grand Canyon", then leap majestically over the raging torrent beneath us. Well, my brother, who was a year or so older than me, with much longer legs, had no trouble with the "leaping majestically" part of the exercise. Over he went every single time, whooping loudly, and he'd land safely on the other side after almost every jump he did. One or two disasters, but they never seemed to put him off. He still operates in exactly the same way on the stock exchange now that he's supposed to be grown up.

'Me, though, I never wanted to jump over that stream. The raging torrent was actually a fairly mildly flowing brook, you understand, but the banks were quite high and there were a lot of angry-looking stones on the bed of that little stretch of water. I was terrified that I'd fall short of the opposite bank and hurt myself badly. I used to stand on one bank and measure the distance with my eye, and ask myself if I really thought I could reach the other side, even if I did my very best, best possible jump. And the answer was always that I couldn't. I knew I couldn't. It was just a couple of feet too wide for me to get across.

'My brother was always very good about it, mind you. We entered into a sort of unspoken agreement that my horse was temporarily lame, and needed to be led gently over the good old raging torrent using some stepping stones a few yards further down stream. He was good like that, my brother. Still is – was – is.'

'Is,' said Philip Hammond helpfully.

'Is, yes. Anyway, what I was going on to tell you was that after my father died I found myself, every now and then, slipping into an extraordinarily vivid daydream, a very silly daydream probably, but it says what I'm trying to say much better than I could. I still have it sometimes, especially when I'm not very confident. What happens is that I'm about ten years old again, grey shorts, knobbly knees and all, and I'm back at the top of the bank that sloped down to that stream where we played when I was young, and it's all more or less the way it used to be except that my brother isn't there, and I'm nervous – really nervous. Because I've sneaked down there on my own to prove to myself that, actually, I *can* do that frightening jump I've always chickened out of in the past. I'm jolly well *going* to do it, so that next time I'm down there with my brother, I shall be able to go sailing over and amaze him.

'So there I am, and I get all revved up, and I clench my fists and gather up all my courage, and away I go running down the slope. But even as I'm racing along I find I'm measuring up the distance I'll have to cover to cross the raging trickle, and I can feel my legs slowing down, and I know nothing has changed. I'm not going to make it. And I never do. I screech to a halt when I reach the edge – just freeze, and feel like a silly failure all over again. The gap is too wide.

'And my problem with believing has been like that. It started at the moment when I saw my father looking so ... so dead. I can't tell you how not-there he was, Philip. The gap between knowing what's true and real about the world and being alive – all the things you can see and feel and smell and whatever the other things you do with your senses are – the gap between that and believing there really is a heaven where individual people go on living and recognizing one another, and having the tears wiped from their eyes by God like the Bible says he's going to, is just too … '

I was quite glad to hear the telephone ring at that moment. I felt as if I could easily have got a bit carried away.

'Excuse me.'

Philip Hammond picked up the receiver and put it to his ear. I listened as he spoke quietly to the person on the other end.

'Yes? … Oh, yes … Excellent! … Yes, that would be just about right, we should be finished here fairly soon … Yes, I'm sure he will … No, not yet, but I'm quite sure the decision will be … Thank you … Yes, I will – goodbye.'

He placed the receiver gently down on its cradle and looked up at me, a little smile playing around his lips.

'Why is my file so thin?' I asked.

'Thin?' he said. 'Oh, well, just the most important things in here.' He picked up the orange folder and flicked through it again. 'Records of a few occasions when you've put yourself second – few but significant. And then, perhaps most importantly, there is the experience you had at six-thirty on October the fifteenth twenty-two years ago. Remember that?'

'My conversion, you mean?'

'I don't know if I'd call it that.'

Oh, dear.

'What would you call it, then?'

'It doesn't matter what I'd call it, Martin. The only thing that matters is that on that day you called out to Jesus and he heard you. He does also, as a matter of interest, hear some who, as far as they are aware, never did call out to him.'

'Philip,' I spoke in a very small voice, 'I did call out to him, and I did mean it, but – well, I don't think I love him as much as you're supposed . . . well, as much as everyone seemed to think you should really.'

'Oh, but Martin,' said Philip Hammond, with something that really did look suspiciously like a tear appearing in his eye, 'wait till you find out how much he loves you.'

A great shuddering sigh of hope and weariness passed through my entire being. 'So, you mean I'm . . . '

'You really do like to get hold of those little ready-made packets of truth, don't you? Aren't you interested to know who that was on the phone?'

'Am I allowed to know?'

'Certainly, it was your father.'

For a full thirty seconds I sat and stared at him. When I did speak at last it only felt safe to whisper. It was like those adventure stories where the trapped hero pulls a length of cotton with enormous care in order to grasp the length of string attached to it, which in turn is connected to the length of rope which is what he really needed in the first place. I didn't want to frighten this fragile possibility away.

'My father was speaking to you on the phone just then? *My father?* Are you seriously telling me that my father is . . . is somewhere near here? Alive, and near here?'

'Just through that door,' smiled Philip Hammond, indicating a door in the wall to the right of his desk that had certainly not been there when I first came into the office. 'You can go and see him now if you wish.'

I rose slowly from the chair I'd been occupying, my eyes fixed, wide and unblinking like a child's, on that insubstantial-looking wooden rectangle which, if this man was telling me the truth, was the only thing separating me from the person I loved so deeply and had so miserably feared was lost to me for ever.

'Just through that door?'

He gestured agreement with his arm. I didn't want to find out if he was right in case he wasn't. It took me an age to cross the room and actually take hold of the door handle. I turned back as something occurred to me.

128

'Is that it? Has the . . . is the assessment finished?'

'Almost. You carry on. I'll see you later.'

'Right – thanks. Thank you very much, err, Philip.'

Still I lingered. 'Tell me, is this normal procedure?'

'Normal procedure?'

I waved a hand vaguely around the room. 'All this. This office and the corridor and all the rest of it. Does this happen to everyone who comes through the . . . the system?'

'Every person is equally important,' he replied, 'but the things that are happening to you are . . . for you.'

'This isn't going to turn out to be a dream, is it?'

'Do you want to wake up, Martin, or do you want to go through that door and meet your father?'

'I . . . I want to meet my father.'

I wasn't actually aware of opening the door and passing through to the other side, but it seemed to happen in a trice. I was conscious only of hearing the door slam behind me, and the sudden impact of finding myself in a completely different and totally unexpected environment. The bright hope in my heart was switched off like a light bulb in a power-cut as I blinked and looked around, for a cruel joke had been played on me. Far from finding myself in an adjacent room as I had imagined would be the case, I had somehow been transported to the very scene that I had been describing to Philip Hammond just now. The door, the office, the grey corridor, the people I had met – all had disappeared without trace. Instead, when I turned my head, I saw the gently sloping field that had once been so familiar to me, its cattle-cropped grass reflecting that bright, motherly species of sunshine that always seemed to adorn Saturday mornings when I was a child. Before me, dropping away directly from where I stood, was the steep slope that led down to the stream where I had known my first real experience of failure. It was just as it had always been.

Where *was* my father? Why was I standing here, instead of seeing him as I had been promised? A sudden fear gripped me.

Suppose I had, in fact, failed this assessment process, or whatever it was called, and the only way to get me out of the office was to promise me something I really wanted, so that I'd go without making a fuss? I gazed down the slope again. From where I was standing the stream looked wider than ever. What if Martin John Porter's bespoke hell was ordained to be an endless repetition of his failure to attempt the leap from one side of the raging torrent to the other? Eternal frustration and disappointment, together with the knowledge that I would be mocked perpetually by this glittering morning, so sweetly fragrant with hope. I shook my head slowly from side to side, longing to opt for the dream, hoping that it was still possible to refuse the fate that seemed to lie before me.

Only one thing possible.

Letting the weight of my body take me, I began to run before I had a chance to change my mind. I ran like the wind, managing to keep my balance only through a succession of small miracles, allowing gravity to carry me down the steep gradient with such exaggeratedly extended strides and at such a rate that I knew there was never going to be any question of stopping on the near side of the stream. I didn't want to. Even if it meant smashing on to those rocks at the speed I was travelling now, I didn't want to.

When my right foot thumped on to the turf at the edge of the nearest bank of the stream, I shut my eyes and pushed my whole self upwards and forwards with every ounce of strength that was left in me. When I opened them a split second later I saw, with a surge of pure joy, that my wild, last-ditch leap was indeed carrying me to the opposite bank of the raging torrent.

The other thing I saw in that eternally fulfilling moment was my father, his arms outstretched, waiting to steady me as I landed on the other side.

Posthumous Cake

Granny Partington died just before eleven o'clock on a Wednesday morning in the middle of the greyest, drizzliest October there had ever been. She caused as little trouble in her dying as she had done in her living. The little self-contained unit, specially built on to the side of her son's house, was as clean and cosy and friendly as it had been since she first moved in with all her bits and pieces ten years ago. There had been no long distressing illness, despite the fact that Granny was only a week short of her ninetieth birthday, and all her important papers, including a will that carefully divided three hundred pounds into four legacies of seventy-five pounds each for the children, were neatly bundled and beribboned in the small roll-top desk next to the television.

Rachel Partington had been shopping on that Wednesday morning. She came straight from the car to the annexe with Granny's old cloth bag in one hand and a half-wrecked umbrella clutched optimistically in the other. Coffee with her mother-in-law was not a duty for Rachel. Mum was the only person who accepted her for what she was. They were best friends.

As she stood in the tiny porch, wrestling her umbrella into subjection and flapping out of her son's absurdly large wellington boots, Rachel chattered happily.

131

'I got you a *Mail*, Mum, 'cause all the *Expresses* had gone, and I found a really nice bit of beef in the cheap trolley – nothing wrong with it at all. Oh, and you do have to sign the form yourself, they won't let me do it. If you sign it now, Bob can pop it in when he gets home, and . . . Mum?'

No comfortable response noises. No oohs and aahs of warm appreciation and reassurance. No flap of slippers on the kitchen floor. No clink of coffee cups and saucers (Mum couldn't abide mugs). No rush of water into the old tin kettle. No Granny sounds at all.

Rachel found her best friend lying on the bed in her slip, one hand cradling her powdered cheek on the pillow like a child. Later, Rachel wondered why she had been so certain that Mum was dead.

'I just knew,' she said to Bob that afternoon, 'and I . . . I lay down next to her on the bed for a minute and said goodbye, and cried for a while. It sounds silly, but I wished I'd stayed in the porch for ever, pulling those ridiculous boots off. Oh, Bob, I didn't even have a chance to give Mum her shopping, and it was such a lovely little bit of beef . . . '

Everyone was in for tea that day, but it was a very quiet meal to begin with. They had all heard by then.

Lucy, the youngest, kept staring into the far distance, her four-year-old brows knitted with the effort of understanding what 'no more Granny' could possibly mean.

Benjamin was eighteen. He had many strong and radical views, but Granny Partington was not an aspect of life. She was a safe place – a secret repository for his trust in human beings. Inside, he wept like the weather.

The twins, Frank and Dominic, had suspended hostilities as soon as they heard about Granny, both of them crying openly, one at the top of the stairs and one at the bottom, curled up like hampsters with their grief. Frank was still sniffling now, as he sucked orange squash through a plastic straw and ate his beans and sausages. Dominic was white and quiet. He ate and drank nothing. The twins were nearly ten.

Rachel looked across at Bob. He was being very strong and supportive with everyone else, but there was a greyness about his cheeks and mouth that she hadn't seen since Lucy had come so close to dying in hospital three and a half years ago.

Rachel stood up. It was time. 'I've got something to show you all,' she announced. Reaching into the larder behind her, she took out a jam sponge on a plate and placed it in the middle of the tea-table. 'Look,' she said, 'Granny made a sponge for us. I found it in her cupboard. She'll have made it this morning.'

'It must have been the last thing she did.' Bob's voice broke very slightly for the first time.

'A posthumous cake,' murmured Ben.

'Can we have some?' said Frank.

Rachel sat down, picked up a knife and began to cut the sponge.

'I'm going to cut it into six pieces,' she explained, 'so that we can have one slice each. But no one's allowed to eat a single crumb until they've reminded us of one special thing about Granny.'

Silence fell. Six pieces of cake lay untasted on six plates. Granny's sponges were famous in the Partington universe. Like so many cooks of her generation, the old lady had produced these delicious creations by throwing what appeared to be randomly measured handfuls of ingredients into a bowl, stirring them up a bit, then sticking the mixture in an oven. The results were always perfect. This was the last one they would ever eat.

'I know a special thing about Granny,' said Frank. 'She gave us two pounds on our birthdays, and we always knew it was a lot.'

Rachel smiled and nodded. Granny had always put two pound coins in an envelope for each of the children when their birthdays came, and because everyone knew that two pounds was a lot for Granny to give, they treated it as a big and important gift. It was one of the things that had reassured Rachel about her children.

'She was very good at enjoying things, wasn't she?'

'What do you mean, Ben?' asked his father.

133

'Well, she always thought everything was really nice and sort of sparkly. If you bought her a cup of tea when you were out it wasn't just an ordinary cup of tea, it was a *wonderful* cup of tea. And if you were walking somewhere she noticed all the flowers and the houses and the people. I dunno, she was just good at being happy. Not many people are, are they?'

'Aren't they?' enquired Lucy, who was a very happy child. 'I thought they were.'

'What do you remember most about Granny, darling?'

'I'm not saying this just because I want to eat my piece of cake, Daddy.'

'Of course not, sweetheart.' Bob spoke solemnly.

'What I remember most about Granny is her cuddles. She loved me,' added Lucy, looking around proudly.

'Her face is like that puff-pastry stuff,' mumbled Dominic, unexpectedly. 'I squeeze it hard with my hands, and she says "Go on with you, you'll squash my nose off", and we laugh and she gives me a biscuit.' A huge tear rolled out of the little boy's eye and dropped with a plop on to the plate beside his piece of cake.

Rachel put her arm round Dominic's shoulders and rested her face on the top of his head. 'The thing I shall always love about Granny,' she said, 'is that she never made me feel useless and silly, even though I am useless and silly a lot of the time. She made me feel good. I'll miss her so much – we all will.' She paused for a moment. 'Bob, you haven't said anything.'

He stirred and spoke. 'I was just thinking – while you were all saying those excellent things – that I've always used Granny as a sort of ruler, a kind of measure, I suppose. Granny loved all of us, but she loved Jesus as well.' He stopped and looked at Ben for a moment. 'I know some of us aren't quite sure what we think about all that at the moment, and that's all right, but she really loved him and she lived her life the way she believed he wanted her to. Every time I went to a talk or heard a sermon or read a book about what we ought to do or how we ought to feel, I used to think about my old mum. She didn't talk about it much, but she lived it. They won't ever put her in one of those Famous Christian books, but she *was* it. She was *doing* it as well as it could be done, I reckon.'

'Can we eat our cake now?'

'Course we can, Lucy,' said Rachel. 'We'll all eat our cake now.' She looked at the ceiling. 'Thanks, Granny.'

'Thanks, Granny,' echoed everybody except Dominic.

Nobody said anything else until the last mouthful of sponge had been eaten. Then Frank pointed at the plate in the middle of the table.

'There's some little bits left, Dad,' he said, his brow furrowed with the effort of trying to remember something important, 'aren't you supposed to eat it all up before you wash the plate?'

'You're thinking of something else,' said Ben.

'No, he's not,' murmured Rachel, as her husband collected the remaining crumbs and put them in his mouth.

Why It Was All Right to Kill Uncle Reginald

My solicitor, Miss Cudlip, has requested that I provide a detailed account of my reasons for executing Uncle Reginald and a full description of the means by which I accomplished the task. This I am more than pleased to do. I would, however, like to make two points first, both of which are crucial to an accurate understanding of my position.

(a) I am not in favour of murder or any other crime. I have, throughout my life, been an exemplary citizen. In forty years I cannot, immodest though the claim must seem, recall a single instance of deliberate illegality. Furthermore, my morality with regard to 'relationships' has been consistently sound. As far as I can tell I have caused emotional hurt to no person, nor have I succumbed to the lure of brief amorous adventures as many men seem to. Miss 'Right' may possibly appear at some point, but if she does not then I am content.

As to my work, I have been employed for the last twenty years as chief assistant (there is one young person underneath me) at a shop which retails smart, traditional clothing, and I should be most surprised if Mr Robards, the manager, were to offer any but positive comments on my behalf.

My original decision to accommodate Uncle Reginald over the last ten years was, furthermore, based on charitable motives. One of my poor mother's final requests was that, when she died, and her room became available, I should invite her brother Reginald to live with me in the house that I would, of course, inherit from her. Mother did not actually frame this as a request, more perhaps in the form of an instruction. After her death I was naturally no longer obliged to carry out her wishes, but a certain mental discomfort prompted me, voluntarily, to remember her words as a plea rather than an order. Accordingly, I invited Uncle Reginald to sell his large house in Eastbourne and move into my much humbler little dwelling near Heathfield. A retired insurance person, relatively fit and of exceedingly regular habits, he seemed an ideal person with whom to share my home, and I experienced none but familial and benevolent feelings towards him for the whole of the first year that he was *in situ*.

My first point in brief, then, is that I am not the murdering type of person and that what has happened *cannot* be classified as murder. Like killing in wartime and the destruction of dangerous wild creatures, my execution of Uncle Reginald was wholly justified and I am quite certain that there is not a judge and jury in the land who, having examined the evidence, would not be anxious to speedily expedite my return to my own little home and the good offices of Mr Robards, who must be severely stretched with a solitary young person on his staff. But what, you may ask, is this evidence of which I speak? This leads me into my second point.

(b) In the bottom drawer of the walnut bureau in the hall at the foot of the stairs, you will find two cardboard containers, each measuring approximately six inches by three inches. Each one is labelled on one of the large sides in thick orange marker-pen. The top one is entitled *Breakfast,* and the bottom one *Lunch,* or it may possibly be *Sunday Lunch*. Each box contains a video tape of Uncle Reginald consuming a meal, and it is essential that this statement should be read in conjunction with the screening of these visual documents. I imagine that it is entirely possible for a large-screened television set to be made available in the courtroom for the benefit of jurors. I would myself not be at all averse to reading this account from the witness-box, while all others present view my two little programmes in the order that I have already listed them. I have no doubt whatsoever that all who see Uncle Reginald in action at the table will not only applaud my subsequent decision, but will heartily wish that they themselves had been permitted to be partakers in his dissolution.

The substance of my second point, then, is that there is more than ample evidence of my complete sanity, the video tapes and this document being the bulk of that evidence. In addition there is my own general demeanour. I make it a point never to express anger or resentment to others, despite (as you shall shortly hear) extreme provocation from Uncle Reginald. I recall, for instance, an occasion when Mr Robards felt it necessary to be quite scathingly critical about a window-display over which I had worked for many hours. Despite the intensity of my inner feelings I merely nodded patiently and agreed to alter completely what I considered to be a most pleasant arrangement. Not only that, but when, later that same day, Mr Robards, in the course of negotiating the very narrow and poorly lit stairs down to our little staff lavatory, tripped over a box that I had inadvertently left on the second step and fell heavily onto the concrete floor below, suffering quite severe bruising, I displayed not a trace of pleasure or satisfaction. On the contrary I helped him to his feet, bade him sit quietly in the easy chair at the rear of the shop, and prepared a mug of hot, sweet tea to restore his nerves. Does an insane person exhibit such self-control? I think not.

If any further indication of my healthy mental state is required, there is the manner in which I set about the preparation of my televisual record of Uncle Reginald's abominable practices. I made the decision to enquire into the possibilities of video tape recording, only after it had become clear that execution was the only appropriate response to the unspeakable things that I was forced to witness and endure day after day.

It seems strange (to digress a little) that a whole year passed before the range and repulsiveness of my Uncle's eating habits began to impress themselves upon me. Certainly I had perceived a remarkable consistency of pattern in his behaviour at the table, but our general relations had been good, if quiet, and I tended to regard his predictability as a virtue rather than a vice. I believe that the first thing to jar unpleasantly upon me was the click in Uncle Reginald's jaw. When I say in his jaw I mean, of course, that it was a click that occurred when Uncle Reginald was using his jaws, when he was chewing in other words. Let me say immediately that it was not a loud click, nor did it occur with every masticatory movement of the jaw. It was the sound one might make by flicking a thumbnail against a fingernail on the same hand, and for some physiological reason that is beyond my comprehension, it seemed to occur on every alternate closing motion of the mouth. When I add that each click was accompanied or instantly followed by an infinitesimal but unmistakable lateral movement of the upper jaw as it met the lower, you will perhaps begin to sense the horror of my position. I do not wish to embarrass the Court with gratuitous obscenities, but I think it important to my case to point out that, occasionally, a fragment of non-solid food would be resting on the lower lip at the moment when the upper lip descended. The effect of the lateral jaw movement in this case was to smear the food along the lower lip and on occasions to spurt a tiny amount of it onto the outer edge of that same lower lip or even, but much more rarely, onto his chin, which was covered with wiry red whiskers.

Naturally, the observation and identification of these details and patterns took place over a period of many months, but certainly, by the time Uncle Reginald had been living in my house for eighteen months, I was occupied for the majority of each meal-time that we spent together with the nightmare of awaiting each individual click and each tiny untoward movement of the jaw. My own eating I developed into a virtually soundless activity so that I should miss no detail of the foul performance before me. I was particularly clever in the way in which I learned to impale and cut food without my knife or fork coming into contact with the plate, thus avoiding those loathsome scraping and clacking noises which notoriously result from the contact of steel on china. Once I had mastered this skill to the point where I could consume meals not only soundlessly but with the barest and most infrequent glances at my own plate, I was able to give my full attention to Uncle Reginald's nauseous activities which, over the next few months, I discovered to my horror, were far from being confined to the details I had already noticed. To my amazement I discovered that every single aspect of my Uncle's ingestive behaviour possessed the same repulsive quality. After more than eight years of studying, listing and inwardly digesting the full facts of the case, I knew that Uncle Reginald should be executed and that I was to be the agent.

I procured my video equipment from a small but reputable firm whose retail outlet is situated in a long, busy road of shops which runs parallel to the promenade in the seaside town that lies a few miles to the south of Heathfield. I was advised and assisted by a most amiable and helpful young man who, very early on in the proceedings, made the false but quite under-standable assumption that I required equipment for the purpose of recording the activities of domestic pets of some kind. It seemed wise to allow this misunderstanding to continue, as the technical problems and demands appeared to be similar, espe-cially with regard to the matter of recording small and not eas-ily distinguishable sounds, such as hamsters squeaking (or jaws clicking). I learned that my best plan would be to arrange what I believe the young man referred to as an 'add on' microphone at a point as close as possible to the sound source in question. As to the all-in-one camera and recording machine, a model was available which combined two very desirable virtues. It was extremely easy for a novice to operate and very little in the way of extra lighting was needed over and above the level of light one might find in an average kitchen lit by the type of strip lighting that is installed in my own house. My adviser suggested that a small spotlight of the domestic variety would be an ideal adjunct

to the normal illumination of the room, and as I already possessed such an appliance, the business of lighting required no further consideration.

In the matter of payment, I received an extremely welcome
surprise. Expecting that it would be necessary to purchase the
equipment, I had taken my building society book from the top
drawer of the bureau and was quite prepared to draw out whatever sum was needed for the purpose. (My account had swollen
at the time of Mother's death, and much interest had accrued
since then.) Imagine my pleasure on learning that it was possible
to hire the camera and microphone for a total of thirty pounds
for an entire weekend. I left the shop with my equipment, a book
of operating instructions, and a deep sense of well-being at the
accomplishment of the first part of my plan.

That evening, after Uncle Reginald had retired to bed at nine
forty-seven as usual, I set up the camera in a corner of the kitchen
and focused on the back of Uncle Reginald's chair. I then connected one end of the microphone lead to the camera recorder,
and having laid the kitchen table for breakfast, placed the microphone itself on a small plastic stand (supplied by the shop) so
that it was pointing towards a spot midway between Uncle Reginald's cereal bowl and the place where his face would normally
be during the act of consumption. When I was satisfied that all
was as it should be, I went up to my own bedroom but was
unable to sleep for some time owing to an excess of excitement
and anticipation concerning the following day. Despite this, however, I am totally sure that if someone had quite suddenly
switched on my bedroom light as I lay on my back in bed, they
could have detected not so much as a flicker on my face or in my
posture to betray that excitement. I believe my fists may have
been slightly clenched, but that was all.

In the morning (Saturday morning) I arose early and unclamp-
ing the small spotlight from the second bookshelf down beside
my window, I carried it downstairs, and after attaching it to one
side of the small cupboard in the top of the kitchen cabinet,

adjusted the angle of its beam until it covered the area soon to be occupied by the top half of Uncle Reginald's body. My sole remaining task before all preparations were complete was to account to Uncle Reginald for the sudden appearance of the appliance facing him from the corner of the room and the microphone standing beside his place on the table. This was rendered quite simple by two things: my uncle's vague geniality (in matters other than eating) and the existence of Cousin Hubert in New Zealand. Hubert is the only child of my mother's older brother Desmond (now deceased). He writes very infrequently and has had no actual contact with relatives at home for thirty years. I informed Uncle Reginald that Hubert had written to me requesting photographs of surviving members of the family, and in particular his Uncle Reginald, of whom he retained very fond memories despite the long period since their last meeting. I had decided, I said, to send Hubert a video tape rather than photographs, and over the weekend I would be recording brief extracts from an appropriately commonplace activity – namely the eating of meals – so that Hubert would be able to witness our ordinary, family, day-to-day living. I added that the equipment would sometimes be operating and sometimes not, thus implying that I had some kind of remote control over the machinery, and that Uncle Reginald should do nothing out of the ordinary for the benefit of the camera. I also pointed out that I would, from time to time, need to leave the table to refocus or adjust the lens, and apologized in advance for the disruption this would cause in our customarily well ordered meal-times.

Uncle Reginald's response to my remarks was precisely as I had anticipated. He appeared pleased, if a little surprised, that Hubert held him in such fond regard, and he was impressed but totally baffled by my television equipment. By the end of Saturday he had become quite accustomed to my occasional departures from the table to make adjustments to the camera, and the constant presence of the microphone no longer seemed to register in his consciousness. The whole day was a perfect rehearsal for Sunday, the day on which I planned to actually imprint Uncle Reginald's crimes onto video tape. That night, lying in my bed, my self-control was severely stretched. It was as though a series of small but thrilling electric shocks were being administered to various parts of my body. How I remained still I shall never know, but my will did manage to triumph over my flesh. I should like the jury to give their fullest consideration to this point. I am sure they will.

We come then, at last, to the recordings themselves. I rather pride myself that, technically, they are really quite proficient, bearing in mind that I have no previous experience whatsoever in this field. I should very much like, when the court proceedings are concluded and my life has returned to normal to retain possession of the tapes for occasional viewing at home. I may even stand a television set on the kitchen table in Uncle Reginald's place so that I am able to view them at meal-times. I must confess to a certain fascination with the prospect of having the power to switch my uncle on or off at will. However, that is in the future. Now to the tapes. I shall not attempt to describe every detail of my little programmes. They are largely self-explanatory. I would, though, like to draw viewers' attention to various items of behaviour under each heading, these items being the ones (in my view) which most clearly demanded that my uncle should pay the ultimate penalty.

Breakfast

As you will observe, my recording of breakfast commences with what I believe is known as a wide-angle shot. This is arranged in order to capture the first teeth-jarring event in Uncle Reginald's daily performance. There is his empty chair and, behind it, the window that looks onto the back garden, and there, after a few seconds, is Uncle Reginald himself, taking his watch from a waistcoat pocket and checking it against the kitchen clock that I purchased by mail-order seventeen months ago. Now he sits down and places both hands, palms down, on the table. He blinks hard and deliberately three times, then looks around as if he had just woken up. At this point I always place a bowl of Weetabix with a scattering of bran over it in front of him. Notice how, as my hand appears on the screen, I lean forwards and smile into the camera secretly (a rather nice touch in my estimation).

Now, this is the moment of that first and quite sickening abomination. It occurs immediately after he has added milk and sugar very sparingly to his cereal. Oh, I can see it! I can see it! He clamps his hands to the edge of the table as if to obtain anchorage, and then it begins. A pendulum-like swinging motion of the buttocks over the surface of his chair, as though he were attempting to settle himself down into something wet and soft. It is a hideous movement of anticipatory relish, accompanied by a sound reminiscent of the sea sucking the tide back into itself on the beach, as he pulls air into his mouth through pursed lips, collecting dribbles and droplets of saliva from the front part of his mouth in the process. I have no doubt that you, viewer, whoever you are, are sensing as I have done so many times, the overwhelming pleasure and satisfaction with which one might take, say, the sugar bowl, and smash it with all one's strength into the face of a man who is guilty of such things! The skin of the aging buttocks, the wool of the underpants, the frayed nylon of the trouser seat, and the brown leather of the kitchen chair, they all move together, do they not? I might rest my case here and walk away a free man, but there is more. Yes, more!

Sunday Lunch

For my Sunday lunch programme, I adjusted the controls on my camera so that it focused directly onto the spot where Uncle Reginald's plate would rest during the course of the meal. You will have already witnessed in the 'breakfast' tape the way in which he suspends his arms at an abnormal height above the food, his hands bending down at a full right angle from his wrists so that his knife and fork are practically in the vertical plane throughout the consumptive process. It reminds me of nothing so much as a praying mantis gobbling some disabled victim, the knife and fork being the probing, scraping ends of the long skinny front legs. Now, it was my intention to concentrate on the plate itself, and the horrendous manner in which my uncle dealt with the food thereon, particularly at the commencement and the conclusion of the meal.

The programme begins with a gratifyingly clear close-up picture of the hot food on Uncle Reginald's willow-pattern dinnerplate. You will note that this consists of three generous slabs of well-cooked beef, four quite substantial roast potatoes, a small pile of peas, a pair of golden-brown Yorkshire puddings, and three or four roast parsnips, all nestling in a shallow pool of thick brown gravy and accompanied on the extreme edge of the plate by a little splodge of horseradish sauce. Now, see how the extremities of my uncle's cutlery appear in the picture. They hover for a moment, then the knife descends. It moves the smallest potato approximately one centimetre away from its fellows and towards the peas. Why? Why has he moved it? There is no reason. It is gratuitous – it is offensive! It is only the beginning.

See now, how he executes two totally random rapid scraping movements with the prongs of his fork on a small portion of exposed china. Do not tell me that this is part of the business of eating. It is a symptom of contained excitement – of salivating, anticipatory greed. I know it! He impales a slice of beef with his fork and begins to cut. Cut, cut, cut, into little geometrically precise shapes, quadrilaterals that not infrequently aspire to genuine squareness. Now he pauses, the end of his knife dangling indecisively as he selects a vegetable. For no reason at all, he suddenly draws a Yorkshire pudding towards him for a distance that must be approaching an inch, then, with unbelievably crass indifference, pushes it back again. Why? The fork now pounces on a large fat potato and holds it firm while the knife saws its flesh. He is cutting it into cubes! God help us, he is cutting it into cubes!

So why – and this is the question that has burned through my very intestines during so many Sunday lunch-times in the last eight years – *why* does he then tear his Yorkshire puddings into ragged asymmetrical pieces using the _back_ of his knife? What strange, twisted aberration can have been lodged in the mind of this person whom I called Uncle, that demanded millimetric precision with meat and vegetables, but a wild, formless approach to Yorkshire pudding? Something in his childhood? Who knows! In any case, I am not one who differentiates between deliberate crime and psychological disturbance. Evil is evil, and punishment is punishment.

The following phase in the preparation of Uncle Reginald's first mouthful of food is not for the squeamish. The fork selects a small square of beef, the knife pushes it crudely back to a lower point on the prongs, a cube of roast potato is added and suffers the same fate as the beef, two peas are affixed and subsequently totally penetrated by twin prongs, a previously shaped rectangle of parsnip is squeezed onto the now quite crowded fork head, and a smear of horse-radish sauce covers and semi-cements the whole. Finally, with a casual stab that, in my view, conceals a peculiar intensity of feeling, a long straggling piece of Yorkshire pudding is fastened to the very points of the fork prongs, and the mixture is transported up and out of the camera's view on its way to Uncle Reginald's mouth. Now, listen! That noise – that sound like wet lumps of meat going round in a washing-machine – that is him! That is Uncle Reginald chewing! And behind it, almost too quiet to be heard, but perfectly audible if one listens very hard, is the click. Yes! I have succeeded in actually recording the click. Hear it now. Chew – click! Chew – click! Chew – click! I hear it even in the silence of my cell, just as it can be heard on the tape. It is so clear.

The rest of my uncle's revolting activities require no further comment from me. The evidence is before you. Note one final point though, if you will. As the meal draws to a close, you will observe that I have left the table in order to widen the angle of the camera lens. This adjustment allows a perfect view of yet another significant piece of behaviour, one that cannot but impress the Court with the utter rationality of my decision to despatch the guilty one. See how Uncle Reginald continues his meal with unabated and ghastly enthusiasm until only a small amount of food remains on his plate. Suddenly, as if out of breath, he lays his knife and fork down on either side of his plate, leans back, puffs his red, whiskery cheeks out, and expels air in a long whistling breath. Next, he places the palm of his left hand on his slight paunch and rubs it round in a clockwise direction, producing a low mooing sound of contentment as he does so. That is hideous enough, but it is followed by an abrupt forward movement as he appears to notice, with a little shock, that he has not completely finished his meal. Picking up his knife and fork he pushes the remaining food into a heap in the middle of the plate, and is (apparently) just about to load it onto his fork when he changes his mind, lays the cutlery down in an exactly parallel fashion on the side of the plate, and in a bluff, genial voice, says the same three dreadful words that he has said at the end of the main course of Sunday lunch for the last ten years: 'An elegant sufficiency, eh? Ha, ha!' He *always* left a little food! He always said those words! How could he have failed to be aware of the fact that I *knew* every time, *every single time*, exactly what he was going to do and say? Of course he knew!

I was anxious that my uncle's execution should not be a painful one. The pursuit of justice does not require inhumanity, and I believe I am, in any case, a kindly person by nature. Accordingly, I spent some considerable time over the selection of an appropriate means of bringing about Uncle Reginald's death. Eventually I settled on simple asphyxiation with one of the spare pillows, and sentence was carried out (with rather surprising ease) on the Tuesday night following that final Sunday lunch. When Wednesday morning came, I made two phone calls. The first to Mr Robards to inform him that I was unlikely to be in a position to continue with my work for some little while, and the second to the local police station. I was, and am, aware that certain formalities will need to be observed before I am released, the most important of which is of course my trial. I might add, incidentally, that from the moment when the two policemen arrived on that Wednesday morning until the present day, I have experienced nothing but polite and caring treatment from all officials concerned. Indeed, I have positively enjoyed the experience of feeling, albeit in a minor sense, that I am by way of being a celebrity, the national newspapers having covered the story of my arrest and subsequent remand in some depth. My only regret is that the journalists involved in the writing of these stories have not had access to this document or to my two video tapes. If they had had such evidence available to them, there would not have been these constant references to 'pleas of insanity' and the like, nor would my name have been linked speculatively with famous 'murderers' of the past, people with whom I have absolutely *nothing* in common. However, the trial will make all things clear without doubt.

In the meantime I wait patiently, and look forward to the day when life resumes its old familiar pattern. Some things I miss. In particular the activity which for some time has constituted my sole form of recreation during the evenings and at weekends. At least once a week after work, and *every* Saturday afternoon, it has become my habit to hire a taxi to take me to Eastbourne. From there I catch the next available train to Victoria Station, and from there pass quickly down the outside steps to the underground station. After purchasing a ticket, I follow the walkway to a point at which one can take a flight of steps down to the Circle Line. I know no happier occupation than to travel on and on, round and round, on the Circle Line, observing people as they board and alight at each station. Why they should want to leave the train I really cannot imagine. It is wonderful to know that, again and again, you will return to the point where you started, and that there is no *need* to alight. It is with the greatest reluctance that I drag myself away on each occasion. Indeed, it has crossed my mind more than once recently, that the day might come in the not too distant future, when I may simply stay on the train, going round and round for ever, and *never* ever get off again.

Friends Coming Round

'Doing anything tonight?'

'Depends what you mean by "anything". Fate has sentenced me to three hours of Ted Sewell. Good behaviour obligatory, but zero remission.'

On Friday the fifteenth of September at approximately three forty-five in the afternoon, whilst preparing to leave the toilet cubicle in which he had been absent-mindedly reading for a little longer than he needed to, Edward Sewell overheard these words. They marked the commencement of a brief conversation that was to result in him feeling very angry, deeply hurt, strangely excited, totally confused, and something else. The anger and hurt were because of what was said, and the excitement was because the contents of the conversation seemed to offer him an opportunity for the exercise of a kind of power he had never experienced before. The confusion was because of what happened afterwards. The something else was – something else.

The two people chatting out there by the urinals and the sinks were David Salmons, a crusty individual of near retirement age who headed up the maths department, and Michael Vinney, a man in his mid-thirties (Edward had just turned forty-three) who was a member of the Physical Education Department.

Salmons, a grey-haired, patched jacket of a man, whose verbal exchanges were famously saturated with growlingly cynical disappointment, had been at the school for years and years, and was reckoned, by common consent, to be a very good maths teacher and a very poor head of department. Those who served under him in the maths department were said to be looking forward to his departure at the end of the next school year with eager anticipation. Edward's relationship with Salmons had always been reasonably cordial but never more than distantly so. Valley Road Comprehensive was an extremely big school employing such a large number of staff that it was impossible to get to know more than a few of one's colleagues on anything but a superficial basis. Edward had nothing against Salmons – at least, not until today.

Michael Vinney, on the other hand, was someone whom Edward knew well. Having begun at Valley Road on exactly the same day five years ago, they had been drawn together from time to time during those first few weeks by a common sense of temporary isolation in the staffroom, the occupants of which, at this early stage in their employment, suggested delegates to a convention of the less probable Dickensian characters.

Edward and Michael were different in almost every way you could imagine. Michael was not tall, but he was trimly fit and firm-bodied, a footballer and tennis player of real class, who, because of the uncompromising toughness of his approach, inspired enormous respect and a fair degree of loathing in most of his pupils, but didn't really care about the loathing as long as they did what they were told and worked hard to reach the limit of their potential. Children judged by him to have no potential simply ceased to exist in any meaningful way as far as P.E. was concerned. It was extremely rare for children to voice formal complaints about Mr Vinney's excesses, which were famous. He could be searingly sarcastic, and occasionally physically punitive, if the practice of hitting children can be described in that way, but somehow he seemed to carry with him such an unassailable right to do what he liked, that he got away with it every time.

On the only known occasion when a boy (Derek Williams in 3DL) had dared to protest to his parents about Mr Vinney clipping him round the ear for being lazy, Michael had survived by the performance of what, to outsiders, must have looked like an amazing conjuring trick. Derek's father turned up at the school to complain, but the P.E. teacher had been so forthright, matey and fulsomely flattering about the qualities of this boy who, it transpired, had far too much potential *not* to be clipped round the ear for the sake of his further development, that Mr Williams had shaken hands cordially with his son's attacker at the end of their meeting and gone home feeling that he had a real ally in the school. The boy himself, who may have been idle, but was certainly not stupid, must have realized that Mr Vinney had now, to all intents and purposes, been granted a licence to clip him round the ear whenever he saw fit. He wisely decided that discretion was the better part of valour, relocating his laziness to the lessons of another, less divinely protected teacher. Derek's father, deeply impressed by the subsequent dramatic improvement in his son's achievements in P.E., declared to anyone who cared to listen that he personally wouldn't hear a word said against Mr Vinney's methods, because, when all was said and done, they worked!

Michael's body, his desk, his routine and his approach to the world were about as ordered and unvaried as it was possible for such things to be. Practical as well as sporty, he was good at making things and mending things. He understood cars and drove them very fast and skilfully.

Michael had only one weakness that Edward knew about. His Achilles heel was situated, as Edward was fond of saying silently to himself, on his head. He was losing his hair, and he didn't like it. All that remained as he approached his thirty-sixth birthday was a light, furry down which, though distributed fairly evenly over the surface of his scalp, was very thin indeed and getting thinner by every baby-shampoo wash. Michael had never actually expressed this concern to Edward, but his wife, Sophie, had mentioned it (in the strictest confidence – Mike would kill her if he thought anyone knew he got worked up about such a silly vain thing, especially if they knew how many times a day she, Sophie, had to reassure him that it didn't really notice) to Edward's wife, Jenny, who had meant exactly what she said, but it had been her habit ever since getting married to mentally exclude Edward from the universe of souls she would never tell, whenever she made that promise. There had to be someone you could tell everything to, didn't there? Besides, Edward would never tell anyone else, so it didn't matter, did it?

Edward was tall, dressed by a committee, more than a little overweight (cuddly, Jenny said), totally impractical, about as sporty as a melting snowman, and blessed with a fine head of thick, dark-brown, usually dishevelled hair. He was an English teacher (mainly for the money nowadays) who really only wanted to be allowed to read books, drink fine wine and eat good food with his wife and friends, go to France and be a poet. Mr Sewell's vagueness and whimsicality in school were so pronounced for most of the time he spent in the classroom that he should have been taken apart by the children he taught. Occasionally he was. But Edward displayed such a genuine and unusual intensity of appreciative interest in the words and works of his pupils, combined with the most confusingly straight-faced irony when the situation warranted it, that most classes seemed to have made a sort of unconscious, corporate decision that there was more to be gained from listening and observing than from misbehaving.

On one occasion, for instance, not long after arriving at Valley Road, Edward had been teaching a notorious fourth-year class, newly elevated from their position as a notorious third-year class. Such classes tend to put a lot of hard work into maintaining their notoriety and this class was certainly no exception. Just after the lesson had begun, a boy called Jackson Ford, who was unofficially responsible for organizing nuisance artillery from the back row, started waggling a stiff arm in the air with all the agitation of an infant urgently needing to go to the toilet.

'Yes, Jackson?' enquired Edward, laying down *A Passage To India,* from which he had been reading the final couple of pages, and giving the boy his entire, fascinated attention. 'What would you like to say to me?'

'Walker and me, Sir,' gesturing towards the grinning youth on his left, 'we're finding this stuff you're reading really boring, and we thought, if it's all the same to you, Sir, we'd take a stroll out to the grass over there and have a smoke until the lesson ends.'

Naturally, delighted laughter greeted this piece of calculated insolence, and all eyes turned to Mr Sewell, each face silently asking that most deliciously anticipatory question of all: 'What are you going to do about that, Teacher?'

Edward seemed genuinely puzzled for a moment, simply because he actually was, then his brow cleared and an expression of bright enthusiasm appeared on his face.

'I wonder,' he said, 'if you could really bring yourself to do that. Most interesting! Here am I, an ordinary, tweedy, conventional schoolmaster who is employed to teach English Literature to, among others, you, Jackson, and here are you, an average to bright fourth-year pupil who is supposed to learn the English Literature that I am supposed to teach. It sounds like a glorious convergence, doesn't it Jackson?' Jackson evinced no desire to offer an opinion. 'But Messrs Fielding and Aziz could tell us how misleading it is possible for such an assumption to be, could they not? How might we both cope with the situation if I were to agree to your request, flippant though I know that request to have been?' He glanced invitingly around the class. 'Perhaps somebody would care to map out for us the trail of consequences that would have its starting point in that agreement. How, for instance, would the headmaster react, on glancing up from his desk, to the sight of Jackson Ford quietly smoking his way through second lesson out on the playing field? What would his response be to the news that he was there with my permission? William Styles, would you care to come out here and be the headmaster, asking me what on earth I think I'm playing at, and Gillian, might you offer us a convincing impression of Jackson struggling to decide whether to take the blame himself or to shop me?'

Jackson Ford, thoroughly bewildered by this experience of seeing his deliberate rudeness turned into the basis of some sort of academic debate and class role-play, found it quite impossible to work out whether Mr Sewell was taking the mickey, or whether he was just loony. Unable to come down firmly on one side or another, he decided to lie low in English for a little while. He spent quite a lot of his lying-low time in chewing over the suggestion that he was 'average to bright'. He'd thought he was no more than average ...

Friendships that have their origins in the loneliness and insecurity of a new situation can become rather laboured later on and perhaps peter out, as those involved find their feet and discover that they have other, more interesting things in common with people who seemed quite intimidating in those first dank days. This, Edward considered, might well have happened with himself and Michael if it had not been for two major factors.

First, the two wives got on extremely well. Michael had invited Edward and his wife to a meal within a week of the two men first meeting, and Sophie and Jenny had taken to each other immediately.

Sophie, eight years younger than her husband, was one of those chatty, good-natured, pretty, pert-bottomed girls who appear to live in a constant state of surprise and alarm over the fact that age and parenthood have relentlessly press-ganged them into the ranks of the grown-ups. The upbringing of her two-year-old boy, Paul, obviously occasioned her the most alarm. Sophie adored Paul, but seemed to regard him as a sort of human crossword puzzle provided without the benefit of clues. Meeting Jenny, whose sons, David and Stephen, were fourteen and ten years old respectively, had been a great comfort to her. From the beginning she had confided recklessly in the older woman, finding in Jenny a quiet, motherly stability that allowed her opportunities once more safely to be the little girl that she was secretly quite sure she always had been and always would be in reality.

Jenny, for her part, enjoyed Sophie's bright, wide-eyed garrulousness and was quite happy, when it was needed, to take a maternal role in her friend's life. Paul was as enchanting and exhausting as only two-year-olds can be. It was a pleasure to offer at least a couple of clues to help fill in the crossword. Apart from anything else, Jenny had never really had what Edward called a 'shrieking with laughter' relationship with another woman before. It wasn't her style, in any case. With Sophie, though, she rather enjoyed the explosions of raucousness that sometimes erupted from the silliest of jokes and situations, often over the sink, for some peculiar reason. Edward said that she must have missed out on some crucially character-building 'raucous phase' in her teenage years, and that it was good to catch up now.

The other major factor in the continuance of the friendship between Edward and Michael was, in Edward's view, the mutual discovery that both of them had been heavily involved at one time in problems connected with what they had both referred to in their early discussions as 'churchgoing'. Michael was obviously not very practised in the business of opening up about himself, but he did tell Edward and Jenny that part of his story in some detail.

Michael's parents had been life-long Pentecostals of the devout but unquestioning variety, who not only expected to remain faithful to Christ until their dying day, but automatically assumed that their only son would follow suit, especially as, to their great satisfaction, he had made his own personal commitment to Jesus when he was a little boy of only seven.

Within days of leaving home to train as a P.E. teacher, Michael told himself that he now knew for sure something he had suspected for a long time, namely, that none of the things his parents believed so committedly had made a real home in his own heart. He struggled quite hard for a little while to make appropriate things happen inside himself, but it was a waste of time. He was definitely not a Christian, he decided. So troubled was he, though, by the prospect of telling his fond mother and father that he was atheistic in his views, that he maintained the pretence of sharing their beliefs for as long as they both lived, attending church when he was at home just as he had always done, singing, praying out loud occasionally, and even raising his hands during the worship as most of the others did.

When both of his parents were killed in a motorway accident two years after he qualified, Michael experienced an odd mixture of pain and relief. The pain was because he loved them and knew he would miss them. He was relieved because, by the very nature of the accident, he could safely assume that their deaths must have been instantaneous, and they had gone together. There would be no loneliness in old age for either of them. And there would be no further need for him to pretend anything about God. There was no God. All that was finished.

Edward's story was similar in one important sense, though very different in others. He had been brought up by his widowed father, an immensely kind, quiet man, who passed his passionate love for books and ideas on to Edward and his older sister, Sandra, a university lecturer, now married and resident in Western Australia with her husband and two daughters.

The similarity between Edward and Michael lay in the fact that Edward's father had also been a devout Christian, although he had not followed the Pentecostal tradition. A life-long and fairly traditional Anglican, he would have felt uncomfortable in the more emotional ethos of the kind of church in which Michael had grown up. Nevertheless, his faith was as important to him as his children were, and he prayed diligently every morning that one day both Edward and Sandra would come to know and love Jesus as he did. Unlike Michael's parents, however, he was a clear-eyed realist, and a man who valued integrity in himself and others. He was perfectly aware that, although Edward had certainly followed him in his love for literature, and his joy in the exercise of mind and spirit, he had not inherited a passion for the Christian faith or the person of Jesus, and he would have hated the very idea of his son feeling obliged to pretend otherwise. Sandra and her husband and family had become very involved members of a big, lively church in the beautiful city of Perth, something for which he thanked God daily, but Edward remained a warmly affectionate, amiable agnostic, a clear target for the power of persistent, faithful prayer, as far as his father was concerned.

Edward greatly respected his father's religious views, and, if it had been at all possible, would gladly have embraced them himself, but he explained that he simply could not find a sufficiently good reason to sacrifice exploration of all the possible horizons of thought and feeling that might appear, to a God who would probably want to fence his mind off into very prescribed and spiritually disinfected little paddocks of inner experience. In vain, on the occasions when he said this, his father offered the mild suggestion that Edward might be reacting to his image of the Church rather than to the actual nature of God. But Edward would just grin and shake his head and say, 'Don't think so, Pop,' and go and make a pot of tea before getting the Scrabble out.

When this happened the old man smiled and nodded, but he never gave up praying.

Edward's father lived well into his eighties and died in considerable discomfort from cancer not long after Edward and Jenny's youngest, Stephen, was born. Jenny and her father-in-law had become very close during the fifteen years that they had known each other, and it was she who had been more than willing to nurse him through the final weeks of his life.

Edward had wonderful memories of his father, but there was one recollection in particular that caused him excruciating pain whenever it rose, always unbidden, to the front of his mind.

One Saturday morning in the middle of summer, not long before the old fellow became ill, Edward and Jenny and the boys had decided to drive up into the hills with the dog and take a good long walk. Edward's father had elected to stay at home and do a spot of very slow 'pottering', as he called it, around Jenny's beloved garden.

After successfully shovelling everybody into the car and setting off, Edward, who was driving, suddenly remembered that although they definitely had one large and very excited dog with them, he had forgotten to take the dog's lead from the hook by the front door. Encounters with other dogs sometimes urgently required the lead to be available, so he pulled up at the end of the road, and walked quickly back towards the house. Letting himself in through the front door, he grabbed the lead, and was about to call out reassuringly, when he heard the sound of a voice coming from the kitchen. It was his father, speaking in passionately imploring tones.

' . . . and heavenly father, I know you always listen to me, and I'm so grateful to you for that and so many prayers answered in my life. I'm . . . well, it's been such a privilege and a joy knowing you, it really has, but . . . ' The elderly, wheezing voice broke a little as it continued. 'I bring my beloved Edward before you yet again, Lord, knowing that you love him more than I do. Grant my dearest wish, and draw him and his family to you when the right time comes. I beg you, Lord, in your great kindness, to hear my prayer . . . '

Edward stole out with the lead, closing the door carefully and soundlessly behind him as he went. He dashed the moisture angrily from his eyes as he walked back to the car. He knew that his father prayed daily for his conversion, but he had never actually heard him doing it before. It seemed so sad and unfair that he couldn't give his father the thing he wanted most in the world. But he couldn't. He simply couldn't lie to his father, and his father would have known he wasn't telling the truth anyway. Blast!

Edward didn't use words like 'Blast'.

Over the years the memory of that painful moment in the hall, when he had discovered the surprising depth of passion in his father's relationship with a God who didn't exist, had become like a slight but chronic physical pain, ever liable to start aching and throbbing when other concerns and distractions faded for a while.

It was on the second occasion that the Sewells and the Vinneys ate together, this time at the solid, four-bedroomed Victorian house in Oxford Avenue that Edward had inherited from his father, that Michael, still feeling new and vulnerable, had talked quite freely about his parents and his 'churchgoing' background. Edward said afterwards to Jenny that he felt Michael had offered this very personal piece of information as a sort of deposit of disclosure into a relationship account that he desperately needed to keep open at that time. Accustomed to such convoluted metaphors, she understood and agreed.

Jenny had been quite surprised on that same evening to hear Edward responding with a detailed description of his own experiences with his father, including the business of the overheard prayer. You were supposed to be careful with pearls, weren't you? Not, of course, she hastily added to herself, that Michael and Sophie were swine. That was not what she'd meant at all.

Invitations to dinner continued to be exchanged on a regular basis after that. Jenny and Sophie always enjoyed these occasions, having become really good friends. They also met for morning coffee and cake almost every week, usually at Sophie's house because of it being easier with Paul, chatting about their children and the jobs they'd done and their houses and what the future might hold. Sophie talked quite a lot about Michael, who, as Jenny soon began to realize, remained more or less in pedagogic mode in his dealings with the pretty, ingenuous girl whom he had married. Jenny made the occasional remark about Edward, but, like her husband, she had never felt the need or inclination to share intimate details of their married life, and there was no temptation to start doing so now.

For Edward, the ongoing relationship between himself and Michael was much more problematical. He was well aware that, since the time when they had both joined the staff group, Michael had gained a great deal of confidence, and a set of friends from among the other teachers who were his own age, and with whom he had much more in common. They tended to be a fairly brash, sporty bunch, who enjoyed beer in large quantities (Edward was all for alcohol, but he and Jenny infinitely preferred the grape to the hop) and spoke loudly in the staffroom about how horrible most of the boys were and how much they fancied some of the girls. When Edward told Jenny about this she asked him if he had ever fancied any of the girls, and laughed when he said, yes, almost all of the sixth form, and particularly Elsie Warningham.

In a sense Edward felt protective towards his friend, or rather, he felt that, in that early exchange of experiences, he had tacitly accepted a responsibility to safeguard a part of Michael that could easily fade and disappear in the company of those with whom he now spent most of his leisure time. He was not always sure about Michael's attitude towards him, but he hoped and believed that one important aspect of his young colleague's personality was fed and nurtured by this periodic exposure to a deeper, more abstract and poetic view of life. Every now and then, he would deliberately bring up the subject of their contrasting religious backgrounds in order to, as it were, re-establish the stamp of their conversational currency. Whenever he did this Michael would listen and nod attentively, apparently thinking very seriously about what was being said, even if he himself tended to say less and less on the subject as time went by.

Edward was certainly a good man, and essentially a humble one, but he had perhaps never quite caught on to the fact that he was slightly unusual, and that other people might not be as enchanted or absorbed by the prospect of sharing his thoughts and fancies as he imagined.

On hearing those initial, devastating lines of dialogue issuing with such clarity from the other side of the toilet door, Edward's first and most automatic reaction was a feeling that he should cover his ears. The voice of his rather old-fashioned upbringing told him that a gentleman does not listen to other people's private conversations, and that, if he does, he certainly should not expect to hear good of himself. But, good heavens above, it was too late for that! Michael's blistering reply to the other man's question had hit him like a punch in the throat before he was given any choice about whether to listen or not. As he absorbed the full impact of what he had just heard, Edward, who was, after all, a perfectly normal human being in most ways, knew that he was no more capable of deliberately blocking out whatever was still to come than he was capable of flying to the moon. He remained perfectly still and listened.

'Thought he was a friend of yours,' he heard Salmons say.

'More of a barnacle on my backside,' replied Michael. 'My own stupid fault. When I first came I was a bit new and green and whatnot, so I latched on to the first human being who'd pass the time of day with me.'

'And you couldn't find a human being so you settled for the resident loony, eh?'

'All my life,' Michael's voice was affectedly weary, 'I seem to have got sucked in by the village idiot whenever I go somewhere new. Must be something about me that appeals to them, I suppose.'

'Best English teacher this school's ever had,' said Salmons, reflectively and rather unexpectedly. He returned to the topic in hand, his voice droningly flat and dismissive. 'I should just cool it off, if I were you. Surely you don't have to spend time with the man if you don't want to, do you? I wouldn't. Three hours of purgatory on a Friday night. What's the point if you're not even a Catholic?'

The two men must have moved away from the urinals at this point. First one tap was turned on and then another. Edward, now in a strange, light-headed state, found himself wondering irrelevantly whether either of the teachers would have bothered washing their hands if the other one hadn't been there. He leaned forward, straining to hear what was said over the noise of water rushing into the sinks.

'The trouble is,' Michael raised his voice as if to oblige, 'we're stuck in one of those blasted "you come to dinner with us, and then we'll come to dinner with you, and then you come to dinner with us" things that go on and on until you emigrate or die. I don't know how to get out of it. I wouldn't . . . ' He dropped his volume as the sound of the running taps ceased. 'Sorry – didn't mean to shout. I wouldn't want to actually upset the old idiot. I suppose he can't help being a chop short of a mixed grill. Besides, Sophie really likes going there and them coming to us – gets on like a house on fire with Mrs Loony. Jenny's all right, actually. Got a lot of time for her. Poor cow.'

One of them had turned on the hot air machine.

'I'll tell you the thing I really can't stand.' Michael was really warming to his theme now. 'Every time we have one of these joyful little gatherings – well, nearly every time – old Sewell seems to feel obliged to go back to stuff we talked about years ago, personal stuff I wish I'd never said.'

'What sort of personal stuff?'

For the first time an evasive note sounded in Michael's voice.

'Aah, just things that happened, you know. I think he thinks we've got some kind of special bond, or something. Reckons it gives him a sort of hold over me. Teach me to keep my mouth shut, won't it?'

'Will it?' whispered Edward involuntarily, but very softly to himself inside his cubicle.

'Still,' continued Michael, as the sound of the hand-drier then started again, 'I suppose I should be thankful for small mercies. At least when he's doing that he's not drifting off into "What if this?" and "What if that?" and "Let's tease out what we actually mean when we describe somebody as a creative person." That was one of his merrier suggestions at the last wake we held. Then, of course, there's "Would you be interested in hearing a line or two of the verse I've been working on?" Mustn't forget that one. If ever he publishes a collection of poems it'll have to be called *Look At My Entrails*. Boy! What I wouldn't give sometimes for a verse or two of "Eskimo Nell" and ten minutes on whether United are going to win the league.'

'I don't think you'd enjoy dinner with me any more than you do with him,' observed Salmons drily, 'not that I shall ever ask you, I hasten to add. My devoted staff would pin you to the ground behind the bikesheds the following morning and force you to divulge my darkest secrets. Not that you'd take much forcing, of course.'

'What makes you say that?'

After the door to the staff toilet block had squeaked open and slammed shut, Edward could still hear the maths teacher's crackling laugh echoing derisively down the corridor outside.

For quite a long time after the two men had gone Edward remained virtually motionless inside the cubicle, focusing his eyes on a small jagged mark near the centre of the green-painted chipboard door in front of him. He was trying to get his breathing under control. For the last few minutes, ever since that conversation had begun, in fact, hardly any air had passed in or out of his lungs. He had never felt quite like this before in his life. It was like being beaten up, as though someone had climbed right into your head wearing boxing gloves and pummelled your brain mercilessly in the places where it was most tender. Bruises everywhere.

Waves of anger and humiliation and hurt began to wash around inside his chest and stomach, making him feel sick with the need for comfort and a chance to hit back. To believe that you were helping, and then to discover that you were being tolerated – patronized! He wanted to see his wife, who wouldn't be back from the hospital just yet, and he wanted to see his sons, who were away on camp, and he wanted to see his father, who was dead. He even felt a sudden painful desire to see his mother, of whom he had no memory at all. He felt about six years old.

'Baldy!' he hissed at the door through gritted teeth. 'I hate you, Baldy! Baldy, Baldy, Baldy, Baldy! I hate you, Mr Michael Baldy Not Much Hair Going Bald And Doesn't Like It Baldy Vinney!'

The sound of someone coming in through the outer door cut short this very necessary release of Edward's overflow of aggression, turning it instead into a quite frightening attack of breathlessness. For two or three minutes he gasped as silently as he could into a handkerchief held in his cupped hands, praying that whoever had come in would hurry up and do whatever they'd come to do, and then clear off.

Able to come out at last a short while later, rather shaky and still battling a little for breath, he leaned, stiff-armed, with one hand on each side of a washbasin, studying his strained, frowning face in the mirror for a moment. There had always been a detached element in Edward's personality that was not just able to, but almost always did, regard all the things that happened to him, however negative or traumatic, as *interesting,* in exactly the same way that Jackson Ford's deliberate act of disruption was an *interesting* thing to observe and contemplate.

'And what are you going to do with all this, Edward Sewell?' he asked his reflection. 'Are you going to confront Michael down in the staffroom in a moment and tell him that you know what he really thinks about you and your dinner parties and your conversation and your poetry and your poor cow of a wife?'

He tried to picture Michael, horrified beyond measure, at the moment when it was revealed to him that all those scathing comments had been listened to by the last person he would ever have wanted to hear them. What sort of flustered, blundering attempts would he make to justify the horrible things that he'd said?

'Oh, n-o-o-o! You didn't think I meant it, did you? Oh, you didn't! I was just having old Salmons on – giving him something to be really miserable about.'

'I knew you were there all the time! Ha! Caught you there, didn't I? Been waiting to see how long it was before you said something . . . '

'Actually, Ted, I haven't been all that well for the last few days, a bit down about some private things as well as some kind of virus – I've been in a funny state of mind. Don't take any notice of what I said, it doesn't mean a thing. Maybe we could have a chat about this private stuff sometime – if that's all right with you, I mean . . . '

Yes, indefensible though his behaviour might have appeared, Michael wouldn't be flustered and blundering at all. He would be bound to come out with something pretty impressive in the way of an excuse. He was famous for it at Valley Road. Probably, by the time he'd finished, Edward would be humbly apologizing for putting their friendship in jeopardy by making such a silly fuss about nothing. Michael would, no doubt, be big enough to accept his apology with good grace.

'In any case,' he argued to his reflection, 'things you say about people when they aren't there haven't necessarily got much at all to do with what you really think about them. You just say things to sound clever, or to fit in with the way you think the person you're talking to feels about things. Or you only mean the horrible stuff that comes out a little bit, but it gets kind of blown up on the way out. Perhaps Michael was just exaggerating. Everyone does that, don't they?'

No, they don't, replied Edward silently to himself, as the burning anger rose once more like bile in his throat, they don't talk like Michael did just now, slicing and crushing and contemptuously flicking from their perfect cuffs, like specks of dust, all the things that mean so much to somebody else. Not when they've been friends, they don't. Not to someone else who's quite likely to pass it all on to the rest of the crowd. No, not everyone does that.

Michael had done, done, *done* it, and a part of Edward that rarely became roused was burning to do something to him in return. His dark thoughts turned to the dinner party planned for seven o'clock that same evening. Perhaps he should just cancel it – tell Michael and Sophie he was sick, or had to go somewhere. Even as he considered that option, though, a new aspect of the situation occurred to him, and the more he thought about it, the more a different and really quite pleasant sensation began to creep over him. The fact was that he knew what Michael thought about him now, but Michael had no idea that he knew. How interesting to observe events from the vantage point of possessing that extra information. Perhaps, thought Edward, it might not be such a bad evening after all.

Downstairs, in the crowded, noisy staffroom, Michael was in the act of lifting his coat from a peg by the door as Edward walked in. He raised a hand in greeting.

'Okay, Ted? What a week, eh? Time to set the animals on the general public and close the zoo for a couple of days. All systems go for seven o'clock?'

Taken aback by the sheer normalness of Michael-the-Enemy's manner towards him, Edward was unable to speak for a second or two. How could this person who was smiling and joking with him now be the same person who had said all those horrible things ten minutes ago? Feeling suddenly cold and confused, he found himself just wanting the whole thing to go away.

'I . . . I was thinking, Michael – if you get home and suddenly wish you could simply flop instead of spending the whole evening with someone you already see all week as it is, you've only got to give me a ring and we can . . . you know, reorganize it. I don't want you to feel – what would the word be? – bound. I would hate you to feel bound.'

Michael froze for a moment, one arm in the left sleeve of his coat, the other poised in mid-quest for the one behind his back. He peered at Edward with narrow-eyed, exaggerated anxiety.

'Are you on something, Edward? Tannin, is it? You've got to watch that school tea, you know. Easy to overdose without realizing you're doing it. What *are* you talking about? I wouldn't miss one of our little get-togethers for anything. Nor would Sophie – you know that.' He paused for an instant. 'Look, is it that you'd rather we didn't come tonight, because . . . '

'Oh, no!' Edward interrupted hurriedly, suddenly seeing Jenny's face in his mind's eye for some reason. He moved forward to help Michael into his coat. 'No, it's just that it occurred to me . . . well, we fix a date for these things quite a long way in advance, don't we, and we ought to, as it were, include a back-out clause, just in case either of us wants to err, you know, back out, or . . . '

Turning, Michael laid a leather-gloved hand on his arm and spoke with mock gravity.

'Edward, we're coming to dinner, not buying your house. Of course we want to come round. What are we having by the way? I've starved myself all day ready for tonight's do.'

The anger surfaced again. Get your hand off my arm!

'Err, I'm not sure – I think it might be mixed grill, that is, assuming we can get the chops without any trouble. I mean, it wouldn't be a mixed grill without a chop, would it? I don't think it would.'

'Without a . . . no, no, I suppose not.' Michael scratched his head in bafflement. 'Look, if I were you, Ted, I'd go home, have quite a sizeable scotch and take it easy for an hour or two. All right? I think you must have overdone it this week. Oh, by the way, there's something serious I want you and I to have a talk about this evening after dinner, if that's okay. See you at seven. Love to Jenny. Cheers!'

'Something you want to . . . ?'

But Michael had gone, leaving Edward wishing devoutly that his ridiculous comment about the mixed grill could be expunged from the history of the world, and feeling in an even greater state of confusion than before. Why should Michael want to discuss anything serious with the barnacle on his backside – the village idiot – the boring holder of wakes? The whole of the encounter he had just endured didn't seem to fit anywhere with the conversation he had overheard – not just in terms of words, but in terms of . . . well, of heart. The Staffroom Michael wasn't the Toilet-block Michael at all. They just weren't the same person. For one irrational moment, Edward really did wonder if he'd got it all wrong and it had been someone else out there talking to Salmons. But he knew he hadn't. He jolly well hadn't got it wrong. It had been Michael, and Michael was coming to dinner tonight.

Driving his battered Volvo home through the busily crowded early darkness of the market town where he lived, Edward changed his mind at least five times about whether to tell his wife what had happened or not. That she would know perfectly well *something* had happened was in no doubt at all. Edward was transparent at the best of times, and Jenny was able to read every one of his moods like themes in a favourite book. He would either have to tell her the truth, or invent something to account for his jittery state. A nasty headache might be the answer. He did actually suffer from them when he was tired sometimes, and a headache was vague enough to account for all sorts of unusual behaviour. He'd have to tell her what had really happened in the end, of course. He'd burst otherwise.

As he pulled off the High Street and turned right into Oxford Avenue, Edward asked himself why he was (temporarily, at any rate) unwilling to share what had happened with Jenny. He usually told her everything as soon as it happened. Two reasons sprang to mind.

The first was a reluctance to ignite one of his wife's occasional, awesome rages. Jenny was quite capable of getting very cross indeed, especially when she felt that her husband was under attack or being treated unfairly. She might – she just might – go straight to the phone and cancel tonight's dinner party using that tight, incensed voice that had always spoilt Edward's day on the rare occasions when it was directed at him. He was pretty sure now that he didn't want the evening to be cancelled. Under the circumstances, the prospect of being with Michael and a couple of bottles of wine for three or four hours on home ground was nerve-racking but ... well, *interesting*. Knowledge certainly did feel as if it might be power. Edward had never really given much thought to the general concepts of having or exercising power before.

The other reason for not telling Jenny had more to do with her wisdom than her rage. In this second scenario she might not cancel the evening, and, in a way, that would be even worse. Edward was virtually certain that once his wife's anger had abated she would begin to take a mature, adult view of the situation. If she hadn't made the cancelling phone-call by the time that inevitable abating stage arrived, he was sure she would express a carefully considered opinion that the dinner should go ahead, and then offer lots of sensible observations about the unfairness of blaming Sophie for Michael's silliness, and the inadvisibility of giving overmuch credence to accidentally overheard remarks, and the fact that the truly grown-up and constructive mode of response was to carry on as if nothing had happened. If the evening proceeded on that basis Edward wouldn't be able to enjoy any sense of secret knowledge or subtle power. Nor would it be possible to manufacture opportunities to taste the (to him) hitherto virtually unknown flavour of revenge, a concept that Edward had thought even less about in the course of his life than he'd thought about power. The mature approach scorned revenge. Jenny would kick him under the table if she saw any sign of it.

As he parked a little way up the avenue to leave his drive clear for Michael's Daewoo, or whatever it was called, later on, Edward made a final decision. He wouldn't tell Jenny tonight, he'd tell her tomorrow, and that was absolutely definite – probably.

Jenny called out from the kitchen as he shut the front door against the cold evening outside. Good! She was back early.

'Good day, love? I can't believe we've got a whole weekend without the boys. Haven't forgotten we've got the Vinneys tonight, have you? You need to put the car up the road, don't you?'

'Done it,' called back Edward in a headache-weakened voice as he hung his coat on the rack in the hall. 'Seems a shame when there's just us for once.'

Jenny was chopping vegetables when he walked into the kitchen. Such a comfortable, familiar figure, thought Edward for the ten thousandth time. A warm and glowing armful. Not a skinny bird. The other day she'd been quite flattered when he told her that she reminded him of the lady who did the Bisto adverts on television. She turned to look at him, her always sympathetic brown eyes registering slight concern.

'You all right, Edward? You sound a bit woozy. What – d'you mean you wish they weren't coming?'

'Bit of a headache – nothing much. No, not really – no, it'll be fine. Besides, Michael says he's got something important he wants to talk about.'

'To us?'

'Me. Don't know what it is.'

'Oh, pardon me for existing, I'm sure. Intriguing. Something to do with the blessed job I expect. Ah, well, Sophie and me'll polish off what's left of the Baileys in the kitchen while you're talking about something important over your brandy glasses. She certainly won't mind. Nor will I. You can tell me what it was afterwards.' She studied his face for a second or two. 'You sure it's just a headache?'

For a moment Edward stood stiffly, his body swaying very slightly. He came very close to blurting out everything that had happened. To see Jenny's eyes darken with anger on his behalf; to immerse his bruised feelings in the warm stream of sympathy that would undoubtedly pour from her spirit to his when she heard the ghastly details; to hear her say how unfair she thought it was to talk like that about someone who was supposed to be your friend; all these things would have been most welcome and enjoyable. He resisted the temptation.

'Mmm, had it all day. I'll take some pain-killers. Shall I do the table? And then I'll have my shower.'

'Please. I'll carry on with the dinner and put your tablets in some squash. I got the wine, so you can open that ready, too.'

After carefully laying the table in the dining-room and uncorking the two bottles of red wine that he found on top of the bureau, Edward went upstairs for a shower, then came back down from his bedroom with a large pad of writing-paper and a Biro. Pulling one of the dining-room chairs away from the table, he sat with one leg crossed over the other, staring into the distance and frowning with concentration as he sucked the end of his pen. After a few minutes he took a determinedly deep breath through his nose, straightened the pad on his knee and began to write. So absorbed was he by this task, that Jenny had to call out to him twice that his dissolved headache tablets were still waiting for him in the kitchen.

'Unless, of course,' she added after the second time, 'you haven't got it any more ...'

By the time the ring on the doorbell came at one minute past seven, Edward had finished his piece of writing, and was in a state of considerable tension. He felt as if he was about to take the leading role in some highly dramatic piece of theatre, but without the benefit of knowing what his lines were to be, or how the other characters in the play were scheduled to speak or behave or react to him. What about Sophie? Did she know what her husband really thought of his 'loony' colleague? What a farce it would all seem if she did.

Whether or not Sophie was privy to Michael's views on Edward, there was little doubt that she was pleased to have arrived that evening. She was the first to trip her way over the doorstep and into the house when Edward answered the bell.

'Eddeee!'

She pecked him brightly on the cheek, dumped her coat with comfortable familiarity over the newel post at the bottom of the stairs, and tottered happily down the hall in her high heels, rather like, thought Edward, a Thelwell pony walking on its hind legs. She really did have calves that were almost edible. Even before entering the kitchen she was beginning to emit the shrill, anticipatory scream with which she invariably greeted Jenny. A moment later Edward heard his wife's deeper, more relaxed laugh sounding in response.

Michael too was all smiles and laid-back familiarity, the very picture of a man at ease finding himself in a place where he was genuinely able to relax. He placed the statutory gift of wine on the hall table.

'Believe this or not, Ted,' he said, as Edward took his coat and scarf and swivelled to hang them on the rack, 'but stepping through this front door of yours makes me feel more at home than just about anything else I know.' As Edward turned back from the coat-rack Michael seized his hand and squeezed it firmly. 'I really mean that.'

What?

For the first time Edward was able to understand what people meant when they talked about being struck dumb. He clutched Michael's hand and stared into his face, completely unable to speak. For goodness' sake! How could the man's voice communicate such engaging intimacy? How did he manage to make his eyes do the warm, crinkly, deeply sincere thing that he was making them do now? How could he possibly have meant what he said earlier if what he was saying now was as genuine as it seemed to be? Aware suddenly that his mouth was hanging open, he shook his head slightly and cast desperately about in his mind for some kind of reply. The result was not, he felt, inspired.

'You do?'

Michael burst into laughter.

'Well, there's no need to sound quite so surprised, mate.' He called loudly down the hall. 'Jenny! This husband of yours is amazed because I said that I like coming here very much. Just shows how clever he is, because I was actually lying through my teeth.' He laughed loudly again.

Edward's polite but feebly expressed protestations that he hadn't meant that at all were lost in a corresponding chorus of laughter from Jenny and Sophie as they emerged from the kitchen with glasses in their hands. He tried to join in, but was conscious of only being able to manage a sickly grin and a vague croaking noise in the back of his throat.

'Anyway,' breezed Michael, 'assuming Sophie and I can bear to stay for just a little longer, there are three things that have to be done right now. First, I have to give the beautiful Jennifer a kiss ... '

He did so. Edward balled his fists, but kept them by his sides. Huh! Right! Wanted to kiss the poor cow, did he? Thought she might like to find out how it felt to be kissed by someone normal, perhaps?

Sophie smiled happily at everybody and sipped her drink.

'The second thing is to ask how you two ladies have managed to get into the booze within seconds of us coming through the front door, whereas we men are so nearly dead of thirst that you probably wouldn't be able to prise our poor parched lips open far enough to get a little moisture in even if you wanted to. Eh, Ted?'

Edward, who found 'chaps and girls' talk difficult at the best of times, forced a smile on to his face and nodded miserably. Light banter was the last thing he felt capable of at the moment. He studied Michael's hair, taking comfort from the sparseness of it. It really was very thin. He realized he should be saying something to Michael, but he couldn't think of anything. Jenny did, thank goodness.

'Ah, well, you see,' she replied playfully, 'it's like this, Michael. I already had a drink, which, as the author of the coming feast, I might add, I've hardly had a chance to touch, so the bottle was already out on the kitchen table. Add the fact that Sophie knows where the glasses are, and that she's got more sense than to wait for me to get round to inviting her, and there you are. We've got drinks and you haven't.' She winked at Sophie and pursed her lips as if debating inwardly. 'What do you think? Shall we let them have one?'

Wrinkling her nose and tilting her head, Sophie closed one eye and stared up at the light-fitting on the hall ceiling with the other, portraying serious thought like a bad actor.

'Yes!' she announced finally. 'Yeah, if they're good we'll let 'em 'ave one.'

More laughter. Ha ha!

'Speaking of the coming feast,' continued Michael, 'the third thing I have to do is to say that ... '

'Are you going to offer Michael a drink, Edward? Sorry, Michael, I just thought you ought to have something to brace you before you do your third thing. I don't know how clever people like you do it. They do it on television don't they? "There are three points I would like to make in this context." I've never been able to think in threes.'

Edward picked up his cue obediently, but even as he spoke he realized just how hard it was going to be to control the words that came out of his mouth this evening.

'Yes, come on Michael, what'll you have? Can I get you an enormous amount of beer and a whoopee cushion?'

Sophie began to giggle uncontrollably but forced herself to stop when she saw that Jenny was not even smiling. Michael seemed quite unruffled, but there was a spark of amusement in his eyes that enraged Edward. Another anecdote to be passed on during his next encounter with a colleague in the toilets, no doubt: 'No word of a lie . . . that loony, Sewell, offered me – and I quote – "an enormous amount of beer and a whoopee cushion". A whoopee cushion, would you believe!'

A short silence ensued.

'Sorry,' apologized Edward, interpreting the message of his wife's raised eyebrow with what he confidently reckoned to be complete accuracy, 'just – just a joke. What'll you have?'

'Well, I think I'll pass on the whoopee cushion if it's all the same to you, Ted, but the enormous amount of beer sounds pretty good. One glass at a time'll do fine, though.'

'Well, the food's very nearly ready,' said Jenny, 'so get a beer for yourself as well, Edward, and bring them through to the dining-room. We'll start the wine a bit later. Come on you two, come and sit down.'

On his way from the kitchen to the dining-room with the beer, Edward met his wife on her way to collect the starters from the kitchen. He had feared he might. A hissed conversation was inevitable.

'Edward, what *is* the matter with you? What was all that about? Why are you in such a funny mood? Something's happened, hasn't it?'

'No.'

'Well, what has happened? Something's happened, whatever you say. I always know when something's happened. What is it?'

'Nothing. Nothing's happened. Well ... '

'What?'

'Not so loud, they'll hear.'

'What, then?'

'No, honestly,' no, he wasn't going to tell her yet, 'I think it's just this headache, Jenny. I'm just a bit ... you know.'

She moved her eyes close to his. 'No, I don't know, and I don't believe you. Go and sit down and look after them. Well, go on!'

At last they were all seated, each with their salad, chicken pâté and toast starter in front of them. Michael spread a little pâté on to a square of buttered toast, popped it into his mouth and chewed appreciatively.

'Mmm, delicious! Made with your own fair hands, Mrs Sewell?'

Jenny nodded and smiled.

'Which brings me to the third thing I was going to do just now,' went on Michael, busily spreading more butter and pâté as he spoke, 'and that was to say how much I'm looking forward to my mixed grill tonight. Wonderful idea! Why don't more hostesses dish it up at dinner parties? I've been dreaming about it ever since the end of school today.'

'Mixed grill?'

Jenny's glass of wine, balanced between her first two fingers, hung suspended half-way to her lips as she stared at Michael.

'I think mixed grill's a reely good idea,' prattled Sophie happily. 'Blokes always like it 'cause there's a lot, and there's a nice variety if you don't like some sorts of meat, so you can ...'

Her voice trailed off as she realized that something was not quite right.

'I'm sorry, Michael,' said Jenny, 'but what made you think we were having mixed grill tonight?'

Edward picked up one of the wine bottles and tilted it, licking his lips nervously as he watched the rich dark liquid fill his glass.

Before he was able to think of anything to say, Michael was answering Jenny's question.

'What made me think ...? Well, Edward told me, just before I left for home this afternoon. He said something about you not being sure you could get the chops or something, but it was definitely going to be mixed grill. Why? Isn't it? Any chance of a spot of wine for the rest of us, Ted?'

As Ted filled the glass in Michael's outstretched hand, he noted that his wife was slowly lowering her glass to the table and fixing him with a stare of utter incredulity. Swallowing hard, he adjusted his face to a setting that might approximate to some kind of normal reading.

'Edward?' Jenny's voice was a rich mixture of therapeutic calm, deep mystification and distant thunder.

'Mmm?' He had deliberately over-filled his mouth with pâté and toast in order to gain a little time.

'Edward, tell me – when you knew perfectly well that we were having seafood lasagne tonight, seeing as you suggested it and you bought most of the ingredients, why did you tell Michael that we were having a mixed grill? Why on earth, Edward? Why? And what, in the name of the great Panjandrum is all this about me not being sure I could get chops? Why would I not be able to get chops?'

Everyone looked at Edward.

Edward, his eyes bulging, indicated his energetically working jaws and flapped his hands in apparent frustration, hoping to convincingly communicate the message: 'I have a truly excellent answer to that question on the tip of my tongue, and I cannot tell you how mortified I am by my inability to produce it at this precise moment owing to a large amount of food that I wish I had never placed in my mouth, but which simply has to be masticated before I even attempt to speak.'

'Well, seafood lasagne certainly suits us just as well,' smiled Michael lazily, 'a real treat, in fact. But I sure would like to know the solution to The Mystery of the Mixed Grill, by Agatha Sewell.'

Edward chewed and swallowed his way through his excuse at last and took a gulp of wine. Why, oh, why had he ever mentioned the *stupid* mixed grill? Why hadn't he kept his big mouth shut in the staffroom and just told Jenny what had happened when he got home, and let her sort it out? What a fool! What sort of ammunition was all this going to present Michael with in the weeks to come? So much for subtle revenge and the exercise of power! It was all going to end up the wrong way round. What on earth was he going to say now?

A brief reprieve came.

'I went on a seafood diet once,' said Sophie, who cherished a sweetly attractive and pathetically indomitable belief that the oldest and most well-worn of jokes would be unknown to her immediate circle. 'Every time I saw food I ate it.' She clapped a hand to her mouth and made little hissing noises like gas escaping. 'Oh, dear, I've messed that up, haven't I? I should have said I *am* on a seafood diet and every time I *see* food I *eat* it.' She looked disappointedly around the table. 'No wonder you all didn't laugh.'

There was a little polite tittering.

Edward tried to sound adult and assured. 'All right, the reason I told Michael we were having a mixed grill is very simple actually, Jenny, and the business about the chops is, if anything, even simpler. I got mixed up between two things. One was tonight's dinner and the other was – well, I can't tell you about it now because it's a surprise for ... well, for a special occasion to do with you and me. I just got the two things crossed in my mind, that's all. I know it sounds mad, but there we are. Sorry, Michael. Sorry, Sophie.'

Sophie, who loved secrets, said, 'Oh, that's all right. Quite exciting, reely.'

Michael inclined his thinly covered head graciously, but that gleam of amusement was there in his eyes again. No doubt, thought Edward, it was all being stored up in readiness for a suitable occasion. As for Jenny – well, the bit about the special occasion had been something of an inspiration. There had always been an unspoken agreement between them that if some hint of a planned surprise was accidentally revealed by one to the other, then no more questions would be asked. He could tell that Jenny was far from convinced, and, sure as eggs, the reckoning would come, but at least he'd said *something*.

They ate for a while. No one spoke. Time to change the subject, thought Edward. The imp on his shoulder made an evil suggestion.

'Tell me, Michael, have you got to know any of the people in the maths department?'

'Why do you ask?'

'Oh, nothing really. I gather they've got real problems there. I wondered if you'd heard anything about it.'

'Well ... ' Michael swallowed his last piece of roast and wiped his mouth with his napkin, 'as far as I can see there's only one major problem and that's the man in charge.'

'Oh, dear, same old problem. Do I know him, Edward?' asked Jenny. 'Plates, please.'

'Name of Salmons,' said Michael, passing his plate and almost turning himself inside-out with a wide yawn. 'Oh, dear, sorry – nothing to do with the company I assure you. Just a little tired.'

Turned out a bit of a wake, has it, Michael?

'No, he's a funny bloke in some ways. Older man. Retires next year. Bit dry and cynical. Never hit it off with his own staff at all. That's the main problem, I should imagine. I don't know him all that well, but we've had the occasional chat over the years. As far as I can recall he's never had a good word to say for anyone. I tell you, the milk of human kindness hasn't just dried up in that bloke – it's curdled.'

'Poor man,' observed Jenny with compassion, as she picked up the plates that the starters had been on and turned to leave the room, 'it must be horrible to end up like that.'

'I'll come and give you a hand with everything,' squeaked Sophie, pushing her chair back, 'I don't want to hear any more about a sad man with a name like some fish. I was useless at maths.'

Edward felt quite scared when he was left alone with Michael. There were so many different strata in this precipice of a situation that he hardly knew who either of them really were. He felt guilty about not telling Jenny, and he still felt angry, and he felt stupid because he was bound to end up feeling worse than Michael. Stupid, stupid, stupid!

'I tell a lie,' said Michael, leaning forward with his elbow on the table and raising a finger, 'old Salmons did say something nice about someone, and I should have remembered, because it was only today he came out with it. I meant to tell you what he said only it went out of my head until just this moment.'

'Is this the serious talk you said you wanted to have with me?'

'What?' Michael's sauvity deserted him for about half a second. 'Oh, no, no, that's something else. We'll do that later. No, this was something Salmons said about you.'

'About me?'

'That's right – now let me just think of the exact words.' He held his thumb and second finger level with his face and slightly apart for an instant then brought them together, snapping his fingers, then shaking a fore-finger in triumph. 'That's it! I'd just been saying that you and I have been friends since we first came, and then I said I was coming to dinner with you tonight and he said: "Best English teacher this school's ever had." Those were his exact words. "Best English teacher this school's ever had." What d'you think of that, then? Quite a compliment coming from a dry old stick like that, eh?'

'Mmm, yes, indeed!' replied Edward, somewhat heavily role-playing surprise and pleasure. 'Yes, that is quite a compliment. Beats me how he would come to that conclusion, mind you. He's never seen me teach that I'm aware of.'

'Well, there's exam results for a start. Speak for themselves, don't they? And these things get around – through the kids, other members of staff, it's a funny little gossipy village, a school, isn't it, Ted?'

Yes, Michael, a funny little gossipy village.

'But how did this come about, then, Michael – you and friend Salmons chatting about me, I mean? Seems a bit unlikely somehow. Have some . . . ?'

He offered the wine once more to Michael, who held out his glass and nodded thanks. For the first time that evening Edward was beginning to enjoy himself. Michael took a sip from his glass and shrugged.

'Oh, we just ran into each other at the end of school and got chatting. I think he asked me what I was doing tonight, and, like I said, I told him that Sophie and I had the very good fortune to be coming to supper in Oxford Avenue with two of my favourite people, and that's when he said that about your teaching. Can't be all bad, can he?'

'Still, I am surprised,' said Edward reflectively. 'I sometimes get the impression that an awful lot of the staff see me as a sort of in-house loony. Do you know what I mean?'

For a moment he thought he might have gone too far. For one tiny fraction of a second Michael seemed to twitch inwardly, as if an unexpected connection had been made, then the moment was past, and, seeing in Michael's face an expression of sternly serious intent, Edward realized with a sense of wonder and horror, that he was about to be encouraged!

'Edward Sewell,' Michael raised his right hand flat in the air, pointing into Edward's face with the tips of his fingers, 'don't you ever let me hear you run yourself down like that again. I don't know if anyone does think stupid things like that, but I can tell you one thing. They'd better not try passing their views on to me, whoever they are. They'll get more than they've bargained for.' He gave a little self-deprecatory laugh. 'In any case, if you're a – what was it?'

'A loony, Michael.'

'If you're a loony, and I'm your friend, what does that make me?'

Well, basically that makes you a lying, treacherous, son of a . . .

'So no more of that, thank you, Mr Sewell. By the way,' Michael glanced at the door before leaning across the table to speak in conspiratorially hushed tones, 'what's this mystery event that won't work unless mixed grill's on the menu? You want to watch it, mate, you nearly let the cat out of the bag there, didn't you? What's going on? Anniversary or something?'

Suddenly Edward was no longer enjoying himself. Oh, what a tangled web ...

'Shush, they're coming back.'

The meal continued in a sort of fog as far as Edward was concerned. Michael repeated Salmons' comment for Jenny's sake (Jenny was really pleased, as he'd known she would be), and he also repeated the gist of that little stern lecture he had delivered, offering to Jenny his considered view that Edward should give himself greater credit for his achievements and be more prepared to trust that his friends would always support him in the event of criticism. Jenny heartily agreed – so did Sophie. Edward nearly brought up his seafood lasagne.

It was at this point that Edward fought, and succeeded in overcoming, a strong temptation to regale the company with an anecdote about his last visit to the hairdresser's, when the girl who always did his trim had complimented him on having such a luxuriant head of hair. She had also expressed a particular interest in, and admiration for, the fact that his hair showed not a trace of grey, despite what obviously seemed to her his relatively advanced age. He fantasized about following this account with merciless repetition of its salient points. 'Luxuriant, this girl said, Michael, meaning a great deal of it, you understand. More than I need. Enough for two. Lots of it. Lots and lots of hair. Lots of thick, dark, luxuriant hair with no grey in it, the sort of hair that pathetic sub-male baldies like you would love to have but can't because they're getting bald, bald, bald!'

He could taste the words, hot on his tongue, but the very thought of losing control and actually saying such dreadful, childish things in front of his wife and the trusting Sophie made him shiver inside. The sooner this farce of a meal ended the better. He knew that there was bound to be instant interrogation as soon as the front door had closed behind their two guests, but at least he would be free to say exactly what he thought then, and Jenny could surely not fail to be sympathetic when she knew what had happened. In the meantime, perhaps assuming that her husband was suffering from some kind of brainstorm, she had obviously decided to take charge of the situation, and, as usual, she really did do a very good job, encouraging Michael and Sophie to talk at length about themselves and their future plans. A topic of conversation, Edward told himself, that never ceases to provide hours of fascination for those who are doing the talking.

It was over coffee that Michael, who had spent some time out-lining the future of P.E. teaching as he envisioned it, leaned back in his chair and said, 'What about the old poetry, Ted? These evenings of ours wouldn't be complete without an offering from the bard of Oxford Avenue, would they, Sofe?'

Sophie, who had never managed to understand a single line of Edward's poetry, smiled and nodded good-humouredly, look-ing forward to the time, hopefully not far in the future now, when she and Jenny would disappear into the kitchen to wash up and gossip while the two husbands drank their brandy in the dining-room.

Edward thought he had made a firm decision not to react neg-atively to anything else that the other man might say in the course of the evening, but this comment simply took his breath away. Why was Michael actually *asking* to hear some of the 'entrails' that he despised and found so boring? He pulled himself together. This time he was prepared.

'Could you pass that notebook, darling, please, just there on the side. Yes, that's the one. Thanks.' He flicked through the pages until he came to the one he wanted. 'There was something I thought you might like to hear actually,' he said. 'It's more dog-gerel than poetry, and it's not really finished, not honed, if you know what I mean, but ... well, you see what you think.'

Sensitivity makes you very sensitive, thought Edward, glancing up in time to register an almost imperceptible tilt of Michael's wrist, as the younger man contemplated a glance at his watch, then thought better of it.

Jenny was looking a little puzzled. Usually, she was asked to read and comment on Edward's new work before anyone else was allowed so much as to sniff at it.

Sophie frowned and leaned forward. She looked as if she was straining to locate those hitherto undiscovered muscles which, when flexed, might aid comprehension.

'Fire away,' said Michael, 'looking forward to this.'

'Right, well, "United In Glory" is the title,' announced Edward. He began to read from his notebook:

> 'Duncan Edwards, once the best,
> Went early to his well-earned rest,
> To find God nursed a secret dream,
> Of managing a football team,
> Seeing Munich made God sad,
> But keen to rescue good from bad,
> Couldn't help but be delighted,
> Most of Manchester United,
> Turned up at the Pearly Gates,
> Good old Duncan with his mates,
> They were offered free salvation,
> Pending full negotiation,
> Contracts stating that the fee,
> Would bind them for eternity,
> (Transfer bans were just as well,
> The only place to go was hell)
> Wages well worth playing for,
> The love of God for ever more,
> Practised kicks and moves and passes,
> Over heaven's shining grasses,
> None more expert than their boss,
> (A long-time expert on the cross)

He laid on boots and kit and towels,
But vetoed all professional fouls,
Aware the team was not complete,
He said he'd need to slightly cheat,
So, doing the pragmatic thing,
He put an angel on the wing.
At last, God's team lined up with pride,
To play Old Nick's infernal side,
And watched by several billion souls,
Heaven won by thirteen goals,
Duncan, who'd put seven in,
Asked God what made him sure they'd win,
Said God, 'No miracles required,
You did it all, a team inspired,
Besides, I knew that, as a rule,
Hell recruits from Liverpool.'

It was one of *the* most gratifying moments that Edward had known for a very long time. All three of the others sitting round the table had been visibly jerked out of their common perception of him by the words he had just read. Michael, for instance, looked, to use an example of modern slang that Edward had tended to abhor in the classroom but particularly relished in private, veritably gob-smacked. Jenny, leaning back in her chair with folded arms, was gazing at her husband with a rare combination of shock, wariness and concern, rather as if she was beginning to suspect that he might be an imposter – an Edward Sewell doppelgänger. Sophie was surprised but delighted. She had heard all about the Munich air disaster from her husband. For once, she felt that she had understood quite a lot of one of Edward's poems. She was the first to make a comment.

'Oh, Eddie, that was reely good, I mean it. The way you made it all – you know. That was reely good, wasn't it, Mike? All about your team too. Reely good!'

'It was excellent,' agreed Mike, looking rather puzzled, but sounding more connected than he had all evening. 'I'd really like a copy of that, Ted, if you don't mind. Completely different from your usual stuff. I didn't know you were a United fan.'

So satisfying, thought Edward, to look into Michael's eyes and see a sudden shift in the foundations of his infuriatingly confident assumption that he knew exactly what to expect from E. Sewell, the old idiot whom, he had very kindly said, he wouldn't want to actually upset.

'Oh, I'm not a United fan,' he replied, 'I was just fiddling around earlier and came up with that. It's nothing really.'

There was a short silence.

'Right!' Jenny smacked the table lightly with the palms of her hands. 'I think it's about time you and I attacked the Baileys, don't you, Sophie? Let's leave these two ... ' throwing a sardonic glance in Edward's direction 'football fanatics to chew the turf together while we get things a bit cleared up in the kitchen.'

'Ooh, yes,' responded Sophie enthusiastically, 'there's something I wanted to ask you about.'

Oh, dear, thought Edward, as the two women left the room, everyone seems to have something to say to someone else. Michael was presumably about to mention the 'something serious' that was on his mind, Sophie wanted to ask Jenny about something, Jenny would undoubtedly be planning to grill Edward intensively just as soon as their guests had gone, and he, himself – did he have anything further to say to this man who appeared to despise him in reality, but continually offered shallow blandishments to his face? Perhaps.

'Ted, I wonder if we could have a little chat?'

It was a few minutes later. An opened brandy bottle stood on the table between them, and a good measure of the precious liquid had been poured into two of the extravagantly bulbous glasses, inherited from his father, that Edward loved to hold and look at and drink from.

'Have we come to the serious bit now, then, Michael?' Edward held his glass in front of his eyes and studied its contents with deep concentration. Perhaps the secret of life itself would be revealed if he were to peer into that twinkling amber world for long enough.

'It's about these evenings of ours,' said Michael, the pitch of his voice very slightly higher than usual. 'There's something – I wondered if we could just talk about one thing that's been part of us getting together like this. Don't get me wrong. As I said earlier, I really relax when I come here, and Sophie gets on like a house on fire with Jenny, so it's not, you know, anything big. It's just that almost every time we have dinner together, round about now, when the girls are out of the way, we – you have sort of been in the habit of bringing up the past. All the stuff about church background and that kind of thing. We do talk about that almost every time we have dinner together, don't we?'

'You'd rather we didn't talk about it at all?' Edward continued to stare into the depths of his glass.

Michael sucked air in through his teeth and rubbed the top of his head vigorously with the tips of his fingers to indicate the intensity of his wish to avoid giving offence. Careful, Michael, thought Edward, you'll rub the fluff away.

'Look, Ed, that poem of yours just now – really good. Like I said, you must let me have a copy – that poem says what you and I really think about religion. It's a game. It's a picture of what a lot of people wish was true. But that's all it is. My mother and father totally believed every word of it because they were fully-committed, born-again types, and even your dad was well into it, wasn't he, although perhaps not in the same way that they were. When I was small I just got caught up and brainwashed like you can easily do when you're a kid, but, well, it was a long time ago, Ed, and – I have to be quite honest with you – I really would prefer to put it all behind me now and just leave it there. Our parents were good people, but – but they were deluded. That's the bottom line for me. I just want to ask if we can leave it off the old agenda from now on because I feel as if I'm being dragged backwards every time we talk about it. What do you say?'

Everything inside Edward had suddenly become very still. He did indeed feel as if an important secret might have been communicated to him, but not from the depths of the brandy. He lowered his glass a little and looked straight into the other man's eyes. When he spoke, his voice was quiet and controlled.

'What did you mean when you said "*even* your dad was well into it"?'

Michael frowned and shook his head, somewhat nonplussed. 'I just meant that he was a traditional Anglican as opposed to a spirit-filled believer, that's all. What difference does it make?'

'And what exactly is the difference between a spirit-filled believer and a traditional Anglican?'

'Well, basically, Christians like the ones in my parents' church are aware that the Holy Spirit is just as important a member of the Trinity as the Father and the Son, and they've been baptized in the Spirit as well as by water, which is what Jesus said had to happen, and they use all the gifts of the Spirit, like prophecy and tongues and healing, all the things that Paul talks about so much in the New Testament. They're true, born-again children of God.'

'Who doesn't exist.'

'Err, that's right.'

'And traditional Anglicans?'

Michael swirled the brandy around in the bottom of his glass and took a tiny sip. 'Well, the general view in our church was that what you might call the mainline denominations, Anglicans, Methodists and so on, were in serious danger of missing the boat, or, to use a different metaphor that our pastor once suggested in one of his talks, they're dead limbs on the Christian tree, and will need to be lopped off in the end.'

'My father was a dry twig on a dead limb?' Edward's voice was still very quiet.

'Well, only if you believe in it all. Look . . .' Michael moved the brandy bottle and a salt cellar like chess pieces as he assembled his ideas, 'you don't have to believe it all to see the sense of it, surely. Much earlier this century God looks around the country and he sees a load of highly respectable, middle-class people trooping along to church every Sunday, purely out of habit, with no real idea of why they're going, and he says to himself, "Right, I've had enough of this. I'm going to set up churches full of believers who are genuinely committed, and anyone from the traditional denominations who wants can leave the church they're in and join one of the new ones. I'll leave spiritual gravity to finish off the old, lifeless ones. They'll just drop off when they're completely dead, or if not, I'll give 'em a little push."'

'So, in your opinion, my father was not a true believer.'

'Well, I didn't know him, Ted, so it's impossible for me to judge. He may have been an exception to the rule, for all I know. But as we know it's all nonsense anyway, what does it matter?'

Edward felt the suspicion of tears pricking the back of his eyelids. 'He prayed every single morning of his life after I was born that I would become a Christian. That's not bad for a dead twig, is it?' Michael just shrugged. 'And your mum and dad, Michael – you're saying, aren't you, that they were totally, one hundred per cent deluded? You are saying that, aren't you? You're saying that the thing they gave their whole life to was nothing but a game. A picture, I think you called it, didn't you?' He waited. 'Well?'

It was a strange moment. Michael's mouth was certainly moving and attempting to frame words, as though there was something he wanted to say in reply, but it was in his eyes that Edward read an admission and a silent pleading, a request for permission to be at peace in this matter. Could it be possible that they had experienced the same revelation this evening? For Edward was reeling inwardly from the shock of knowing something now that he had never known before, although the truth of it was a part of him. Perhaps it always had been. Michael's absurd distinctions had provided the final clarification. His father had not been deluded, or rather, he was not a man in whom such a delusion could find a lifetime's home. Of course he wasn't! The spirit of his father, as real to Edward today as when that dear man had been alive, that warm amalgam of gentleness, kindness, generosity and faith could never have been dependent for sustenance on a picture or a game. There was no delusion, except in the subtle denial of his own true responses. What Edward was experiencing was not a conversion, but a restoration of clear sight. And those who can see are more easily able to choose which path to take.

Michael's eyes had lost the battle with his mouth. 'It was a good enough game as games go,' said the mouth, 'but that's all it was, and I don't want to think about it any more if it's all the same to you, Ted.'

'Okay, Michael, I promise I won't mention it again unless you do. All right?'

'Fine – thanks,' said the mouth. Hold on to me, said the eyes.

Edward took a risk. 'There's one condition, though.'

'A condition?'

'Yes.' Edward tore a clean sheet of paper from the pad which was still lying on the table, and passed it across. 'I want you to write the truth on this piece of paper, then fold it up and give it to me to keep.'

'The truth?'

Michael's very visible attempt to pretend that he had not the faintest idea what Edward was talking about failed almost immediately. The sardonic smile simply would not be resurrected. For a second or two he stared at the blank sheet of paper in his hands, then, laying it down on the table, he took a slimly elegant Biro from the inside pocket of his jacket, clicked it, and wrote busily for about a minute. Finally, after stabbing the paper with a final full-stop, he put his pen away, folded the sheet neatly three times, and handed it back to Edward.

'I have a feeling we must have both gone stark staring bonkers,' he said with weary resignation, 'but there you are – take it. You can read it if you want, but only after I've gone. And we don't talk about it any more, right?'

'Right,' agreed Edward, 'I promise,' and he poured a little more brandy into both their glasses.

Half an hour later, when the usual twittering goodbyes and assurances of reunion had been completed, and the front door had finally closed behind Michael and Sophie, Edward put his arms around his wife in the hall. She stayed there for a few moments before drawing back and studying his face at arm's length.

'What happened today, Edward? If you say "nothing" I shall get a large, flat kitchen implement and beat you with it.'

'Promises, promises!' Edward smiled, feeling very tired suddenly. 'I was in the toilets at school today and I overheard Michael talking to that bloke Salmons about me and you and tonight's dinner party.'

Jenny gasped. 'What did he say?'

Edward repeated the conversation as accurately as memory would allow. 'He was nice about you,' he said in conclusion, 'said he'd got a lot of time for you, Mrs Loony.'

'Oh, Edward, darling, what a little rat. You must have been so upset. Why on earth didn't you tell me when you got back?'

He thought for a moment. 'Mmm, lots of bad reasons. I suppose I should have done really, shouldn't I? But, in fact, as it's turned out ... ' He laughed. 'You never did believe in my silly headache, did you? What did Sophie want to ask you, by the way?'

'Oh, yes, she said that she and Michael were wondering if we would be willing to do one of those things for little Paul where we agree to take him in and bring him up if his mum and dad get killed in a car crash or something. But after hearing about your toilet experience I can't understand why. Why us? Why Mr and Mrs Loony?'

'As far as Sophie's concerned it's obvious. She thinks the sun shines out of your back door ... '

'Edward!'

'So who could possibly make a better substitute mum for Paul if anything happened to her? And she's right. I agree with her. As for Michael ... ' he shook his head slowly from side to side, 'well, much more complicated, I think. Jenny, something happened this evening that we need to talk about. Not now, I don't mean, but soon – I haven't really sorted it out for myself yet. Tomorrow, perhaps.'

She yawned. 'Tomorrow will do. Do you think you'll ever tell Michael you heard all those things he said?'

Edward thought for a moment then shook his head. 'Too late – should have told him today if I was going to. No, I shan't.'

'Let's go to bed, Edward. Nothing matters much till the morning, and it's blessed, wonderful Saturday tomorrow, so we can sleep in if we want.'

Edward and Jenny were both asleep by eleven thirty. At three o'clock in the morning the extension telephone in their bedroom rang. Edward always said that when the phone rang at that time of night it could only be bad news or an Australian. Jenny answered it. This time it was bad news. Michael had suffered some kind of massive heart attack during the night, and had been rushed by ambulance to the hospital where Jenny did her part-time job, the nearest with an accident and emergency unit. It was the hospital on the phone now, passing on a message to say that Paul was safely with a neighbour, but Sophie had asked if Jenny could come and be with her at Casualty.

'Oh, poor, poor Sophie!' said Jenny, with tears in her eyes, as she struggled into her clothes, 'she'll be like a little wet handkerchief.' She put a hand over her mouth. 'Oh, Edward, I called him a rat last night. I wish I hadn't. You will come with me, won't you?'

The cold, dead weight of shock kept them both silent as they drove down the virtually deserted main road to the hospital. All that Edward could think of was Sophie's open, pretty face crumpled with grief, and Michael's worry over his thin hair. Thinking of the hair especially kept making him want to cry. They arrived at the hospital just before half-past three.

Michael died at six thirty that same morning, having failed to regain consciousness sufficiently to communicate with anyone. The next few hours were all about Jenny looking after Sophie, who alternated between silent, blank puzzlement and floods of tears throughout the morning. In the early afternoon she fell into a troubled sleep on the sitting-room sofa, exhausted by grief and lack of sleep. Jenny and Edward, worn out themselves, sat over strong coffee in the kitchen, letting whatever was in their heads come out in words.

'At least, wherever Michael is,' said Jenny, after a while, 'he knows his little boy is safe.'

Edward nodded agreement, but at Jenny's words an abstracted look came into his eyes. He pushed his chair back and stood up.

'Look, I think I'll go for a bit of a stroll,' he announced, 'just round the block – get some air. You can go when I get back if you want.'

It was a bright, frosty day, sparkling but cold. From the end of Oxford Avenue, Edward took the short cut through to the main road, turned right and walked briskly past the High Street shops until he arrived at the bottom of a flight of stone steps leading up to the austere frontage of St John's, the parish church where his father had been a regular worshipper for many years. Climbing the steps, he hesitated for a moment, then turned the handle of the big front door and pushed hard. To his slight surprise, it was unlocked. Slipping quickly into the church he leaned back against the door, clicking it shut behind him.

Inside, the hushed silence was almost a shock, the temperature even lower than it had been in the open air. Shivering with cold and vague apprehension, he made himself walk purposefully up the wide central aisle between row after row of long, dark-stained Victorian pews towards the east end of the church. Ascending two shallow steps to the cloth-covered altar, he stopped and rubbed his chilled hands together for a moment. Before him, one at each end of the altar, stood two majestically large brass candlesticks.

'I could steal those if I wanted to,' he murmured quietly to himself, 'but I don't think I will.'

Undoing two top overcoat buttons he reached inside his jacket pocket with numbed fingers, to locate and draw out the folded piece of paper that Michael had left with him the night before. Carefully unfolding it, he studied the words that had been written with close attention, nodding gently, as if not at all surprised by what he read. Refolding the sheet, he closed his eyes, and held it up in front of him in both hands for a few seconds, before laying it gently down on the flat surface of the altar.

After backing slowly down the steps, Edward sat huddled on the front pew for a little while. One stumbling prayer for Michael and Sophie, and one for himself and Jenny, then, suddenly embarrassed, he hurried out of the church into the brittle winter sunshine and the ice-cream air.

(A little girl runs up to a very satisfyingly police-manish sort of policeman.)

GIRL: *(Very breathless.)* 'Scuse me . . . oh, 'scuse me . . . Mr Policeman . . . Sir . . . 'scuse me!

PC: 'Allo, 'allo, 'allo. What's all this then, young feller-me-lad?

GIRL: I'm a girl! And I've found a flower.

PC: *(Laughs.)* You've found a flower, 'ave yer? I see. Well that's 'ardly a matter for 'er Majesty's police force now, is it?

GIRL: But you don't understand. It's not an ordinary flower – it's . . . it's . . . it's beautiful and it's tall and it's special and . . . please come and look!

PC: Well . . . I don't know . . .

GIRL: *(Rustles a paper bag.)* I'll give you a rhubarb and custard sweet if you do.

PC: Bribing a police officer, eh? All right then, just a quick look.

GIRL: It's over here. Come on!

PC: All right, all right. *(They move to the flower, looking up.)* Well, blow me down!

GIRL: Don't you think it's lovely? I think it's lovely. Do you think it's lovely? I think it's –

PC: *(Interrupts worriedly.)* Oh, it's er . . . lovely all right, but I am bound to point out in my official capacity that *(firmly)* it can't stop 'ere. Lovely and all that it may be, but it's blockin' the path and is therefore what we in the police force term a public nuisance. If it 'ad 'ad the sense to grow four feet away, over there, it might – I say might – 'ave been all right. Apart from that, it's too blinkin' big!

GIRL: *(Aghast.)* Too blinkin' big for what?

PC: Well . . . it's obvious isn't it? It . . . well, you imagine one of them petals falling off and 'itting someone on the 'ead. Besides, you'll 'ave everyone walking along 'ere with their 'eads in the air not looking where they're going, and before you know where you are they'll be crashing into each other all over the place.

GIRL: Please . . . you can't hurt it. It's too –

PC: Let's 'ave a look at the old rule book. 'Ere we are. *(Clears throat.)* Section thirty-six, paragraph twelve, line eight. "On encountering strange, abnormal or obstructive growths, the officer present shall summon a detachment of 'er majesty's armed forces, horticultural division, with three long blasts of his official whistle. He shall then relinquish 'is post to the military officer in charge." Right! 'Ere goes! *(Blows whistle three times. Army squad enters – one officer and two men.)*

HIGGINS: Left, right, left, right. Halt!

PC: Ah! That was quick. Now, as you can see, *(laboriously)* we 'ave a case 'ere of what you might call –

198

OFFICER: *(Interrupting briskly.)* All right, Constable, carry on. The army is here now, we'll handle things. Where's the flower? Ah, yes. Right, men. I don't know what it is, and I don't understand it, so I think we'd better blow it up. The enemy are devilish cunning, and I think what they've faced us with here is an unexploded flower. Corporal Higgins!

HIGGINS: Sah!

OFFICER: When I give the word you will place a small explosive charge at the base of the suspected object. Detonation of said charge will cause said device to explode, thus rendering said device harmless to the general public.

HIGGINS: Sah!

OFFICER: Private Hoggins!

HOGGINS: Sah!

OFFICER: Clear the area of all civilians until the danger's over. Shoot any who resist.

HOGGINS: Sah!

OFFICER: Right, men. Move!

HOGGINS: Right . . . back . . . back . . . Move along if you please, sir . . . Now, what have we here? . . . I'm sorry, miss, but you can't stop here. *(Rising impatience.)* We have a job to do, miss, and that involves you moving right away from that . . . that flower. Will you let go of it? Right, if that's your attitude . . . 'Mission to speak, sah!

OFFICER: Carry on, man.

HOGGINS: Sah! This person, sah! Refuses to move, sah!

OFFICER: I don't think you understand the danger you're in, miss. When that thing goes up, it'll take you with it.

GIRL: But it's a flower, not a bomb ... and even if it is a bomb, it's beautiful and frightening. You're ugly and frightening. Can't you please leave it alone?

OFFICER: Her mind's gone, Hoggins. Hold her back till we've finished.

HOGGINS: Sah! Right – you heard the officer – *(shouts)* Move!

GIRL: Ow! Let go! I think you're all horrid!

OFFICER: Right. Everybody down! Ready, Higgins?

HIGGINS: Sah!

OFFICER: Ignite on the word of command. Ignite! *(Small explosion.)*

GIRL: *(Running joyfully to the flower.)* It wasn't a bomb! It wasn't a bomb! You see! You see, sir! It wasn't a bomb! The flower's still there!

OFFICER: When you grow up, little girl, you'll hear about something called logic. If the army says that an object is a dangerous explosive device, and steps are then taken to destroy the device, then logically said device can no longer exist. I see no flower. Do you see a flower, Higgins?

HIGGINS: No, sah!

OFFICER: Hoggins?

HOGGINS: No, sah!

GIRL: But it is still there. It is isn't it? You can see it, can't you? Oh, do look! *(The soldiers prepare to move away.)*

OFFICER: Right, men – let's move!

HIGGINS: Left, right, left, right ... *(Fades into distance.)*
(Fade in to news.)

NEWS-READER: Here is the news. In a heated debate in the Commons tonight, Mr James Bland, Minister for the

Environment, sought to give assurances to the opposition spokesman on horticultural affairs that a large flower which has recently appeared in a small provincial town does not constitute a serious threat to national security. Mr Bland said that although contingency plans did exist for dealing with such a crisis on a national level, he had no reason to believe that the local authority concerned was not fully competent to deal with the situation, and that interference by central government in local affairs was not a feature of the manifesto that had brought this party to power. At the same time, he added, the government was fully up to date on the crisis and prepared to intervene if and when it became necessary. Replying to suggestions that the troops had in fact already tried and failed to subdue the flower, Mr Bland said that he was unable to comment for reasons of security. Meanwhile, observers report that the flower continues to flourish.

Now, the Middle East conflict, and after this week's fresh outbreak of hostilities . . . _(Fade out. Fade in – stirring, insistent documentary music is heard. It is the introduction to the TV programme Focus.)_

PRESENTER: Good evening and welcome to _Focus_. Once again we are zooming in on a subject of current national concern. Our aim as always is to reveal the truth behind the rumours, to ask the important questions, and, if possible, to provide some of the answers. Tonight – it's the flower problem. Not flowers in general, but one flower in particular: the flower which stands behind me here. In a very short space of time this 'growth from below the ground' has threatened to undermine the very fabric of our society. Why has a single flower, admittedly an unusual one, given rise to so much controversy and debate? The alleged failure of the armed forces to deal with the situation raises serious questions about internal security, and indirectly the effectiveness of the present government. Should the flower go, or should it stay? People everywhere are demanding an answer.

Tonight, we have invited four experts to join us here on the spot – a comparative horticulturalist, a cabinet minister, a minister of the church, and a child psychologist – to give us their ideas on the implications of, and possible solutions to, this pressing problem. We are hoping – everyone is hoping – for some answers here tonight. But, first of all, could our children be in danger? For an answer to this question we turn to a child psychologist, Miss Olga Fink.

PSYCH.: I would like to say straightaway that I believe this flower to be a serious threat to the healthy mental development of those children who encounter it, and there are good reasons for this belief. I think everyone would agree that the flower is abnormal in many ways. For the developing child an encounter with such abnormality can grossly disturb and disrupt that perception of an ordered world which is so necessary to the maturing infant, and in some cases could cause serious damage. We can only achieve real security by seeing ourselves as units in a world where the laws of nature and human behaviour have never, and will never be, altered to any great extent. Clearly, then, the child who is suddenly exposed to such a phenomenon as this absurdity will begin to develop the dangerous notion that *(dramatic pause)* ... things do not necessarily have to remain as they are. Throughout his life that child would be expecting, perhaps in serious cases, even hoping, for something more than the real world has to offer. Such an outlook can only lead to fantasy, depression and a paranoiac dissatisfaction with life as it really is. If we persist in allowing our children's minds to be filled with false ideals, they may become as obsessive as this child here, who originally found the flower and now seems hopelessly ensnared by the mutation. Unless I'm very much mistaken her responses will already be heavily conditioned by exposure to this plant. Let me show you what I mean. *(Approaches little girl as though visiting a dying relative.)* Little girl, what do you think about this flower? What do you see there?

GIRL: *(Puzzled.)* A flower.

PSYCH.: *(Indulgently.)* Of course, yes ... but I mean, how does it make you feel inside?

GIRL: Happy.

PSYCH.: Happy?

GIRL: Yes, happy.

PSYCH.: Happy? Happy? *(Annoyed.)* What is happy? I want to know why you keep staring at this ... thing.

GIRL: Because ... it's beautiful. It's just ... beautiful. I just love looking at it – it's so beautiful.

PSYCH.: But ... *(Gives up in despair.)* As I thought, this sad little girl is already almost incapable of rational conversation. She sees only what appears before her, her feelings are dictated by her emotions, and her thinking is governed almost

203

entirely by her thoughts. To use an old-fashioned term, she is ... simple. If this flower can have this effect in so short a time, we *must* decide how best to protect our children in the future. In my view, there can be no doubt – the flower must go!

PRESENTER: A grave warning indeed, and one which I am sure will cause parents everywhere to ask of the authorities, 'What are you going to do? What is the official view of the situation?' To answer these questions we have with us tonight the Minister for the Environment, the Right Honourable James Bland. Minister ...

BLAND: Well, I think everyone will agree that there has already been too much beating about the bush on this issue. The time has come for somebody to make a committed stand on one side or the other. There has been quite enough talk – more than enough discussion. What is needed is the courage to put forward a definite viewpoint and stand by that viewpoint, whatever the consequences.

The flower must go! So say those who take that particular line, and I am in full agreement with any action which ensures that such an option remains a viable alternative. The arguments put forward in favour of preserving this plant are equalled in potency only by the highly respected views of those who do not take that particular stance. Let us not consider personal feelings, except to the extent that they guide us to a solution based on certain facts which must be ignored if the truth is to be served. The government is quite clear on this issue. We intend to pursue a firm policy of action until that policy is rendered obsolete by virtue of its inability to fulfil those objectives which caused it to be put forward in the first place. This kind of consistency, involving as it does a healthy refusal to equate theory with mere practice, will result in the flower staying within the boundaries of a situation which is defined by its insistence on a strong decision concerning the removal of restrictions on the flower's ultimate fate. Our position, then, is clear. We both oppose and support resistance to measures which are exclusive of either side of the argument. To those who do not welcome this kind of straight talking, we simply say, 'Leave it to those who do.' Thank you.

PRESENTER: Well I don't know what our viewers made of that, but I'd like to ask you a straight question, Mr Bland. Are you in favour of removing the flower, or allowing it to stay?

BLAND: That is exactly our position, yes.

PRESENTER: I'm sorry, Mr Bland, but can I press you a little further on that? What is the government going to do? What are your immediate plans? Where do you go from here?

BLAND: *(Pause.)* To the station. So sorry. Train to catch, must run, so sorry. All under control . . . *(Fades into distance.)*

PRESENTER: Well – so much for the government view. That was Mr James Bland, minister for the environment. Now, let's turn to the church for the spiritual angle, and I want to ask the Reverend William Cuthbert, vicar of the local church, how he sees the situation. Reverend, what do you think of this flower?

REVEREND: I must start by saying that I have personally examined this flower very carefully, and I have no hesitation in saying that it is one of the most beautiful things I have ever seen. The flower is, in fact, so stimulating *(a dangerous word for him?)* that I think it must be approached with care. The effect of such a bloom on both children and adults is very difficult to predict.

PRESENTER: What should we do?

REVEREND: I believe that a period of waiting is indicated. In, let us say, ten years time, it should be more possible to assess the implications of this lovely object and perhaps even to give the go-ahead for free and general enjoyment of such unusual beauty.

PRESENTER: And in the meantime?

REVEREND: My suggestion is that the flower should certainly *not* be destroyed. Rather, let the church remove the plant and keep it carefully during the next decade in a secure part of one of our church gardens where it can neither harm nor be harmed, as might be the case if it were left out here in the open. At the end of that period the situation could be reviewed and the whole matter reconsidered.

PRESENTER: And in the meantime the flower would not be on view at all?

REVEREND: I am sure the church would have no objection to selected groups viewing the flower with the co-operation of the clergy involved. To this end one could prepare a viewing rota which might be concentrated on weekends, and also include one or two periods during the week.

PRESENTER: So what would the next move be?

REVEREND: I think that our priority must be to remove this beautiful thing from general circulation, both for its own safety and for the safety of those who may falsely interpret its meaning. We cannot be hasty in these matters. We may, *(pauses as he becomes increasingly absorbed by the flower)* like this little girl, feel … greatly attracted in a very simple way to the sheer loveliness of the flower, but perhaps in a sense *(comes to his senses)* she has started at the wrong end. We have a wonderful thing here. Let us not spoil it by relying too hastily on our initial responses to what we see. We have made one or two mistakes of this kind in the past. The result has been division, argument and disharmony. I hope that we have now learned our lesson. *(Increasing in confidence.)* We need to develop a universally accepted system of formal appreciation with regard to this flower before we allow passion or excitement to cloud the issue.

PRESENTER: Thank you very much, Reverend. Miss Fink, what do you think of the vicar's suggestion? Do you agree with him?

PSYCH.: Oh yes. If the flower is taken over by the church I think we can all stop worrying. It will be forgotten within weeks.

PRESENTER: Well, we seem to have an uneasy agreement there. Now, before we turn to our last speaker, I'll see if I can get a comment from the little girl who first found the flower. *(Goes to her.)* Hello, there! All the people listening would like to know what you think about this flower. Would you like to tell everybody?

GIRL: *(Pause.)* I think … I think … it's so lovely. I can't think of anything else to say.

PRESENTER: Okay, well now, you've listened to what all these people have been saying about what should be done with the flower. What do you think we should do with it?

GIRL: I think ... perhaps ... we should water it and then look at it some more.

PRESENTER: *(Touched.)* We should water it. I see. All right, you go and get some water while we go on with our programme. *(Girl leaves.)*

GIRL: All right, but you will look after it, won't you?

PRESENTER: Yes, yes of course. *(Turns to camera.)* If only it was that easy, but it's not. So let's turn to our last expert, Dr Harry Winter, an internationally known comparative horticulturalist who has done much to bring horticulture to the people in a way that can be accepted and understood even by those who find it difficult to appreciate flowers of any kind. Dr Winter ...

WINTER: Right, if we could just gather round the flower. Good. Thank you. Well, you know, I think this whole thing has got rather out of hand, and I want to show you how a proper horticultural perspective will invalidate most of the myths which seem to surround this so-called flower. The fact is that in a very real sense, this flower simply cannot exist. It goes against all we know about plant growth. Let me say categorically that this is *not* a new species of plant. I've seen it all before. Everybody screams, 'New flower, new flower!' and within a few days it turns out to be artificial or poisonous or freakish. This growth cannot exist in any known type of soil or climatic condition, and it will certainly never reproduce itself. And yet some people, including myself, do not feel that the flower should be totally destroyed. It has a certain ... potential ... charm, and I believe that any qualities that this plant possesses should be available to everybody. I suggest, therefore, that we preserve the flower, but in an acceptable form, in a form that will allow people to say, 'Yes! This is something I can enjoy without having to abandon my common sense.' Let me show what I mean. *(He produces a pair of garden shears and prepares to cut.)*

REVEREND: Are you sure that . . . *(Sound of first cut.)* Oh dear!

WINTER: If I just snip off this branch here . . . and this one . . . Cut a little more off this side . . . Now, let's shape these petals . . . and again . . . *(Lots of vigorous snips.)* There! I think that deals rather neatly with the situation. The flower now conforms to normal expectations, it can no longer harm the minds of little children, nor can it exhaust the wits of our politicians.

PRESENTER: Well, there we are. The flower problem seems to be a problem no more. Thank you, Dr Winter, Miss Fink, Reverend Cuthbert, and thank you for joining us. From *Focus*, goodnight.

(Everybody leaves except the vicar.)

PSYCH.: Are you coming, Vicar?

REVEREND: Er, no . . . I think I'll just wait for . . . that is wait until . . . oh dear, oh dear, oh dear!

(The little girl arrives back with her water.)

GIRL: I've got the water . . . I . . . oh . . . oh no! *(Pause.)* Oh look, look at your poor, poor petals! Oh, I'm so sorry!

(Silence.)

REVEREND: I'm afraid we . . . I didn't think they'd actually hurt it. *(Pause.)* I wish . . . I wish I could have stopped them. I just didn't have the courage, I'm afraid. *(Pause.)* Do take your head out of your hands. Please don't cry.

GIRL: *(Raising her head.)* I'm not crying.

REVEREND: Oh ...?

GIRL: I'm remembering.

REVEREND: Remembering ...?

GIRL: My flower. I thought someone might do something to it, so I looked and looked and looked at it so that I'd remember every bit of it.

REVEREND: And do you ... remember every bit of it?

GIRL: Yes. I do. Every bit.

REVEREND: Hmmm ... I'm afraid that although I remember it was very beautiful, the details are rather hazy. What with all the speakers and the discussions and ... well. *(Pause.)* I wish I could see it again.

GIRL: Well ...

REVEREND: Yes?

GIRL: I could tell you about it.

REVEREND: Would you? Please.

GIRL: Well, it was tall, and very unusual, and very, very pretty – and the colours – they were ... they were blue and red and yellow. They were the best thing ... *(They walk away hand in hand.)*

The Cellar

'And now – I'm going down into the cellar.'

Weighing the heavy old cast-iron key in the palm of her hand, Lucinda marvelled at how light and relaxed her own voice sounded. In fact, she thought, her whole being felt clothed in a robe of peace. A foolish fancy, but it really was difficult even to imagine the old fear regaining ascendancy over her.

During the last three years, the period when her mind had been in such a sadly unhappy state, Lucinda had never once dared to take down the big old-fashioned key from the hook under the stairs in the hall, let alone use it to open her cellar door. That subterranean place had somehow acquired a negative significance that was really frightening. The merest, vaguest thought of actually going down there had been enough to shorten her breath and displace other emotions with sheer panic. Panic was a very bad thing for Lucinda. It triggered the endless cycles of delusion that, at the best of those terrible times, threw her into torment for most of her waking hours. Organising the world in her head so that thinking about the cellar never came to the front of her mind had been a secret, tiny little achievement unknown to anyone else, and that included her friend Sally from the shop in the High Street. After hours of patient listening, Sally knew more about the inside of Lucinda's head than people like Doctor

Poole or even Janet, her counsellor. The cellar thing was something she had done herself, all on her own, something to slip into a very private place and feel proud of, even if she could only afford to glance quickly at it out of the corner of her mind before hurrying out again, as it were.

But now she was going to do it. She was going down into the cellar. Why? Well, simply because – because she could.

It had been heart-warmingly, tearfully good arriving back home to her friendly, semi-detached Victorian house, still equipped with its wonderful, ponderous old sash windows, the sort that brought hopeful double-glazing salesmen panting lustfully and in vain to her door at least once a fortnight. For the first time in years she was able to see and appreciate it properly. It was her place – of *course* it was – decorated and furnished since her father's death half a decade ago in all the russets and browns and careful greens that she loved to surround herself with. Only the cellar had been left as it was.

Lucinda had forgotten how warm and enfolding and attractive she had made these small rooms with their high ceilings. Every picture, every ornament, every single item of kitchen and bathroom equipment had been chosen with the same, lingering, meticulous consideration. Who had done it? Remind yourself. Well, she had done it. Lucinda Evans had done it, and done it well. Every creative moment given to the task had been pure pleasure.

During those last three dark years everything of that sort had become empty and meaningless – irrelevant and silly. The house had stopped being a home. It turned into a cave with locks, a place where you crouched fearfully when the powerful people in charge at the hospital 'decanted' some of the patients out of the psychiatric ward for a holiday weekend or something equally alarming. Lucinda never invited anyone round, other than Sally very occasionally, and the place became dusty and untidy. In the end it was a real mess. She hadn't cared, and hardly noticed anyway, because there wasn't enough space in her head for trivial things like cleaning or polishing.

Now, unexpectedly, miraculously, everything had changed.

Getting out of hospital in time for Christmas had been sur-prising enough, but, in contrast with past experiences, leaving the institutional confines of the ward and then feeling so extra-ordinarily optimistic and clear-headed on the outside was like walking through a door labelled Hell and finding yourself in heaven.

Sitting opposite Lucinda in her bedspace with the curtains drawn Doctor Poole had explained that it did sometimes happen like that. It could take months or even years to get the medica-tion absolutely right, he'd told her, but at this point in time he felt extremely hopeful about her case, and thought she should go home and not do anything too stressful, just relax and simply enjoy not being tortured by those black fears that they had talked about on so many different occasions. He reminded her that there had been times in the past when, for a few days or weeks, she had felt quite a lot better, but had then had to return to the hospital because everything slumped into being as bad as before or even worse. He hoped – no, he honestly believed that this time was dif-ferent, but she must be careful not to upset herself. Wherever pos-sible, she must steer carefully round the things that had been a problem in the past, he advised, and return regularly as an out-patient so that he and his colleagues could keep an eye on her.

Then he had made his eyes twinkle as he usually did at the end of an interview, slapped his knees before getting up, and said, 'I think the chemicals in that head of yours might really be getting their act together at last. Let's hope so! Have a wonderful Christ-mas, Lucinda.'

Lucinda had thanked Doctor Poole and promised she would be careful. She had not told him – she had never told him – how much she always loathed and hated any talk about chemicals in her brain. How could the way you behaved and thought and felt be determined by little globules of this and that slopping around inside your head and being good or bad for you depending on what happened when they met and mixed together and what their proportions were? How could that be so? She very much did not want that to be so.

Of course, as in the past, there had been people to say good-bye to before leaving the ward. Tommy, who always sat in the corridor by the door waiting for his mother to come, although Lucinda knew she never would because she was dead, had cried when she told him she was going, so had wheelchair Martha, who was very friendly and kind, made tea for everybody and had been in places like this for more than twenty years. Daniel, a tall, thin, older man who was always telling Lucinda he fancied her, asked to be remembered in her will for obscure but probably quite logical reasons of his own. And beautiful, sad Miriam who spent all day drawing daisy-chains and fairies and weeping because she was not allowed to be a little girl any more, had pressed a little silver locket on a chain into Lucinda's hand, and said she hoped Lucinda would be back very soon. Then she had thrown her hands up, flushed and said 'You know what I mean!' and they had both laughed.

Later, about to walk out through the double-doors behind the reassuringly plump and familiar figure of Sally, who had kindly come to collect her in her little car after lunch, Lucinda had paused and looked back over her shoulder past Tommy down the ward corridor for a moment. All those patients and their chemicals. She had felt a bit sick as she pushed the doors open and walked down the wide stairs towards the bright entrance hall and the car-park just outside.

For some time Sally had been amazed and delighted at how well her friend was.

'The last week or two I've stopped being careful about what I say to you,' she said, as they drove along the main road away from the hospital.

'Good,' sighed Lucinda, 'just carry on like that.' She smiled and patted Sally's arm. 'You know how grateful I am to you for putting up with so much of my rubbish, but I'm much happier not being a loony, if it's all the same to you. From now on a loaf of bread and a pound of sausages is all I'll be asking you for – I hope.'

'You'll be fine, love,' murmured Sally comfortably, 'I think you'll be just fine.'

And that was precisely what she had been. She had been fine. From the moment she stepped out of Sally's car and turned the key in the lock of her own front door Lucinda had remained utterly, almost disconcertingly fine. It was, she reflected with wonder, like the electricity coming on after a night-time power-cut when you've been stumbling and groping around in the dark searching for just one live match in a box and any old fragment of candle. The world – her world – was unexpectedly flooded with light, and it was bewilderingly difficult to remember just how tough it had been in the darkness. Suddenly it was ridiculously easy to be alive. Chemicals getting their act together. Perhaps.

That night, after taking a shower, she had dared to look at herself naked in the mirror in her bedroom for the first time for months. Not too catastrophic, she'd thought, for someone in her late forties. A little overweight in all the wrong places, but a bit of exercise might sort that out. Perhaps she'd start going up to the gym in the new year. What a thought! Smoothing her dark, shoulder-length hair around her face to make it look less round, Lucinda wondered if it was too late for her. Not Daniel, though. Not anyone like Daniel. Not anyone who had ever been on a ward.

She spent her first two days at home working in the house. The rooms were not large, but there were a lot of them, and the months of neglect had left a sort of crust. A week of hard work would only just begin to touch it. She had relished the work, though, putting her gloves on and cleaning and scrubbing and dusting and hoovering and throwing stuff away with a concentrated energy that seemed to grow and multiply on the culture of its own use. She would save sorting out the garden as a treat for when the house was finished. By the end of the second day the hall and quite a bit of downstairs was beginning to look halfway reasonable. Tomorrow she would walk up into the town and reward herself for her hard work with some fresh flowers and one or two little new bits and pieces to brighten up the living-room.

That night Lucinda's sleep had been long, sweet and dreamless. She had woken feeling at peace but slightly confused, until, with a little rush of joy, she remembered.

'I'm at home – and I'm well!'

The cellar idea had come into her mind at that very moment. She was well, and when she'd finished her work today, she was going to go down to the cellar to prove it. It didn't need proving, of course, but she was going to do it anyway.

Later that morning she had found the town awash with folk making last minute purchases for Christmas, but there had been a bright, excited amiability among the crowds of shoppers and in the shops themselves that made Lucinda glad, and in a funny way proud, to be part of such bustling ordinariness once more. She bought a beautifully detailed porcelain model of a country cottage as a gift for Sally, and a card for Janet, who would be expecting to see her tomorrow.

That evening, just as she was finishing her tea, the phone went. It was Janet.

'Just rang to see how it's going and check if we're on for tomorrow.'

'Oh, Janet, I can't tell you how – I feel _so_ well!'

Janet's role in her life was quite different from Doctor Poole's. They had spent most of their sessions working through problems about things that had happened much earlier in Lucinda's life, private things connected with her father that had been very hard to forgive – not that it had stopped her virtually giving up a life of her own in order to nurse him during the last years of his life. The counselling sessions had started and been going on long before the onset of Lucinda's delusions, but Doctor Poole's professional opinion had been that the trauma in her early life had little bearing on or connection with the illness that he and his fellow-doctors had been treating. Although her counsellor never said so directly, Lucinda had been able to tell that Janet was by no means sure she was in agreement with this. She had felt pleased. It was better than chemicals.

'See you tomorrow – you be careful,' Janet said at the end of the call.

'I will be,' Lucinda replied.

But she had not mentioned the cellar.

At the precise moment when she turned the key to gain access to the cellar somebody knocked loudly on the front door. It made her jump. Clasping one hand against her chest, she automatically turned the key clockwise again, almost as if – despite her beating heart, Lucinda couldn't help smiling to herself at the thought – almost as if she was making sure someone or something couldn't get out before she returned.

It was only a man collecting for some children's charity. Lucinda fetched her bag from where it hung on the newel post at the bottom of the stairs, took her purse out and dropped a pound coin into the man's box. He thanked her and turned away with a wave. She closed the door. Good. Good. Good! Just look at that. She was a perfectly normal person who went to the front door, dealt competently with whatever needed dealing with, and then returned to the thing she had been doing before being interrupted.

Cellar.

The door opened inwards onto a little landing from which a flight of steep stone steps led down into pitch-blackness. She peered into the gloom, wrinkling her nose. An unpleasant smell rose from the depths, not damp, but dry and musty. A tiny stab of fear pricked her confidence. A faint fluttering of the heart. Well, why not? Presumably dark, long-deserted cellars were less than attractive to the toughest of people at the best of times, and this one had its own very distinct challenge for her. Okay, she was nervous now that the moment had come, but that was not the same as being neurotic.

Lucinda had armed herself with a heavy rubber torch unearthed from the back of a cupboard in the kitchen, and was about to switch it on when she noticed the old-fashioned, black plastic switch just inside the door on her left. Stretching out her hand she pushed it down, but without much hope. To her surprise a light came on somewhere below, illuminating the area that had been so impenetrably dark a moment ago. Gripping her torch tightly (three-year-old lightbulbs were surely not to be trusted any more than indefinable fears), she made her way slowly and carefully down the narrow flight of steps, then paused at the bottom, wide-eyed with apprehension, and looked around her. Heartbeat and breathing began to settle down almost immediately. Something of an anticlimax really. In one way the cellar was more or less as she recalled it, a largish, brick-walled room with a naked lightbulb hanging from the very centre of the low ceiling. The only difference was that it was far more cluttered than she remembered. Instead of the few old empty cement bags and lengths of wood piled in one corner that she had expected, the four walls were stacked from floor to ceiling with everything from dusty old odd pairs of wellingtons to broken deckchairs. She must have just dumped loads of things down here without thinking before her illness. She shrugged. It didn't matter. That was it. There was nothing else to see. It would have to be sorted out one day, but there was no hurry. Get upstairs sorted out first. She felt fine.

If anything, thought Lucinda, perhaps because of that single, cobweb-festooned bulb, the place had a slightly artificial atmosphere. Filmic. It reminded her of underground chambers in those melodramatic pre-war thrillers in which the hero gets incarcerated by the arch-villain and has to devise an ingenious escape plan before his underground prison fills up with poisonous gas or water or something equally improbable. The cellar was vivid in that rather unreal way. But no, there was nothing to fear here. It was just a space where unwanted things were stored. In the future, after she'd cleared the rubbish out, maybe she'd fix it up – do something clever with it.

As she closed and locked the cellar door behind her and hung the key back on its hook in the hall, Lucinda hummed contentedly. She had done it. She had faced a major symbol of her old fear and discovered that the fear itself was an impostor – a delusion.

She had to tell someone. Sally. Just ten minutes. Sally would still be at work. Slipping on her thick winter coat she buttoned it up against the cold of the December evening and let herself out of the front door.

Sally was stacking shelves in the off-licence section of the Early to Late shop when Lucinda came in. The stuff fell off the shelves as fast as you put it on at this time of year. Genuinely pleased to see her friend, she offered to take her next break early so that the two of them could have a cup of tea and a chat together in the little rest room at the back.

'I want to tell you about something I did today,' said Lucinda once they were settled.

Sally sipped her tea and smiled encouragingly, shaking her head from side to side in amazement once more at the sight of her friend so bright-eyed and confident. How many times in the past had Lucinda arrived in the shop looking painfully drawn in the face and physically rigid, filled with a frantic, completely non-distractible need to be told, to be reassured, that the elderly, harmless music-teacher who lived next door to her was in fact *not* inviting people round with secret listening devices to pry into the most intimate activities of her neighbour, or that most of the people who passed by her in the street were not already dead and beginning to rot away. This was not that deluded person. This was Lucinda as she was meant to be.

'You tell me what you did.'

'Okay, but – well, I'll have to start at the beginning.'

Lucinda explained all about how the cellar had become a sort of focal point of her fear, and how she had managed to temporarily put that fear in a part of her mind where it could do her no harm. And how, now that she was feeling so much better, she had wanted to face this final dark area, and so today – just now – that was exactly what she'd done.

So engrossed did she become in her own narrative that she had finished speaking before it dawned on her that the encouraging smile on the older woman's good-natured face had faded. Instead, she was gazing at her friend with a troubled, perplexed expression.

'Lucinda, sweetheart,' Sally said very softly and gently, laying a hand on her arm, 'there is no cellar. You haven't got a cellar in your house – you know you haven't, darling.'

Silence.

In the street outside, a choir started to sing carols through the sound system that the council had set up in the High Street.

> 'Silent night, holy night,
> All is calm . . . '

Lucinda frowned, and the pupils of her eyes seemed to flicker as a spasm passed once right through her body. Then she was completely still, her gaze as untroubled as it had been when she first walked into the shop, her manner as serene as an ocean becalmed between storms.

'Oh, of *course*,' she said, 'how silly of me.' Leaning forward a little she contracted her brows, wanting to understand, anxious to be sensible. 'So, what you're saying, Sally, is that you don't think I should go down there any more.'

Bethel

Between Black Carn and Logan Rock lived a snail called Bethel, who became proud. Heaven frowns on a vain snail, and Bethel had become just a little too big for his shell.

Yes, one admired the polished chestnut brown of him, the pearly, whirly, swirling cream of him, and the pin-line midnight black of him.

And, oh yes, one was enchanted by the bright, intelligent eyes, ever alert on their majestic, grey, swaying stalks, eyes that were full of passion with just a hint of pain. Bethel's trail was broad and shining. He had loved and lost and learned and loved again. Always intensely, and always . . . slowly.

But a day came when poor Bethel, blinded by ambition, said rash things near Frenchmen, birds and children.

'I shall never be consumed on licensed premises.'

'I shall never be smashed into succulence on a thrush's stone.'

'I shall never be condemned to absent-minded death in a child's glass prison, on a pile of dead leaves, beneath holes that let air in but will not let me out.'

The world reacted.

A failed restaurateur named Dupin, a thrush with a past called Mulligan, and a fat-kneed child whose name was Wallace, formed a gang and, in a wooden shack behind St Levan's Church, swore an oath to crush the spirit – if not the life – out of brave, foolish Bethel who, in their hatred, they nicknamed 'Slugpot'.

The gang was armed and vicious.

Dupin carried an onion knife as long as his arm.

Mulligan had a leather quiver full of sharp, bright nails, hanging from a stoatskin belt around his neck. Dip'n'spit was his obsession. He could pin a butterfly to a tree-trunk from ten feet.

The child Wallace carried a container shaped like a sneering face, into which he put things until they died. There was quite a lot in it.

The gang was very nasty indeed.

One day, Bethel chanced upon his own grave. The gang had done it to panic him, to soften him up for the kill.

Buried in the emerald dusk of a leafy wood near Trevilley was a small clearing. Here, beneath a notice-board fastened three feet above the ground to a young beech tree, two terrified lizards hacked frantically at the ground with silver cruet spoons, relics of some long-forgotten holidaymakers' picnic. Their small stupid mouths dropped open in horror as Bethel streamed easily into the glade, a favourite haunt – until now. By the sheer magnetism of his personality, he forced the trembling creatures to meet his steady gaze.

''Snot us, Gov,' jittered one, his eyes little black beads of fear. A pulse jerked and jumped under the yellow skin at his throat.

'Froggy an' Frush an' Fatty made us done yore 'ole,' said the other desperately. 'We likes yer, don' we, Micky?'

'Said they'd scrush us impletely,' squealed the one called Micky, his whole spotted skin stretched with apprehension. 'Else bung us in Fatty's pot. So we adder dig yore 'ole, else . . .' His shrill voice trailed off miserably.

But Bethel was no longer listening. He was reading the words that had been picked out on the notice-board in tiny silver nails. And as he read and understood, he no longer felt proud. He felt only fear.

IN BAD MEMORY OF SLUGPOT
REST IN PIECES
(... of shell. I ate the soft bit – signed, Mulligan)

Bethel felt the need for prayer and counsel. The hidden sanctuary in crumbling Penbar Cliff came to mind. A grinding journey for a pilgrim snail, but there, between sky and sea, was a place of peace and meditation. There he could seek advice from fat old Mutton-cruncher, shrewd and kind, the last wolf in England. Converted years ago, the ex-carnivore worked out his penance as a minister to those in need, assisted by three white novice ewes who, protected by the depth of Mutton-cruncher's conversion and his complete lack of teeth, served silently and devotedly in the candle-lit depths of the Penbar Chapel cave. In the velvet hush of this holy place, Bethel, weary but strangely calm, prayed a simple prayer before he approached the wheezing pile of dog-collared darkness seated beside the altar.

The huge wolf's crimson tongue flashed out and round and back as Bethel spoke with quiet urgency. The ancient yellow eyes snapped open for a startling moment, two tiny windows to the furnace of his brain. The snail waited, nervously sensing other, stranger supplicants in the deeper shadows of the cave behind him. He recalled strange tales of creatures so rare or ill-formed or wretched that the darkness of the cliff sanctuary offered the only safe home they would ever know.

At last the wolf stirred and spoke, his voice impossibly deep, unexpectedly warm.

'Are you brave and good, little snail?'

It was a time for truth.

'I have been proud. I fear for my life. I hate the gang ... especially Wallace.'

What would Mutton-cruncher suggest? What weapons? What strategies?

It seemed an age before the wolf spoke again.

'Have a party. Invite all three of them ... especially Wallace.'

Bethel stared. Party? What did he mean?

The old grey head bent forwards. The wolf's last whispered words were for the snail's ears only. As he listened, Bethel nodded gravely. Soon, he turned to leave. The fear remained, but there was a new and better resolve in his heart.

Evening sunlight turned the dust into tiny specks of gold on Bethel's polished drift-wood desk, as the snail sat staring thoughtfully at three sealed envelopes propped in a row before him.

His home was a converted hip-bath at the bottom of a dried-up pond out towards Porth Loe. Bethel was not rich as molluscs go, but he was a lover of beautiful things. He had one of the best collections of blue china fragments in the whole peninsula, each piece neatly drilled with a small hole and suspended from the ceiling by a barely visible length of fishing line.

Then there was the quite unique framed set of dawn webs, somehow preserved intact with their original dew, just as they had appeared at the magical moment when the legendary joy spiders of Logan Rock completed their ecstatic morning dance.

Over the window hung a portrait of Bethel's maternal grandfather, Dicken, a great traveller who had been painted in oils by Salvador Dalì. The great artist had later presented the finished work to Dicken in gratitude for a discreet personal service of unknown nature. It was a strange painting, but it meant a lot to Bethel.

It all meant a lot to him, this special place that had taken so long to find, furnish and make his own.

His eyes lingered fondly for a moment on his little personal library, a row of birch-bound volumes standing between two big pebble book-ends on the pine shelf beside him. He knew them all so well.

I Dared to Call a Slug 'Friend', the great liberal classic by Ambrose, the martyred pond snail.

Is God a Gastropod?, the controversial best-seller of the sixties.

The Whelk and the Spanish Dancer, by an anonymous winkle.

And Bethel's favourite, *Out of My Shell,* a light-hearted call for freedom of expression by the Gwennap Head philosopher, Caliban.

All these things, the china, the webs, the picture, the books – they were all so dear and so familiar. Now, he was about to invite those whom he feared most in the world to come to his home for – of all things – a party! Would they not smash his home and all that was in it? Would they not smash him also? Glancing up at his grandfather's picture, he could almost hear old Dicken's careless chuckle: 'If a snail's got one foot in the grave, laddie he's in the grave!'

Bethel's heart nearly failed him. Only the memory of the wolf's head, dark and heavy beside his own, and the echo of the old minister's last whispered words, made him pick up the invitations and take them to the door where Micky the Lizard's youngest brother, Alf, was waiting to make the delivery to Dupin and Mulligan and Wallace.

Alf was very quick. Lizards had to be. It was their only talent, some claimed. A slow lizard was a useless lizard – a dispensable lizard. Alf hurried.

The first delivery took him up onto the St Buryan road where Dupin was busy in the greasy kitchen of *Le Cochon Mort,* a restaurant which an Egon Ronay agent had once described as 'La scum de la scum'. As a business it was dead, but Dupin was planning a private dinner for three. The invitation amused him. He spat into the milk pan and laughed in a gallic manner.

In his hollow oak armoury, Mulligan was sharpening nails with leisurely expertise on a flat, oddly discoloured stone. As he read Bethel's note, the expression of cold competence in his eyes did not alter in the slightest. He examined the point of a nail closely. It was not quite sharp enough.

Wallace was in his bedroom, squeezing super-glue onto the window-sill for sparrows. When his Aunt Pearl slid the invitation hastily under the door, he opened it slowly with his plump, raw sausage fingers, read it twice, licked his lips once, and glanced at the sneering pot in its special place beside the bed. His eyes gleamed, then disappeared as his fat face split into a smile. His lips moved silently, framing the word – 'Slugpot'.

Every morning and evening, Bethel carefully filled the old brass oil-lamp that balanced on a bracket by his door. It was a matter of routine. It burned night and day. This evening, his head full of troubles, the snail had forgotten to carry out this small but essential task. In the very early hours of the following morning, the comfortable yellow flame flickered for a moment then, with a series of little popping sounds, died completely. Bethel, still wide awake with worry, went rigid with fear as the darkness slammed into him from all sides.

When snails panic they simply stop thinking. Bethel panicked badly now. It was the dark – he was terrified of the dark. As a very young mollusc there had been an unfortunate incident with a cockroach in the pitch-black bend of a wet and echoing drain-pipe. Little Bethel, exploring recklessly despite his mother's warnings, had cowered back into the angle of the drain as the huge glutted roach lurched heavily past chanting the same words again and again in a horribly flat, dead voice:

> 'Satisfied
> to rot inside,
> we eat and eat
> but don't excrete.'

The loathsome creature hardly noticed the shivering snail. It was already far too bloated to bother with such a scrap.

Later, at home, Bethel's distraught mother had comforted the trembling podlet, while Grandpa Dicken, more than ready to take on the entire cockroach world single-handed, offered good advice: 'Roaches? Kick 'em in the legs – that's where their brains are!' Dicken knew a lot.

Nothing had ever removed the horror of the memory, though. Now, in the black silence, Bethel relived his childhood terror, and for an instant was unable to move. Then, like a crazy clockwork toy, he began to blunder from wall to wall, blindly seeking release from his own fear and from the army of phantom cockroaches that hunted him in the angry darkness. Things fell and smashed unheeded. Above his head, china pieces tinkled and jingled together as the whole house swayed and shook. At last the latch on the door was knocked loose and Bethel, feeling the flow of cool air on his body as the door swung open, turned instinctively in that direction, and was soon outside on the damp grass, his eyes drinking in the faint light from the cloudy night sky.

Those – and there are many – who label snails 'slow' should have seen Bethel that night as he urged himself, body and shell, up the grassy slope to the highest point of the cliff. There he rested beside a curiously shaped smooth stone slab, and, as if to reward his efforts, the moon, full and friendly, stepped from behind a cloud to illuminate the lonely cliff-top and the rock-strewn beach of Fool's Cove far beneath him.

Suddenly Bethel knew that all he wanted was escape from what awaited him on this day that had already begun – the party, the gang, the possibility of death. Never mind being good or brave – all that mattered was getting away. He looked up. The moon was very bright, the air as still as a sitting bird. Why should not tonight be the night for The Drop? It was early in the year. Usually he saved it up until late summer, but surely there would never be a night that was more ideal than this. The beach below was bathed in silver; in the far distance the ocean rumbled and whispered quietly in its sleep. It was perfect.

Excitement thrilled through Bethel's aching body – the same excitement that possessed him every year just before the descent. In a fever of decision he levered up the flat stone beside him and dragged out the back-pack in its thick cellophane cover. No lizard on hand to help with the straps this year, but he managed some-how, and after a pause for breath he slipped over the tufted grass on the cliff-edge with a little gasp of exhilarated abandonment and felt himself falling like a stone through the breathless air.

'One – two – three – four – five!'

There was the familiar jolting tug at his body as Bethel pulled the rip-cord, and the parachute opened like a huge upside-down flower. That moment of blossoming safety seemed a special kind of miracle, and the dream-like experience of floating down in the moonlight was the most magical sensation he had ever known. But it was over *so* soon. Less than a minute later he was carefully adjusting the angle of his descent in order to land as near as possible to his destination. Seconds later he made a good landing on a small patch of wet sand, shrugged off his harness, and moved quickly towards the base of the cliff where a glowing patch of artificial light marked the position of Oscar Wild's Mollusc Repair Shop.

He passed the sign saying NO HERMIT CRABS – HOW MANY TIMES DO I HAVE TO TELL YOU? and in the entrance to a natural cave, surrounded by tools, spares and the general paraphernalia of his trade, he found the old mole busily burnishing a cockle by the light of a single electric bulb, powered by an ancient generator chattering away somewhere in the cave behind him.

Oscar was a well-spoken, rather classy old mole, who after years of small-time shell repair and synthetic slime production had seen his life and work revolutionized by the development of fibreglass. He was the best in the business and could have become rich, but for some reason he chose to turn his back on financial gain to set up a workshop here at the bottom of the Fool's Cove cliff, where he served, serviced and repaired all manner of shelled creatures with great skill and discretion.

Bethel did The Drop once a year, partly for the obligatory slime and shell check, partly because he relished the whole experience, and partly because he enjoyed talking to old Oscar. The parachute had been Dicken's idea of course. Dicken and Oscar had enjoyed a very special friendship.

'How now, my brave Bethel?' greeted Oscar with a smile of surprise and pleasure. 'Early this year, are we not? How are we? Cracked, crinkled, crumpled, crushed? How goes it?'

'It goes not very well,' confessed Bethel as the cockle oozed away, and he climbed onto the work-pad. 'My big mouth, really.'

He told the greying mole about the gang, the trip to Penbar Chapel, and the party that was due to begin in less than twelve hours, if it happened at all. Oscar nodded slowly as he tested a sliver of artificial shell against a small nick in Bethel's left side.

'Seen the wolf, have you? Ah!'

'Grandpa Dicken always said I should visit Mutton-cruncher if things went seriously wrong,' explained Bethel, grimacing as the mole rocked him gently, listening for telltale creaks or rasps. 'So that's what I did.'

'Dicken . . .' Oscar chuckled richly at the mention of his old friend's name, 'Dicken never told you, I suppose, that it was the wolf's advice that brought me down here instead of – anything else?' There was a strange warm sadness in the mole's voice. 'And he was right. The wolf knows. Do what he says, you hear?' He patted the snail's shell affectionately. 'Off you go. You're finished, completed, repaired, mended. Pot of slime? No? Good to see you, little Bethel-Dicken. See you next year. Don't forget what I said now.'

A queue of claw-clicking, muttering creatures had built up behind Bethel. Much as he would have liked to talk more with Oscar, he knew that it was just not possible. Turning away from the warm glow and bustle of the repair shop, he saw in the distance Oscar's lizard gang folding and repacking the parachute. Before next summer they would have replaced it under its clifftop stone. The system worked well. Nearby, Jacktar, the seedy middle-aged cormorant, was waiting to give Bethel his usual lift to the top. The overweight bird was just about able to flap that far. Not for the first time the snail wondered what kind of hold Oscar had over the black oily creature. Whatever it was, it certainly worked. A few unsteady minutes later, just as dawn arrived over the peninsula to chase the darkness into the west, Bethel arrived home safely, only to experience a shock of dismay on seeing the extent of the damage caused during his earlier panic. After filling and lighting the brass lamp, he wearily set about the task of restoring order among his precious things until, finally exhausted, he simply leaned his weight against a wall and slipped into unconsciousness.

For many hours his sleep was deep and dreamless, but eventually a dream did come, the strangest and most vivid nightmare that Bethel had ever had.

At first there was only mist – thick, yellow and chill, blotting out everything but itself. Bethel found himself in the midst of an alien, muffled world, listening intently and nervously as he waited for – what? He dared not move. Who could say what traps and terrors were lying in wait behind the swirling wall that surrounded him? He could not, in any case, have moved more than an inch even if he had wanted to. Wide leather straps were tightly criss-crossed around his body and fastened at his back to some kind of pole or stake. He shivered with fear and cold in the menacing silence, knowing, as one does in dreams, that someone or something was coming for him – something bitter and cruel.

It began as a slight thickening of the mist directly in front of him, gradually gaining substance until Bethel became aware that a form of some kind was making its way towards the spot where he had no choice but to wait. Slowly the form began to take on a definite shape – tall, thin, square-shouldered and stooping, two little black eyes glinting malevolently as the figure finally emerged from the mist and stood over the terrified snail, its face wolfish with grinning malice and triumph.

It was Micky the lizard. Taller, different somehow, full of an ugly sneering arrogance, but undoubtedly Micky. The long leathery body was dressed in some kind of military officer's uniform, with polished leather jackboots and a high-fronted peaked cap. The grey material hung in baggy folds around the lizard's scaly form. He looked all wrong – like a skeleton in evening dress.

'You have two minutes left, snail. If you have not told us what we need to know by then, you will be shot.'

The creature's voice was high and grating, totally confident, full of relish. Bethel's brain was spinning. What was he supposed to tell them? Who were they?

'Micky, I ...'

'You will not call me Micky! You will call me "sir"! Go on, say it! Say "sir"!'

The lizard raised a thin, vicious-looking swagger-stick above his head, his narrow face contorted with fury.

'Errr ... sir,' said Bethel hurriedly, 'I – I can't quite remember what ...'

The creature lowered his arm, then bent from the waist until the smooth tip of his snout was almost touching the snail's face. As he spoke, a long-twig-like tongue flickered to and fro, gently pricking Bethel's flesh each time it slithered out to its full extent.

'We want the Frenchman and the thrush and the fat boy – especially we want the fat boy. Now that we have become the master race we intend to do to them what they did to us. We have suffered at their hands, now they will suffer at ours.'

The lizard's breath was hot and rancid on Bethel's face.

'We shall make the Frenchman run errands for us on his hands and knees. Hundreds of little trifling messages and tasks all day and all night. If he stands up he will be shot. We shall make him go on and on way past the point where his skin is raw and bleeding. Eventually, we may cook him and serve him in his own nasty little restaurant with a nice green salad and a suitable French dressing.'

The tongue vibrated excitedly as the creature went on.

'As for the thrush ... the thrush will never submit to our authority, nor will he show fear, but that will not matter. We shall imprison him in a large cage and use him for target practice. A moving target is useful – a fluttering one even better. We may invite the butterflies to join us. They too have suffered.'

Bethel very much did not want to hear what the lizards were planning for Wallace, but there was no escape. The harsh voice continued, tinged with the craziness that is fuelled by lust for revenge.

'We are going to be very, very fair with the fat boy. We shall do to him exactly what he has done to many of us. We shall pull his legs off to see if he grows some more – just out of interest, you understand?'

Snails do not go pale. They tremble. Bethel trembled now.
'But why . . .?'

'You know where they are, snail, and you are going to tell us immediately, or face the firing squad. The choice is yours.'

Bethel started to protest that he had no idea of the whereabouts of the gang, but stopped abruptly as it was borne in upon him that, in the context of this other dream world, he *did* know where Dupin and Mulligan and Wallace were hiding. He *knew*, somehow, that the three gang members were cowering abjectly in the attic of *Le Cochon Mort*, waiting for an opportunity to flee the peninsula. Assuming the lizard was to be trusted, he could free himself with a few simple words. And why not? He had no reason to love the evil trio – on the contrary. He would be perfectly justified in sacrificing them to save himself . . . surely?

'Very well!'

The creature stood up and drew back to one side. Behind the place where he had been standing the mist was beginning to disperse. Through the coiling wisps that remained, Bethel could now make out a tall wooden structure, supporting a platform on which a vaguely reptilian figure crouched behind a mounted gun of some kind. Stretching away from the corners of the tower to form a right angle were two high metal fences topped with tangled masses of barbed-wire. Most chilling of all, though, was the line of a dozen lizards, uniformed and metal helmeted, who stood motionless, their rifles already raised and aimed at the very centre of the snail's body.

'You have until I count to five,' hissed the lizard officer, drawing a pistol from the holster on his belt as he spoke.

Five! Five seconds in which to decide whether to hand over the gang or not. An easy decision of course. Why should they live and he die? And yet . . .

'. . . two, three, four – another second, my fine snail, and it will be too late . . .'

Go on, Bethel, he screamed inwardly, *tell them! Open your mouth and tell them, you stupid snail! In less than a second it will be too late!*

BANG!

Bethel was woken by the sound of his door slamming, as Micky the lizard's brother, Alf, tried yet another ploy to wake the deeply sleeping snail.

'Gotta wake up,' insisted the lizard in a high-pitched nasal voice, ''snearly time fer the party! Gotta geddup – 'sgettin' late. Gotta geddit all ready.'

From a sleeping nightmare into a waking one. Bethel stared at the hand-wringing creature for a moment, trying hard to focus on what had just happened, what was happening now, and what was going to happen this afternoon.

'I've goddall the stuff outside on the 'andcart like you said. Ice buns fer Fatty, seedcake fer Frush, an' onion rolls fer Frenchy. Got the drinks an' all. Dun good, din I?'

Bethel looked at the expression of quivering eagerness on Alf's face and remembered his dream.

'You've done extremely well, Alf. I had no right to ask you to do all that. You're very kind – thank you. Er ... do you know what time it is? I invited them for about four o'clock, so -'

Alf was unable to answer for a moment, so shocked was he by the warmth and gratitude displayed by the snail. No lizard expected more than the odd word of curt approval. Pulling himself together he poked his head out of the door for a second and glanced up at the sun.

'Free twenty-free,' he called, 'eggsackly!'

'What?' Bethel was aghast. 'I've been asleep for hours and hours! Come on, Alf, let's get busy!'

'Right!' said Alf. 'Less get busy!'

By three fifty-five everything was done. Standing in a little group beside Bethel's house were three makeshift tables, each one laid with a member of the gang in mind. Alf's upturned cart bore a plate of onion rolls and a glass of wine for Dupin. A huge wild rhubarb leaf was anchored to a hillock by the seedcake, neatly sliced and laid out, together with a glass dish full of pure fresh water. That was for Mulligan. On Bethel's desk, dragged out of

233

the hip-bath after a tremendous combined effort by the snail and the lizard, lay a plate of iced buns and a tall glass of lemonade for Wallace.

'Whaffor you doin' this?'

Emboldened by Bethel's new attitude to him, Alf asked the obvious question. Bethel looked at him and slowly shook his head.

'I don't really know,' he said, 'I'm not sure . . .'

Alf glanced meaningfully at his tail. 'Fink I'll be orf,' he twittered nervously, 'don' want Fatty ter see me.' He looked up. 'Free fifty-nine eggsackly – see yer later.'

Bethel waited alone by the tables, listening to the far murmur of the sea and wishing that he was as aggressively courageous as Grandpa Dicken had been. A snatch of careless laughter made his heart race suddenly. They were here. Seconds later the gang appeared over the rim of the old pond, and Bethel's heart, far from racing, nearly stopped altogether.

The next half hour was very strange. In a peculiar way it reminded the snail of Dalì's painting of Dicken. Things were almost too vividly real to *be* real. And it was all so very quiet. The only thing that Bethel had said (in strangled tones) was 'Welcome. Th-thank you for coming. Please help yourselves to anything you – you want.' And the gang, without saying a word, had proceeded to do just that. As they ate they stared fixedly at Bethel, unpleasant anticipatory smiles on the faces of Dupin and Wallace, while Mulligan remained coldly expressionless.

They ate and drank everything on the tables. Every crumb. Every drop. Finally, Wallace wiped the back of a fat hand across his icing-smeared mouth and spoke for the first time.

'Party games now?' His little eyes glittered. 'What's inside?'

Mulligan ducked out of his leather strap, leaving the quiver of nails on the desk beside Wallace's sneering pot. 'I'll look,' he said shortly. He disappeared into the hip-bath, reappearing after a minute or so with a cluster of blue china fragments suspended from his beak by their lengths of fishing line. He dropped them on the desk in front of the fat boy. Wallace picked one up and looked, first at it, then at Bethel.

'Pretty!' he sneered, then handed it to Dupin. 'Chuck 'em, Frenchy.'

Dupin laughed raucously. *'Oui, je les jetterai!'* he cried, and one by one he threw the pieces high into the air over the edge of the cliff and out of sight. Wallace beamed. Mulligan watched.

Snails do not cry. They slump, and their horns droop. Bethel knew that the gang were about to destroy his dearest possessions, bit by bit, enjoying every little flicker of response that could be elicited from their victim. He slumped and drooped. It was heart-breaking. Wallace dropped the framed webs onto a stone and Dupin ground the resultant mess into the mud with his heel. The picture of Dicken was propped up against Alf's cart and shred-ded by half a quiver of nails, spat with unerring accuracy by Mul-ligan from a distance of nearly ten feet. That was what finished Bethel off really – the clatter of heartless laughter as his only per-manent reminder of Grandpa Dicken was destroyed. It was too much. For the first time in many months, he withdrew into his shell and yearned for oblivion.

Resentment burned brightly in his soul. Why, oh *why* had he ever listened to what anyone else had said about what he should do? It was all very well for old Oscar and the wolf to give advice. They weren't about to be murdered after watching their most pre-cious things being systematically demolished or thrown away. He could hear them out there now, those ... those cockroaches! They were throwing stones at his house – heavy, mindless, denting stones. Soon it would be his turn to feel the keen edge of Dupin's knife, the agonizingly sharp points of Mulligan's nails, and what-ever unspeakable torture the fat boy had in store for him. Alone in the clamping darkness of his own shell, Bethel felt as if his mind was slipping out of gear. As if in a fevered dream, his head seemed to be thronged by a host of faces and voices from past and pre-sent, struggling and jostling to gain his attention. His own mother was there, pleading with him about something, but he couldn't quite hear what she was saying. Dicken, too, was urging him to act in a particular way, while old Oscar the mole just stared sadly at him from somewhere behind the others. There were other friends – and enemies, other sounds and voices. He wanted to turn his back on all of them – give up and simply sink into nothingness. If only they would let him.

Then, one face suddenly filled the space where all the others had been. One voice spoke quietly but clearly in his mind. It was the wolf, repeating the words he had whispered into Bethel's ear just before he left the Chapel cave. And now, for the first time, Bethel understood what he had to do, understood the strange dream of earlier, and understood that there was only one possible way for him. But he must do it now or it would be too late. Thrusting his head into the light, he cried out in a voice that echoed around the cliff-top like the notes of a golden trumpet: 'I forgive you! I forgive you! I forgive you!'

The effect was startling. Dupin, who had been advancing on the snail, knife in hand, turned a deathly white, let his weapon clatter to the ground, and turned and ran as though pursued by devils. Mulligan, who had just selected a spot from which to fire his deadly nails, rose abruptly on panic-stricken wings, and was very quickly just a dot in the pale sky to the east. Wallace was green and paralysed, his little fat mouth the only part of him that moved. It jabbered soundlessly. When he did finally stir, his was a backwards walk in slow motion. Slipping and stumbling, but apparently unwilling or unable to turn his back on Bethel, the flabby child retreated over the lip of the hollow, until even his fat green face bobbed out of sight, and a great silence fell over the cliff-top.

Behind the amazed snail, Mutton-cruncher signalled to the line of grotesque and terrifying creatures whose heads had appeared above the edge of the dried-up pond as soon as Bethel's cry reached their ears. As silently as they had come, they left, to return to the sanctuary of the Penbar Chapel. By the time Bethel happened to look behind him, there was nothing to be seen.

But he had sensed the power.

The Second Pint

As a teenager Flynn had hated Sundays. They offered him none of the things that he knew he wanted and believed he needed.

He wanted cafés, for instance, where he could sit and discuss life with friends and acquaintances in a cosy, hypothetical glow. In the little market town where he lived, only one café was open on the sabbath, and that was a place of dirty lino and clanking pin-tables, used with brutal exclusiveness by leather-jacketed bikers and a smattering of older men with crudely chopped hair and grubby personas whom Flynn had unconsciously classified as child molesting types. He was too fragile for all that; too frightened of facing his own dread of violence. He only really lived in his head, enjoying periodic conversational adventures in the clinking safety of chintzy tea-rooms.

Poor Flynn had never done anything except think and talk and smoke, but he had been quite an impressive sixteen-year-old for all that. Many of the contemporaries with whom he chatted in the Little Cottage Café on a Saturday morning (his favourite time) left, feeling that this untidy, faintly Irish person really did have a quite remarkable grip on the business of living. Little did they realize that even their most humble attempts to grapple with the realities of day-to-day problem solving were quite beyond the capabilities of Flynn, whose attractively pungent way of putting things was just the flashy label on an unspeakable can of worms.

Occasionally it would be a girl sitting on her own with him at one of the circular oak tables. He would be extra casual then. Girls terrified him, but he had developed a number of self-titillating ploys which he was able to enjoy in absolute secrecy. Sometimes he would manipulate the talk round to the subject of art and then say with airy nonchalance, 'Of course, Picasso always maintained that he painted with his testicles.' The sort of girl that Flynn liked best would perform a perfect double-take, blush warmly, and do her utmost to match his nonchalance with a sophisticated nod and a half-smile of relaxed amusement. 'Interesting and highly athletic,' he always added, looking as bored as possible, and inwardly relishing the intrusion of what he thought of as a grimy sex word into what he supposed was the freshness of her mind. Sex itself was out of the question. Far too horrendously, complicatedly close and real. All about skin and touching and giving and abandonment. Not Flynn's scene. Perhaps it would never happen – not outside his head anyway.

The other thing that Sunday lacked was an appropriate number of people distracted by their own busyness. Flynn's favourite part of the week (other than Saturday morning) was Monday. No longer at school and unemployed himself, he knew no higher pleasure than that of setting out with a sufficient supply of cigarettes and money for a day's café dwelling, to stroll in a carefully nurtured trance-like state through streets peopled by busy workers and glazed-eyed housewives mentally listing and computing between shops. It was an intoxicatingly delicious sensation to be in, but not of the active world, to use the grey and granular backdrop of other people's daily grind as a means of finding colour and sharpness in his own image of himself. He moved and thought and felt in pockets and patterns of sensation-related place and time and environment, very defended, and very alone. Sundays left him stranded like a twitching fish on a beach, wait-

ing for the tide of weekday ordinariness to turn and refloat him – to make him exist again.

When Flynn was seventeen he found a solution to the sabbath problem. He became a Christian. It began at eight o'clock one evening after a long and particularly bleak Sunday in autumn. He happened to walk past the open doors of a tall red-brick building set back from a small road which turned humbly off from the steep high street. People of his own age were going in, laughing and chattering in twos and threes. They looked clean and harmless. One of them noticed Flynn watching and invited him in. He went, unusually daring, and found himself in an after-church youth club where coffee and biscuits were served over a semi-circular bar set in a corner of the large church hall. He started to go every Sunday, becoming something of a group celebrity with his quick wit and carefully judged and controlled air of worldliness. Eventually, he started going to church until, in time, it was assumed that he had undergone some kind of conversion. He went away for weekend house parties with the rest of the youth group. He had views on things, and even occasional revelations. Sundays were transformed. Church-related activities and encounters provided a perfect filling for the Saturday-Monday sandwich. Was he really a Christian? Flynn didn't quite know, but it didn't matter. Sundays were all right now.

The years passed. Minor changes and adjustments became necessary in Flynn's life, but by the time he reached his forties, unmarried, living in another but similar town, and employed in an undemanding job which had altered very little over the years, he had established a pattern for Sundays, and Sunday evening in particular, which was as near perfect as he could imagine.

Every Sunday evening at six o'clock, for the last fifteen years, Flynn had put on clothes of a carefully average nature and walked the mile or so from his house to Portland Road, where two large and important buildings confronted each other from opposite sides of the street. That they were large buildings was an objective fact. That they were important was a matter of opinion.

Flynn was unusual in that he was the only member of his church who used the pub, and, as far as he knew, the only pub regular who used the church. They had been twin habits of his for a long time now, and he had managed to extract considerable satisfaction from both environments, especially as he had consistently succeeded in keeping the whole thing well under control. He had always managed to escape real commitment to the church as a spiritual or a physical body (albeit sometimes by the skin of his teeth) and you could easily leave a pub if it looked as if you were going to be asked for something that you didn't want to give.

Altogether, it was a very comfortable arrangement for the head-locked Flynn. Into the church at six-thirty for an hour of stimulating and pleasantly dangerous observation of other people being vulnerable, then over to the pub at about seven forty-five to play, equally pleasantly, with the Lego-like guilt that he allowed this to cause in him. He saw no reason why this should not have gone on indefinitely, but he was playing a very dangerous game, and one Sunday things went badly wrong.

The church which Flynn attended was a very lively one. People sang loud joyful choruses as though they really meant the words. Some put their arms in the air as they sang, others held their hands out in front of them, palms upward, a few even danced on the spot or, more freely, out in the centre aisle. Prayer time was long and intense, sometimes involving the use of spiritual gifts such as 'speaking in tongues', or prophecy. All of the prayers were extempore and heartfelt in tone; frequently a member of the congregation would start to weep and be surrounded by a little knot of elders or sympathizers laying a hand each on the sufferer, and praying him or, more usually, her through to a release from grief. The sermon, or 'message' as it was called, tended to be far longer than one would expect in the more traditional churches and was almost always related in some way to the themes of repentance and salvation. Communion was called 'coming to the Lord's table', and happened every other Sunday. It was a central event in the lives of the people in Flynn's church, but they used cherryade instead of wine, so as not to offend those whose consciences were troubled by alcohol, or tempt folk who had problems with restraint in that area.

Flynn used the church and its members as he had used them since that night more than twenty years ago when he wandered into the red-brick building in his home town. He was able to be vivid and significant among people who were predominantly mild and anxious to be good, and it was safe in an edgy sort of way. Inside him two strands of response had remained unaltered throughout the years. One was a dull, unspecific yearning, the other a rigorously maintained and largely defensive cynicism. The two ran parallel like live wires. Flynn knew that they must never touch. There had been dangerous moments, chances, invitations, opportunities, but they had all passed without him being shocked out of himself.

On the Sunday in question the service was led by Maurice Daniels, a large, energetic, boy-like man, whose talents lay more in the areas of organization and practical application than in encouragement and exhortation to worship. Flynn knew that Maurice always experienced a little crisis of confidence at about the midway point of the service and that he invariably perceived this as a problem in the congregation rather than in himself. The big man's equilibrium could only be restored (so Flynn's observer's logic told him) by something blatantly spiritual happening among those whom he was supposed to be leading. Today was no exception. Halfway through 'He is Lord', Maurice signalled to the musicians to stop, and addressed the congregation in a low, but confident voice, only his eyes dancing a little with the fear of failure.

'I sense that there's a spirit of heaviness in the room,' he intoned, his mouth very close to the microphone. 'I think the Lord would have us open our hearts and spirits to him and each other for healing this evening.'

There were two or three 'amens' and a loud 'hallelujah' in response to this. Flynn mentally rehearsed certain well-used procedures in preparation for what was about to come. Encouraged by the verbal assent to his diagnosis of the problem, Maurice went on, his eyes steady now.

'We will sing that chorus through twice again, and as we sing, if you feel you need ministry, just catch the eye of a brother or sister nearby and they'll come and pray with you.'

He signalled once more to the musicians. Piano, violin, guitar and metallophone swung into mellow action again, but more quietly this time. Maurice raised one hand high in the air above his head as he led the singing.

Flynn had two alternative coping ploys for situations like this. One was the eyes-shut-praying-for-others ploy. Simple but effective, all it involved was sitting with a straight back, eyes lightly closed, with a small smile of faithful serenity to indicate that no ministry was needed *here*. The other was only possible when the words of a relatively uncommon chorus were displayed on the overhead projector screen. Then, Flynn would peer fixedly at the screen, apparently too concentrated on the unfamiliar words to be concerned with catching or being caught by anyone else's eye. That one would be useless today. Everyone knew 'He is Lord' by heart. It would have to be the closed eyes and seraphic smile. Above all, don't look around, don't risk a glance in any direction at all. Flynn had become an expert in the art of avoidance. Perhaps he had become a little too confident in his techniques, because now, in the infinitesimal moment between the commencement of the chorus and the lowering of his eyelids, he knew that an almost non-existent engagement of the eyes had occurred between himself and Arnold Fuller, one of the most fervent and devoted members of the congregation. Alone in the darkness, he knew that Arnold would be upon him in seconds. He braced himself. It wasn't the first time. It wouldn't be the last. He could handle it. He had handled it before.

'Bless you, brother. Let me pray for you.'

Arnold had come round behind Flynn so that he could lay his hands on his shoulders. He was leaning forwards and speaking into the left ear of his needy brother.

'I saw you looking at me, my friend. I think the Lord is going to do something really wonderful for you tonight.'

Flynn clenched everything and concentrated on his voice. He knew he could manage his voice.

'That's great, Arnold. I don't know what it's all about, but it's always good to be prayed for.'

He was a master of the defusing response, but it didn't work this time. Arnold was starting to pray, and he was doing it quite loudly.

'Lord, I believe you want to really break into this life tonight, in a completely new way. I just know that your Holy Spirit is waiting to fill our brother with all the love and joy and peace that you promise to those who follow you, and that's what we're praying for right now!'

To his horror Flynn, his eyes still closed, heard the scraping of chairs as others got up to assist Arnold. A hand was laid on his head, an arm was placed around his shoulders, someone in front of him was holding both of his hands, fingers rested on his knee. The music had stopped. Flynn was in the centre. Arnold's voice rose a gear as he went on praying.

'O Lord! I really believe that you are going to release your child from bondage this night! That you are wanting to do a mighty work of redemption in this man's life! Break down the barriers, Lord, and just let your Spirit have his way with our brother! Oh, hallelujah!'

Arnold and several others started to pray in tongues, and the hands resting on various parts of Flynn's body pressed and quivered with powerful intention.

Inside his head, Flynn was shouting and screaming and panicking and pleading and longing and hating and arguing. Outside, he continued to smile quietly and acceptingly. He had still not had sex with anyone. He was not skilled with passion. All this was forcing him to feel extravagantly. He might burst into tears. He would hate that. They would like it. Good sign. He might shake them all off, stand up and shout obscenities, then rush from the church into the wonderful open air. Very soon those parallel wires were going to touch and then anything could happen. If he could just hold on a little longer, just a little longer ...

'Amen! Thank you, Lord!'

Arnold leaned forward to whisper in Flynn's ear again.

'Okay, brother?'

Flynn's warm smile and gentle patting of Arnold's hand as it rested on his shoulder were absolutely perfect. Costly, but perfect.

'Thanks, Arnold – really appreciate it, brother.'

Everyone sat down again and the service continued. Maurice swung his arm exultantly as he conducted the opening verse of 'Bind us together'. There was an atmosphere of joy and achievement.

Flynn was a pallid, sweaty, trembling wreck, but he looked fine as he joined in with the singing. For some reason, difficult to define, he comforted himself inwardly with his knowledge that the last few minutes were solely a product of Maurice's insecurity, Arnold's need for spiritual excitement, and the congregation's tendency to follow like sheep. He could see through Maurice and Arnold – and the rest of them. He could see under people's skins. Others couldn't. He could. That's all there was to it.

But Flynn was shaken. He had always been very careful not to be drawn in any real way into what he saw as the carefully organized spontaneity of the services, but for once he had not been vigilant enough. He had been lucky to escape with as little attention as he had, but there was still the possibility that they would get him in the social period after the service was over. Luckily, he was sitting at the back, near the door, always the safest place to be in any church, Flynn reckoned. As soon as the last prayer had been said, and the roll and clack of the kitchen hatch heralded coffee time, he did a back-in-a-minute walk through the door, and headed straight for the pub.

He needed time and beer. Lots of time to recuperate from this disturbing experience, and lots of beer to assist any necessary process of self-justification, or if that didn't work, to provide the courage not to care.

It was beginning to get dark outside. He shivered slightly as he crossed the road to his other habit, the Britannia Arms, a majestic Edwardian establishment whose massive landlord, Edgar, served perfect beer to Christians and pagans without discrimination, or indeed, any apparent interest. He employed a number of minions who did bob and smile and hurry around, but they only served to highlight his huge indifference to the world in general and customers in particular. It was the perfect place to recover and chew over his sins, but – there was a problem. The Britannia had three bars, two large and one small. Flynn hesitated outside the pub for some minutes, knowing that whichever bar he chose, would, with the consistency of natural law, contain Trev.

Trev was an elderly alcoholic whose life revolved around the maintenance of his status as a regular at the Britannia. Actually, he was more than a regular. He was a constant. Trev was *always* there, smiling, winking, ready and willing to advise Flynn on any aspect of his life that, in Trev's opinion, needed attention. Flynn was diseased with politeness in certain relationships, and had allowed the old man to feel that he saw him as a sort of wise elder, without whose words of wisdom he would never dare to make any major decision. Flynn was fond of him in his own limited way, but it was a curious fact that whenever he particularly didn't want to see Trev, he was invariably ensconced in the bar that Flynn decided to use. It was rather like the old magician's trick with the three cups and a ball. Flynn never managed to guess right. Sometimes he tried to cheat fate. He would approach the saloon bar at speed, veer sharply to the left at the last moment, and crash through the door of the Snug, to the considerable alarm of all those present, except, of course, Trev, who would wave and smile as usual in happy anticipation of another counselling session with his inadequate friend.

Today, Flynn didn't want to talk to Trev. There was something so appallingly real about the defeat and decay behind the old alcoholic's pub brightness. Flynn knew it would prevent him from moving smoothly towards an enjoyment of his own problems. He decided to opt for the saloon bar, usually the quietest part of the pub. Tonight was no exception. There was only one other customer. Sitting in an armchair in front of the imitation coal fire beneath a huge picture of the Queen, Trev lovingly caressed his early evening pint of mild, and gestured invitingly at the chair beside him. Accepting defeat, Flynn closed the door behind him. One of the minions supplied him with a pint of old ale, and soon he was settled comfortably by the fire, anticipating with relish the familiar illusion that the beer, defying gravity, was draining upwards through his brain, putting out all the little fires of tension and guilt.

'All right,' said Trev, wiping his mouth with the back of his hand. 'What's up?'

Flynn took another mouthful of beer without answering. He was feeling better already.

'Let's 'ave some nuts,' suggested Trev. 'Dry roast. Then we'll sort you out.' He leaned back and smiled benignly. 'I'll gettem if you like.'

Flynn sighed as he heaved himself out of his chair and returned to the bar. It was one of the sacred traditions of their relationship that he never accepted any offer from Trev to buy him anything. The unspoken understanding was that Trev's contribution of wisdom and guidance was worth far more than Flynn's humble offering of beer and nuts. In any case, Trev's slender finances were organized down to the last half pint necessary to remain a bona fide customer at the Britannia for the whole of the week.

'Let me get you another pint as well, Trev. Same again?'

Flynn quite enjoyed this bit usually. Trev's brows would knit and his mouth would drop slightly, as though his companion had made some totally novel suggestion. Then his face would clear, and he would smile wonderingly, as though fascinated by his own response to a unique invitation.

'Jew know, I honestly think I will,' said Trev, sounding like someone who has lost a battle with his principles for the first time. 'Yes, I will!' The decision was made.

For Flynn, there was something very special about the second pint. He was invariably awash and at sea after the fourth or fifth, but the second represented that point at which he was committed to neither sobriety nor drunkenness. He was neither innocent nor guilty. Part of him could swear that there would not be a third. Another part knew with purring assurance that there would. All was well. All was peace. Morality slept. It was a beautiful but neutral pint, the second one. If, in addition, there was a little pile of dry-roast peanut dust in front of him, ideal for consumption by means of a wet forefinger, then, for a short time, the world could not hurt him, and God could only frown, fold his arms, and tap his foot. All of them – man, God, spirits of the air, denizens of the deep – all were obliged to suspend operations while Flynn finished his second pint. All, that is, except Trev.

'Why jew go to that church?'

Flynn was stunned. It was a question that really meant something. He was so used to Trev's wholly predictable, half-baked philosophy that he was temporarily incapable of answering. Despite his curse of politeness, he had always known that he was really only humouring this sad old alky. Now, with one deft step, Trev had arrived at the centre of his immediate inner life, and Flynn had to decide whether to kick him out or not. He stalled.

'What do you mean, Trev? Why does anyone go to church?' Panic filled him. It was as though something had pursued him across the road.

'Them at your church, an' me. Little beggar at playin' games, aincher? Playin' games with us. Them an' me. Aincher?'

This was awful! Had Trev gone completely mad? Had he forgotten that he was just a broken-down alcoholic and Flynn wasn't? Didn't he know that Flynn secretly despised him; that he could switch him on or off in his life like a television programme? Good grief, the man seemed to be getting the idea that he existed!

What did he mean, 'Them an' me?' What could Trev and the people at church possibly have in common? Playing games? The eyes of Flynn's mind narrowed. There was no way he was going to get turned over again this evening. He had no words. He surveyed all the possible avenues of escape, and rejected the honourable ones. Beer would do it. Trev's geniality could be bought back with more beer. A bottle for the baby – something like that. Flynn laughed lightly as he stood up.

'You're in a funny old mood, Trev. Let me get you another pint. Cheer you up.'

Battle raged in the rheumy old eyes, but after a few seconds it looked as if Flynn had won. Trev's swan song as a genuinely involved human being was cut short – extinguished – by a single pint of beer. He licked his lips, swallowed hard, and twisted his face into a fair imitation of the old familiar grin. He said nothing, just nodded and slapped his hand down on the arm of his chair. Time enough later, Flynn thought, for profound regret, self-criticism, and all that. Right now, he felt only relief that, once again, he had found a way to safety.

Turning away from the fire, he jumped a little as he saw that Edgar, the landlord, was watching impassively from behind the bar. The huge man said nothing as he served the beer, but there was a stillness in his gaze that left Flynn feeling vaguely uneasy as he made his way back with the drinks.

He had some difficulty fitting two more pint glasses onto the shiny surface of the little wrought-iron table that stood between them. He was still only half-way through his second pint, and Trev had only just finished his first. But never mind. The panic was over, and it was comforting to see the glasses of dark brown liquid nestling together, winking and gleaming in time with the repetitive patterns of light thrown out by the flames of the artificial fire.

'Cheers, Trev.' As Flynn drew the other half of his neglected second pint fondly towards him, he glanced up at the old man's face. Oh, no! He was crying! Two large tears were rolling down his face, his eyes blinking furiously as he fought back whatever was trying to come out. A few sniffs later he seemed more or less all right, and after a couple of explosions into a big off-white piece of cloth dragged from the side pocket of his crumpled jacket, he sat quite quietly for a minute or so, gazing into the fire.

Flynn? Verbal paralysis. He finished his second pint.

'I'm saved, yer know.' Trev's hands trembled slightly as they rested flat on his knees. For the time being he seemed to have forgotten his beer. 'Salvation Army. Just 'fore the war. Saved in the street, I was. Saved for Jesus.' His right hand rose an inch or two, and swung gently from side to side, perhaps conducting some dimly remembered gospel tune from the past.

Flynn put the empty glass down softly on the table, and picked up his third pint. Trev saved? He didn't look very saved. He looked lost. Old and lost. He was intrigued. Now that the pressure was off he could afford to be interested. He had a number of scintillating insights into this particular topic, and he was more interested in impressing the old man than he had been before. He snuggled back into his chair and addressed the other man lightly and reasonably, waving his right hand occasionally to emphasize a word.

'All right, Trev, granted that all those years ago you did have some kind of conversion experience – and don't get me wrong, I'm not saying you didn't – but . . .'

'To hell with yer buts!' The old man turned on Flynn, his face working with anger and some kind of ancient frustration. 'You listen ter me! One day 'e's gonna pick me up an' dust me down an' look straight in my face an' say, "Trev, you're an old soak an' you ain't never done nothin' fer me, all you've done is get drunk, an' sleep – but Trev, mate, you – are – saved!" An' you –' Trev suddenly stuck his arm out towards Flynn and wagged his finger in his face. 'You'll get spat out, because you ain't even a soak. Fish nor fowl, you ain't. You ain't nothin'!'

He stood up, shaking with emotion, and without taking his eyes from Flynn's, picked up the pint he had just been bought, and half dropped, half threw it against the stone surround of the fireplace. There was glass and beer everywhere, and a fierce hissing as the liquid penetrated to the heat source of the fire, sending a cloud of steam up around Trev's angry figure as he leaned forwards to deliver his final speech.

'I'm gonna drink a lot more beer tonight, but I ain't drinkin' that one!'

It was another nightmare. Flynn sat through this outburst, quite unable to move, helpless as ever in the face of raw emotion, and especially violence. It was a relief to hear the calm, determined tones of the landlord breaking into the silence that followed the old chap's last words. He spoke from somewhere just behind Flynn.

'I'm not having this. Come on, you. Out!'

Poor old Trev. Flynn felt what he supposed must be a genuine twinge of sympathy at the thought of the old man being thrown out of his beloved local, but he felt so shaken up by what had happened, that he couldn't help looking forward to being able to relax when he'd gone. Trev was still standing, the top half of his body bent forwards, his eyes glaring into Flynn's. He didn't seem to have registered Edgar's words at all. Flynn tried to be kind.

'Come on, Trev. No point making trouble. Best if you just go really. What d'you think?'

Flynn's heart leaped with shock as a heavy hand landed from behind on his shoulder, and Edgar's voice, slow and sure, sounded once more.

'I'm not talking to Trev, I'm talking to you. Out!'

Flynn hadn't even started his third pint. He passed through the door in a daze, and stood for a few moments, quite terrified, gnashing his teeth in the outer darkness.

Father to the Man

It was very difficult to sleep after seeing my son so distant and miserable that evening.

I was still awake at two o'clock in the morning, having read almost half of *Biggles And The Black Peril* to take my mind off the dreadful bleakness in Dan's eyes as he said goodnight. Violet had always hated me using my old children's books as emotional teddy bears, but I couldn't think of any other way to cope with the feeling of hollow panic that arrived with the night.

Eventually, worn out by tiredness and the constant effort needed to keep the image of Dan's face away from the front of my mind, I left Biggles, Algy, Ginger and Bertie to their own world-saving devices and drifted off to sleep. It seemed only seconds later that I was awakened by the sound of the bedroom door opening.

'Daddy,' said a small frightened voice from the other end of the room.

I sat up. My daughter, dimly visible in the half-darkness, stood just inside the doorway, a fluffy friend clutched firmly under each arm. Her feet, two little frayed ends, were brightly lit by a narrow shaft of yellow light from the streetlamp outside the landing window. Curly wasn't too big to be helped, and wouldn't be for a long time. I could give her everything she needed on this particular night.

'Hello, darling,' I said softly, 'what are you doing here?'

'I woke up an' was a bit scared of the dark, Daddy.'

'Come and get in with Mummy and Daddy, sweetheart. We won't be afraid of the silly dark then, will we?'

The feet disappeared as Curly pattered across the two yards between her and the bed, clambered up with a helping hand from me, and threw herself into the gap between Violet and me like a soldier jumping into a foxhole.

'Is that Curly?' mumbled Violet sleepily. 'Are you all right, my love?'

'Bit scared, Mummy,' said Curly, taking her thumb out of her mouth to speak, then putting it back again.

'Well, you're okay now, aren't you, Curly-Poops?'

Curly nodded briskly on the pillow as Violet kissed the back of her head before turning over to go back to sleep. I lay awake for a while watching sleep and safety chase away the fear from the little girl's face. Finally the sucking motion ceased, Curly's thumb dropped from her mouth and she began to breathe deeply and evenly. The darkness had been defeated once more.

It could be Danny lying there, I thought, as I studied Curly's serene features by the light filtering through the curtained windows above the head of the bed – it could easily be Danny lying there. It had been Danny many times when he was a little boy, when he was as openly vulnerable and frightened as his sister had been tonight, when Violet or I could solve just about every problem he was likely to face with a cuddle or a distraction or one of those academic explanations that he enjoyed so much, when he was Danny instead of Dan, and his life had seemed so happy that I really wasn't able to see how he could be anything but content when he grew older. I had poured so much of myself into that child – the best of myself. Me without the manipulation and the sulking and the subtle neglect that I had been capable of in all my other relationships. How could he not be all right now, when I had given him so much then? Was I going to go through it all over again with Curly when she was older? Grief and pain passed through me in waves as I waited for sleep to come.

'I find it very difficult to forgive Dan for being unhappy.'

That was the remark that got the following day off to such a bad start, and I suppose I knew, if I'm honest, that it wasn't going to go down at all well with Violet. She had been up since about six-thirty with a very excited child. Curly's eyes popped open every morning like bubbles bursting. She saw no point in wasting a single moment of any of these wonderful days, that happened like magic again and again, on dozing or lying awake in bed. Besides, today was one of her two play-group days, and Valerie, the lady in charge, had promised they would do finger-painting on Thursday. Today was Thursday. What joy! Curly had been sharing this joy of hers generously with Mummy for two and a half hours by the time I made my bleary-eyed way downstairs to the kitchen. Violet was slumped over yesterday's paper and a depressing-looking piece of toast when I made my opening statement. She didn't even look up when she replied.

'I don't mind getting up with Curly and seeing Dan off to school while you're doing your corpse impression upstairs, but I do object to playing audience when you talk like some third-rate Oscar Wilde. If you're trying to convince me that you're a writer, then I suggest the most persuasive argument would be a sheet of paper with something actually written on it. You'll still have a couple of working hours left today if you take half as long over breakfast as you did yesterday.'

I almost fell over. I never had been able to handle Violet's ability to slice me in half with words when she really wanted to. Various replies chased each other round my mind. I wanted to point out that I had talked like a fourth-rate Gilbert Chesterton, not a third-rate Oscar Wilde. I wanted to tell her that I had a brilliant idea for a comic novel, so well developed that I could begin writing it today. Most of all, though, I wanted to tell her that I really had meant something when I spoke just now. It was true that I had spent some time preparing what I was going to say as I washed and dressed and hid my Biggles book, but that was only because I needed to invest my vulnerability with a little dignity.

If I'd let my feelings out in their raw, undisguised form I might have ended up on the floor sobbing my eyes out. No one had ever seen me doing that, and Violet was not going to be the first. Nevertheless, I wanted her to know that I really was feeling bad. I dropped a slice of bread into the toaster.

'I wasn't just trying to be clever, Violet, I was quite unhappy last night, you know.'

Leaning back, Violet pushed both hands heavily through her hair before answering.

'Dan is a perfectly normal teenage boy, Paul. Last night he revealed that he's going through some of the perfectly normal problems that perfectly normal fifteen-year-olds go through. There's no tragedy about him getting a bit low sometimes. He's growing up and changing, that's all.'

'I know that, but ... '

'What you're really talking about is you. You can't accept that your relationship with him is changing as well. You can't solve everything for him any more and neither can I. Why should we expect to be able to? You don't want him to be some sort of pre-adolescent dependent for the rest of his life, do you? Or perhaps you do. Well, I don't!'

'Of course I don't want ... '

'In fact, if anything, Dan needs you and me even more now than he did before. He's unsure about who he is or where he's going. He needs us to be strong and supportive in the background, not feeling sorry for ourselves because he's failing to make us feel good in the same way. I'm sorry if you feel I haven't let you be unhappy, but I think you've got to face reality for Dan's sake.'

Violet would have been astonished if she had known how close I came to collapsing emotionally at that moment, how near she was to hearing about the feelings of desolation and bereavement that were crippling my peace since Dan opted to continue his journey without my close and intimate companionship, and how impotently furious I was that the battle raging inside me between adult and child was depriving my son of the kind of father he needed so much at the moment.

'Anyway,' said Violet, 'I must go to work. Your toast is done. I'll see you later.'

'So, who,' I asked nobody in particular as the front door shut behind my wife, 'do I talk to about feeling more miserable than I've ever felt in my life?'

Locked, as I was, into my own failure to communicate, it seemed impossible that such a question could ever be answered satisfactorily.

I didn't write anything for the rest of that day, although guilt kept me at my post until the hour when your average respectable working man would feel it right to down tools.

People who have never written for a living find it very difficult to understand the most pressing daily problem for scribblers. The plain and awful fact is that, on every single working morning, you must freshly create a universe which will distract, enthral or otherwise absorb you to the exclusion of all the real, day-to-day considerations that are tugging at your attention. This 'universe' simply doesn't exist until you construct it yourself out of ideas and inventions that can be found only in your own head, and not, sadly, at any shop in the High Street.

As I sat at my study window, a piece of A4, feint-lined, narrow-margined paper leering emptily up at me from the desk, my head was full of Dan, and the gap that seemed to have opened up so abruptly between us. I fantasized conversation after conversation between him and me, in the course of which all was healed and settled and restored to the sweet and sunny way it was. Pain filled me as each imaginary dialogue ended, and the false relief that it brought ebbed away to reveal the stomach-lurching truth that was robbing me of peace.

I had one consolation. It was a book recently presented to me as a sort of symbol of friendship by my best friend, Greg Parker, a reluctant coach-driver, who suffered, as I did, from advanced cricket mania. _The Book Of Cricket_ by Plum Warner was a rare prize unearthed by Greg in the local second-hand bookshop. Published more than sixty years ago and containing a rich mixture of fact, opinion and photographs, this satisfactorily fat and faded volume was almost as powerful a distraction as Biggles, and represented an act of heroic sacrifice on my friend's part. Greg valued and studied our relationship as misers do their gold, and he liked to celebrate it from time to time with the sort of gesture that had resulted, last week, in my ownership of this treasure. He had brought it to the pub at the usual time on Friday wrapped in very carefully chosen paper, presenting it to me between our first and second pints, and saying only, 'I thought this might appeal to you.' Inside the front cover he had written:

To Paul, a gift from your friend Greg.
May we continue to speak the truth to one another.

Reading a paragraph or two from Warner's book every now and then and peering at the quaintly posed, old-fashioned action photographs did bring some relief from my feelings, but I found myself coming back again and again to that inscription on the title page.

Central to the friendship between Greg and me was the mutually accepted and frequently stated fact that we always told each other the truth. Nothing was too dark, shameful or distressing to be withheld, because we were prepared to own each other's problems. In the same way, any joy or good fortune that occurred to one of us was invariably shared and celebrated by the other, usually at 'The King's Head', which was our regular meeting place on Friday evenings.

Perhaps because I was unusually sensitized on this particular afternoon, I became aware of something I had known, but never managed to acknowledge before, namely, that this so-called 'fact' about our relationship was not a fact at all – not as far as I was concerned, anyway. I had no doubt that Greg had been unsparingly vulnerable and open in his dealings with me. All through the long period when his ridiculous marriage had been falling to pieces, for instance, he had shared personal problems and insights into his own behaviour that I knew I would have had the greatest difficulty in even mentioning to anyone at all. Many of our Fridays still consisted almost entirely of Greg describing and analysing and seeking reassurance about aspects of his life and personality that had been troubling him during the week just past. All that was really required of me was the occasional nod, a few encouraging noises, a round of drinks when it was my turn, and the vaguest of vague acknowledgements that we were very similar people, and that, therefore, I couldn't fail to understand exactly how he felt.

Somehow, I had managed to avoid sharing any important part of myself with Greg, and yet, if you had asked him how well he knew Paul Williams, he would have smiled happily and said that he knew everything there was to know about me. Greg's marriage had been of the type that scatters previous friends like some sort of social hand-grenade, and its failure after five years had left him lonely, lost and severely lacking in self-confidence, so I knew how important I was to him, and for reasons of my own I valued the need he had for me.

Sitting there at my desk, holding the token of friendship that he had given me, I realized for the first time how much Greg's dependency had become part of my own security. I enjoyed and looked forward to that sensation of hiding inside my head on Friday nights, secretly feeding his mistaken belief that we were genuinely close. It was cosy and unchanging. It made me feel tall and deep and relaxed and wise. I felt sorry for him, and gave myself little pats on the back for tolerating such a sad character. It was suddenly borne in upon me that I even enjoyed the occasional flush of annoyance that I felt on those evenings when he'd spoken about himself solidly for an hour and a half, without ever seeming to feel it necessary to ask how I was, or how my life was going. Not that I would have told him much if he had asked. I would have made some general, fairly whimsical point about the problems of being a human being, and set him off again with a question carefully designed to trigger a new monologue on strictly Greg-related subjects. It was easy to manipulate him.

Violet's response to my friendship with Greg was resigned, but slightly scornful. She said that I was using him to postpone genuine contact with people, and that I should invite others to join us on a Friday night to prevent both of us from getting away with the pointless games we played with each other. She was probably right, but she didn't really know how cataclysmic a revolution like that was likely to be.

I didn't want any revolutions tonight. I wanted business as usual. I wanted to take my misery about Dan down to 'The King's Head' and hug it to myself as I listened to the list of problems that Greg was likely to produce. I felt quite excited, in fact. There was something about the effects of a few pints of beer that ennobled misery, and allowed a mellowing of the sharp emotions that were so unbearable in a strictly sober state. Yes, that's what I'd do – float sadly along on an underground river of melancholy, bravely withholding the pain that my needy friend would be unable to cope with if I exposed it to him.

My disappearance to the pub each Friday was usually preceded by an uneasy passage of arms with Violet. If I had worked well and productively during the day I was quite confident in my casual announcement that I was 'off to the pub' for the evening, but if, as was the case on this particular day, I had actually produced nothing at all, then my carefree cry had a hollow ring to it. Unfortunately, Violet had a very discerning ear.

'You would say that you had earned the price of an entire pint today, would you, Paul?'

That's what she said – always a new line from Violet, who should have been a writer herself – and, as usual, it had the effect of gutting me. I laughed, but it came out sounding squeezed and unconvincing. Then I felt confused. There was anger boiling up in me, but was I right to feel angry? There was hurt, but was genuine hurt a justification for doing no work at all for an entire day just because I was a soppy writer? If I'd been a roadmender I'd have just gone and done it, wouldn't I? But then, why shouldn't I go for a drink with a friend once a week – I mean, why not?

'It wasn't a bad day,' I lied, adding more truthfully, 'I need to go out tonight.'

But she wasn't going to say the magic words of permission: 'Off you go, then. Have a good time. Don't drink too much ... ' I had to leave heavy-footed, with the sour taste of disapproval in my mouth, but it only lasted for a few hundred yards. After that I began to sense the inward effects of that first pint lightening my step and drawing me onward. Soon I would be sitting opposite Greg at the corner table that we had pretty well made our own. There I would cuddle my private chaos and he would express his. I almost skipped as the coloured lights of the pub came into view around the next bend.

Nothing could have prepared me for the double shock that I experienced when I finally entered 'The King's Head' and glanced expectantly in the direction of our usual table. Greg was certainly there, but he was not alone – that was the first part of the shock. He was engaged in earnest conversation with a man I'd never seen before. The second was when he suddenly spotted me and hurried across, his face shining as though the dusty old forty-watt bulb inside his head had been replaced by a new hundred-watt one, to grab my arm and whisper in my ear.

'Paul, it's fantastic!' breathed my poor, unhappy, dependent friend, 'you've got to come and meet Steve and let him tell you what he told me. Paul – it's _so_ great – I've become a Christian!'

Have you ever experienced the feeling that a vital supporting wall in your life has suddenly collapsed? That's how I felt as I followed Greg back to the corner table in the saloon bar of 'The King's Head'. What a betrayal of our relationship if he actually had made a move into some kind of commitment or belief with absolutely no reference to me, and without any thought of how our friendship might be affected. And what in God's name was all this 'come and meet Steve' business? If the wretched individual who was now rising and extending a hand towards me was really responsible for poor Greg's new delusion, then he was the last person I wanted to meet. How could my so-called friend have brought him here to *our* place without at least giving me some warning? Everything in me tightened and tensed as I took the hand that was offered to me. I gripped it more tightly than necessary to show who was boss. He spoke first.

'Hi, my name's Steve – I work with Greg. He's been telling me that you two make a habit of this.'

Steve was an ordinary-looking sort of bloke, quite tall, dark-haired, casually dressed and with a pleasant, crinkly smile, although I wasn't very interested in the pleasantness or otherwise of his smile at that particular moment. I decided to regard his comment as a critical one.

'A bad habit, you mean?'

'Not at all.' Steve's smile was undimmed. 'Jolly good habit, if you ask me. I wouldn't mind getting into the habit myself. Sit down and join us. Can I get you a drink?'

Like a sealed kettle I bubbled with silent fury. How dare this man invite me to sit down at a table and in a place that were more mine than his? I set my face in what I hoped was an expression of calm and steely independence – and sat. Yes, he could get me a drink.

'Okay, I'll have a pint of Directors and a large scotch chaser with nothing in it.'

He didn't turn a hair, damn him. 'Directors and a large scotch with nothing in it – right. What about you, Greg? Have another shandy?'

'Shandy!' I couldn't believe my ears. I laughed with exaggerated harshness. 'You're drinking shandy? Please tell me I'm dreaming!'

Greg blushed purple.

Steve spoke easily. 'What d'you usually drink, Greg? I'm only having shandy because I like it. You have what you want.'

'He drinks Directors like me,' I said sardonically, 'at least, he did up to last Friday. I'm not quite sure what's happened since then.'

'Pint of Directors, Greg?'

Greg nodded, his face still flaming, as Steve set off towards the crowded bar.

For a few moments neither of us spoke, then Greg leaned forward over the remnants of his small Christian shandy and spoke pleadingly.

'Paul, I know you're feeling stroppy because there's someone else here and all that, but everything's changed, and ... '

I hated him being right about how I felt. I interrupted as crudely as I could.

'Greg, just tell me what's happened, and please, please promise me you haven't brought that man along here to convert me, because if you have I'm going home right now, if not sooner.'

The excitement that had been lighting up my friend since I first saw him a minute ago was far stronger than his embarrassment over the drinks. I couldn't remember a time when I had seen such life in his face or heard such animation in his voice.

'I've asked Jesus into my life, Paul! I've been born again!'

So loudly did Greg make this appalling announcement that the whole bar went quiet for a second or two. Then several people laughed and the noise level returned to normal. I didn't know where to put myself. I could have died.

'You don't have to shout your head off about it, do you?' I hissed. 'The whole bloody pub knows about it now!'

'Yes, but isn't it great!' hissed back Greg in a horribly penetrating whisper, looking like a kid who's just been given what he wanted for Christmas. 'I've never felt so good – Jesus has saved me!'

'No, it's not great,' I replied, with cold, intentional cruelty, 'it's sad – pathetic. You've let some Bible-bashing loony get you all worked up about something that doesn't exist, and now you want me to have my brain washed so that I'll end up as demented as you. You were just the same when you got talked into that pyramid selling thing a couple of years ago – that lasted about ten days as far as I can remember. It was going to be *the* answer,

261

remember? All your money problems were going to be solved within a month. It was just as obvious then that you'd been taken for a ride. Let's face it – you're easy meat for these dream-merchants, Greg. They must think it's their birthday when they see you coming.'

Greg's face clouded over. Good. He was still within my reach. He looked at me like a puppy the first time it's been smacked.

'You told me you thought that was a good idea at the time,' he said. 'Didn't you mean it?'

'Of course I didn't mean it,' I snapped, hating myself, 'but sometimes you have to let people find out for themselves that they're up the creek. You wouldn't have listened if I had told you what I thought. People don't.'

Greg looked at me with his head on one side and said nothing for a little while. The expression of slowly dawning comprehension on his face made me want to grab all my words back and pretend that I'd never said them. Sometimes, though, when, for better or worse, you set out on a new way, you can almost hear the sound of gates clanging and locking behind you. Maybe all roads were going to be new ones from now on.

That bulb was suddenly switched on inside Greg again as he remembered his new faith. I just felt plain, bright-green jealous.

'Paul, believe me – this really is different.' Greg clenched and unclenched his fists with the frustration of being unable to convey the passion that he felt. 'When Jesus . . . '

I couldn't stand it any more. I spoke through gritted teeth. 'Greg, will you stop saying that word! I have to be absolutely honest with you – it makes me feel physically sick in my stomach. I don't know why, it just does. It's so – yukky! And you sound so stupid when you come out with it.'

Steve reappeared with a tray. 'Pint and a scotch for you, Paul – one for you, Greg. And some crisps. Sorry it took a little while. Cheers!'

My first gulp from that first pint was *so-o-o-o* good. It slid down my throat like a rabbit running from a hound. I concealed a sigh and relaxed a little. Greg sat and stared at his beer, blinking in thought. Nobody said anything for a moment or two.

'Penny for 'em,' said Steve at last, placing his glass carefully down on to a mat on the polished surface of the table.

Greg looked up abruptly as though he'd suddenly regained consciousness. 'I was just thinking,' he said, 'about how different people can be. Paul was just saying while you were up at the bar that hearing the word Jesus makes him feel really sick, and ever since Tuesday evening it's made me want to cry with happiness every time I say it or hear someone else say it. Isn't that weird?'

Steve looked at me with nothing but calm interest in his expression. 'That's how it makes you feel, eh?'

I was none too pleased with Greg for repeating what I'd said. There are things you say to stir your friends up that are way too excessive to be passed on to anyone else. Embarrassing. Still, in for a penny, in for a pound. I'd show this smoothy God-follower that I wasn't a pushover like Greg. I finished my pint in one long swallow and downed a good third of the whisky.

'I'll answer your question when I've got myself another beer,' I said, standing up with my empty glass in my hand. 'What about you two? Ready for another one?' Childishly, I injected the merest trace of contempt into my tone as I glanced at Steve's half-full glass, and Greg's pint of Directors that, incredibly, hadn't even been started yet.

'I'm okay, thanks,' smiled Steve, 'you carry on, though.'

'Oh, I shall do,' I muttered to myself under my breath as I made my way to the bar, 'I shall carry on whether you give me permission or not, thank you very much indeed.'

Waiting at the bar, I tried to analyse the nervousness that had crept into me. There was something about this bloke Steve that was threateningly unflappable. I knew how shaky I was inside over the whole business of Dan, and I didn't want to be prised open in some way by the conversation that was about to take place. I'd just have to be careful. When I was served at last I had a secret extra whisky to give me confidence before returning to the table with my fresh pint. To my annoyance Steve and Greg were speaking quietly with their heads close together when I got back. They stopped talking as I sat down, and Steve turned to me with that same imperturbable smile.

'Right,' he said, 'you were saying – about Jesus.'

I drank the other two-thirds of the whisky in front of me before replying.

'I was saying that the name of the person you claim to follow makes me feel physically sick.'

My words climbed out of my mouth with the exaggerated clarity of incipient tipsiness. Those first three drinks had gone down far too quickly. I was still just about in control, though, and beginning to feel rather clever. Thank goodness Violet wasn't here. Greg looked expectantly at his new friend, trustingly convinced that some kind of lofted spiritual straight drive would smash my secular full-toss for six. But Steve just nodded his head in an interested sort of way, leaning back and considering for a moment before he spoke.

'Mmm, I fancy you wouldn't be alone in thinking like that.'

Bastard! I wanted to be alone in thinking like that, not just one of some boringly predictable crowd who all felt the same about everything. Still, if he was determined to make himself feel safer by placing me in some common atheistic category or other, I'd make damn sure I represented my 'group' as forcefully as possible. I took another mouthful from my glass of bitter and licked my lips.

'Why, does that surprise you, then?' I asked, with what I hoped came over as nonchalant scepticism. 'I really don't see why it should. As far as I can see the church is a place where people who are already nearly dead go along to practise being completely dead for an hour or so every Sunday. No wonder the bloke who started that makes people feel ill. Pathetic state of affairs, I'd say, wouldn't you?'

I was rather pleased with this little speech. The stuff about nearly dead people was really quite good. I glanced at Greg to see if he was impressed, but he was wearing his dying frog expression, staring at Steve as if disappointed that Steve's straight drive had been intercepted and caught with such ease by the bowler. Excellent! With a bit of luck this whole situation could be normalized before too long.

'I'd have to agree with a lot of what you say,' said Steve. 'There are loads of churches like that, but not all, by any means, and I don't think that actually explains why people react so strongly – almost violently – to Jesus himself. I mean, you were talking about feeling physically sick, weren't you? That's a very extreme way to feel, isn't it? What do you think are the real reasons for you being so violently anti-Jesus?'

I opened my mouth as if I couldn't wait to answer, but actually I was quite pleased when Greg broke in before I had a chance to speak. I hadn't wanted to look as if I was stuck for a reply, but the truth was I had no idea what I was going to say.

'Drink up, Paul, I'll get you another one. Steve? No? Same as before, Paul? Right . . . '

Greg's early enthusiasm was ebbing away. I had the distinct impression that he was trying to prevent or at least deflect our conversation from the course that it was taking. Perhaps, I thought, he was worried that his new hero, and consequently his new faith, could crumble under the onslaught that I might be about to unleash. As Greg disappeared into the crush around the bar, Steve made an encouraging gesture with his hand.

'Carry on, Paul. You were about to say . . . '

'I'll wait for Greg,' I said, my manner suggesting that Steve was trying to cheat in some subtle way.

Another silence fell. I didn't know what he was thinking, but I was trying to get my brain into some sort of reasonable gear for negotiating an answer to the question that I'd just been asked. It was nice to have two fresh drinks in front of me when Greg got back. After these two I was quite likely to get silly, but I still had enough control left for one major speech. I sipped carefully from the overfilled pint glass and wiped froth from my top lip with the knuckle of a forefinger.

'Steve's into cricket like us,' said Greg somewhat plaintively. He must have known perfectly well that we weren't about to embark on a friendly discussion of last summer's batting averages.

'Hold on, Greg. Steve asked me a question. It's bad manners not to answer questions. Why am I violently anti-Jesus? – that was it, wasn't it? Okay, well – here goes.' I counted the points on my fingers. 'First, he was a failure. Getting nailed up on a bit of wood at the age of thirty-three can hardly be counted as a winning move, can it, especially if you've been claiming to be God and have miraculous powers? Secondly, it hasn't worked, has it? It's caused more wars and trouble and torture and killing than just about any other movement in history. Thirdly, as I was saying just now, people who do call them- selves Christians seem to specialize in being boring or hypo- critical, or both. And fourthly . . . ' I felt the muscles in my hands and face contract as I searched for words to express the only genuine problem on my list, 'I dunno – there's something so mealy-mouthed and . . . and cringingly gruesome about this goody-goody wafting around in a dress like some hippie, telling everyone that life isn't important and we've all got to be nice to people we don't like. It all seems so weak and spine- less and useless. That's why most people despise him, I should think. It's why I do. He was just a pathetic twit. Does that answer your question?'

Another silence fell. Steve seemed to be peering down into his drink, so I couldn't see his face. Greg was sitting upright, fingertips on the edge of the table, staring at me in disbelief, as if I was a complete stranger. When Steve looked up at last I searched his face for a reaction. It didn't take much search- ing. Not so imperturbable now. His eyes were wet with tears. What on earth was going on? I felt uncomfortable suddenly, hot and heavy and crass, like a child who's experimented with a dirty word without knowing what it really means. Perhaps I'd been a bit harsh. But then, I told myself, I hadn't started any of this. All I'd done was come out for a drink with my best friend, and found myself confronted by this shandy-drinking, scaled-down version of Billy Graham. No, I had nothing to feel guilty about.

'Well, you did ask me,' I said, 'so I told you. Being a Christian you wouldn't want me to tell anything but the truth, would you?'

Steve shook his head slowly. 'No, you're absolutely right, Paul,' he replied quietly, 'I'd much rather you said what you really thought.' He paused for a moment. 'Do you . . . do you mind if I tell you why I got a little upset?'

Unwisely, I downed the whole of my third whisky in one gulp. Sledging in the dark from now on. I shrugged my shoulders with studied unconcern, last of the great democrats.

'Fair enough.' A bit slurred. 'I've had my slay – say, you have yours.'

I looked at Greg. He was a dismal lump, hunched miserably over his drink. For a fleeting moment I thought *I* was going to burst into tears. Too much alcohol, I thought, that's all it was.

'I got upset, Paul, because . . . well, because the things I believe are not just a set of ideas or a way of living or anything like that. For me it's all about the Jesus that you think of as a spineless twit.' He raised a hand to ward off objection. 'No, I'm not complaining about you telling the truth. You only said what an awful lot of other people think.'

Bastard!

'No, the thing is that . . . well, I love him, you see. I love Jesus. I don't just believe in him, or think he made some good points, or told good stories or any of those things. It's gone way beyond that. I really love him, and when you were saying about him being weak and silly I felt like crying, because he's here and he's listening, and he's had two thousand years of being despised by the . . . the people he did so much for. He wasn't weak, Paul. He was strong and obedient, even though it meant dying in the end. And can you imagine how his father felt?'

'God, you mean?'

'Have you got any sons, Paul?'

The wound inside me opened. I answered in a whisper.

'Yes, one son – called Dan.'

'Can you imagine how your heart would break if Dan was separated from you because of what other people had done? All that father's love raging with pain and grief until he was safely back with you again. Because that's what happened with Jesus on the cross, and it's still happening over and over again when people can't see what he's done for them. That's why I got so upset, and I can't help it because it means everything to me.'

The light had come back into Greg's face in the course of this speech, and now, as Steve stopped speaking, he turned hopeful, expectant eyes towards me. I put my empty beer glass down, knowing that I had only enough sobriety and self-control remaining for one reasonably coherent piece of communication. I spoke slowly and distinctly.

'Could I please ask you to do something for me – both of you?'

They nodded. Greg leaned forward eagerly.

'Would you please go away – right now, without saying anything else, and just leave me alone.'

They sat and stared at me for what seemed like a long time, but then they did go. I stayed and got very drunk. At around eleven-thirty I somehow managed to get a coin into the slot in the phone-box outside the pub.

'Violet, c'you come and pick me up?'

'Literally?'

'Please.'

'Start staggering and I'll meet you half-way.'

I've often felt wrecked, but not usually on every possible level. I woke up on the Saturday morning with a hangover in my heart as bad as the one in my body. Physically, mentally, emotionally and spiritually – whatever that might mean – I felt coated and streaked with the indelible marks of some species of shame. I tried to wash it away under a scalding shower, but that only woke me up a bit and made me even more conscious of my wretched self. Hot, sweet coffee revived me to an even higher level of dismal awareness, and four pain-killers cleared my head just enough so that I could begin to focus on how miserable I really did feel. Violet had said almost nothing when she picked me up from the pub after closing time the previous evening, but, like good old Biggles when bandits appear at two o'clock, her mouth had been set in a thin, grim line. I knew that the reckoning was to come. After an eternal night spent in a bed half occupied by my indignantly malfunctioning body, and half by the silent mass of disapproval that was my wife, I was not looking forward to the weekend.

There was one small mercy. By the time I dragged myself downstairs, Violet had taken Curly to her swimming lesson, and Dan was nowhere to be seen. I presumed that he'd taken himself off to his Saturday job at the local Eight Till Late shop. I had the house to myself for an hour or so. Thank God!

'No, don't thank him,' I muttered to myself, 'he doesn't exist. And if he does, he's not very nice. He causes trouble between friends.'

I made some more coffee and tried to work out what I was going to say to my wife.

I was still sitting at the kitchen table when Violet and Curly arrived back. Dear Curly burst through the front door and rushed along the hall towards me with undisguised joy, throwing her arms around my neck and kissing me on the cheek.

'I did really well at swimming, Daddy! Mummy says I'm doing the breathing for the crawl exactly right now and we had a slushy drink and a chocolate biscuit afterwards' cause I didn't take too long getting changed. What have you been doing? You should have come, Daddy. Daddy should have come, shouldn't he, Mummy?'

Enthusiasm and innocence worry and disarm me.

'I wish I had come, Darling. I love watching you swim. Perhaps I'll be able to come along next ... '

'Daddy looks very *tired*, Mummy,' interrupted Curly solicitously, placing her hands on my shoulders and drawing back to study the puffiness under my eyes and the general limpness of my demeanour. 'He does, doesn't he, Mummy? Poor Daddy looks ever so tired. Why don't you make him a nice cup of tea?'

I avoided my wife's sardonic eye.

'Yes,' said Violet dryly, as she filled the kettle and plugged it in, 'poor Daddy does look rather tired, doesn't he? But he may not want anything else to drink this morning because he did rather a lot of that last night, didn't you, Daddy? Perhaps that's what's making you so sleepy today. *Shall* I make you a cup of tea now, or do you think you'll be too tired to drink it?'

'Err, yes,' I replied, 'thank you very much, Violet. That would be very nice. Curly, darling, why don't you take a drink and a biscuit into my study and do me a really nice drawing of your swimming class, eh? I'd like that.'

Curly pretended wide-eyed puzzlement. 'I can't draw a picture with a drink and a biscuit, Daddy. You have to use colours.' She went into peals of laughter at her own brilliant joke. 'Can I use your special pens just this once?'

'Yes, make sure you put the tops back on each time you finish with one, though, won't you?'

'Course I will.' Sensing that her absence was being bought, Curly decided to up the price a little. 'Can I use your very, very special paper as well, if I don't waste it, please?'

'Yes,' said Violet firmly. 'Shoo! Here's your drink and your biscuit. Now go!'

Curly departed serenely, aware that our unwritten contract involved her staying out of the kitchen for at least a quarter of an hour or so.

Violet placed tea in front of me and sat down at the other end of the table. I studied the flower design on my mug with narrow-eyed, intense concentration. This very satisfying item of unusually thin china was the sole remnant of a batch of four we'd unexpectedly come across on an East End market-stall a few months earlier. Both of us preferred our hot drinks in this particular mug. The difference between Violet and me was that, whereas when *she* made the drinks she always gave me the good mug, when I made them I usually awarded the prize to myself, and the chipped Manchester United mug to her, or else she got the one that was annoyingly small with a handle too little for your finger to go through. After Violet had pointed out this difference to me a few weeks ago the flowery object had become to me a sort of symbol of my own selfishness. Ever since that day I'd made a point of always giving my wife the nice mug, but I didn't really want to – I just wanted to claw back a little of my self-esteem.

There's a limit to the time you can convincingly spend staring at mug designs, however pleasant. It was time for me to say something.

'Better get the shopping done, I suppose.'

This sparkling conversational ploy was a pathetic attempt to steer Violet's thinking away from the specific subject of my drunkenness the night before, and the current, general cloud of gloom that was suspended immediately above my head.

'Why did you get drunk last night?'

I can never decide, when a row is brewing, which of various possible options to select. Self-justification usually springs to the front of my mind before anything else, but this can be very hard work, involving, as it does, the racking of memory to recall occasions when Violet has committed similar or equally heinous crimes. She doesn't commit many. Nor was it as if I could plead stress due to an excessively heavy work-load. My output had dwindled to almost nothing recently, despite quite a reasonable flow of commissions. There was always the 'I'll do what I want – you don't own me, you know' tack, but such a response is easier in theory than in practice. Violet was more than capable of dealing with that one. Less devious, but certainly potentially more dangerous, was the option of exposing real resentments – genuine, unresolved feelings of hurt that would be heavy enough to club my wife's complaints about drinking out of existence. Something inside me still trembled with child-like rage over the way Violet tended to shut down my agony about Dan because it wasn't quite rational enough for her liking. I didn't really want to go down that road at the moment. Where might it end?

I decided to opt for a kind of truth.

'I got drunk last night because Greg's become ... well, he thinks he's become a Christian. He's got religion. I don't know how you say it. He's met this bloke called Steve something-or-other, who was in the pub with him last night when I got there, and all they wanted to talk about was Gentle Jesus, Meek and Mild, who drinks shandy rather than bitter.'

My voice was full of scorn, but I suddenly realized that if my attitude to Greg's conversion really had been as dismissive and laid-back as I must be sounding now, there was little if any justification for my claim that it had precipitated my descent into inebriation. I was right. Violet put a finger to her chin and moved into Perry Mason mode.

'Let me see if I've got this right. Greg's had some kind of religious experience which you – despise? Is that too strong a word? I want to get this right.'

I shrugged. 'Yes, more or less, but ... '

'And he came along with the man who talked him into this despicable state, or led him there, or whatever, and on hearing about this you immediately had no choice but to get expensively, stinkingly drunk. Is that a fair summary of what happened?'

'No-o-o!' I went through my tongue-clicking, head-shaking, sighing routine. 'It wasn't that. It was just that ... well, he was making such a fool of himself. You know what he's like when he gets an idea into his head. Nothing else matters for a week or two, and then suddenly he loses interest and he forgets he ever was interested. He's always been like that. Remember the shopping thing – the pyramid selling thing? That was almost like a religion. He just gets taken in so easily and – I don't know ... It upset me.'

'So why didn't you get drunk on the night when he told you about the pyramid thing?'

'Because,' I explained, speaking with great clarity as if to a half-wit, and dropping blindly into the pit I had so efficiently been digging for myself, 'like I've already said, I knew it wouldn't last.'

'Whereas this time ... ?'

I stared at Violet in silence for a moment, and then, to my own horror, a sob burst from me and I started to cry.

I imagine that people who cry easily in front of others will find it hard to understand why this was such an earth-shaking experience for me. The fact was, though, that I had been brought up never to display excessive emotion in front of anyone. For me, the idea of shedding tears in a public place, even in such a limited and domestic public place as the presence of my wife, was the equivalent of walking naked along a crowded street. Violet and I had, for a variety of not very good reasons, avoided open discussion on the subject of my repressed nature for some years now, although I knew that it was a source of great sadness to her that I so rarely expressed affection, and virtually never shared other, deeper feelings.

My little sob of grief was, in fact, so unprecedented in our relationship, that neither of us knew what to do next. I pulled myself together almost immediately, but the damage, if that was what it was going to turn out to be, had already been done. I have to confess that the detached observer in me, the sharp-eyed watcher who saw all new experience as potential writing fodder, waited with interest to see how Violet would react to such an unusual display of emotion. The other me, the one who had lost control for a second, was horrified that she should have seen me in such a vulnerable state, no matter how brief that glimpse had been. I took a few deep breaths and said nothing while she stared at me with a warily puzzled expression on her face.

I was struck suddenly, and for no particular reason that I was aware of, by how much I still secretly loved my wife's face after years of marriage. I loved her large, dark, serious eyes, and the way her mouth kinked humorously at one corner, and her handsome grown-up nose and the way her dark hair tumbled in ringlets on to her shoulders. I wondered for the thousandth time why I was incapable of telling her things like that, when it would have assuredly been *such* a very good thing to do.

She said nothing for so long that, in the end, I couldn't meet her gaze any more and had to resort to further mug-studying.

'Paul . . . ' Violet took in a deep breath and blew it out again like a stream of cigarette smoke before speaking quite gently. 'What is all this really about?'

I found that, unconsciously, I'd begun a slight backwards and forwards rocking movement in my chair, perhaps trying to establish some sort of pattern in the midst of chaos. Now I had to decide whether or not to make contact with Violet. How about a postponement? I looked up at her.

'What is all *what* really about?'

She twisted back in her chair, and, after considering me appraisingly through narrowed eyes for a moment, seemed to make a decision, one which to my troubled perception had 'RISK' written all over it. She leaned forward, resting her folded arms on the table, and spoke just as gently as before.

'All right, if you're really asking me, I'll go through it, and you can tell me where I'm getting it wrong. Work, first of all. You're doing hardly any writing at the moment, which would matter very much if it went on for a long time, for obvious reasons, but only matters at the moment because it shows that your mind is so busy wrestling with something else that you can't concentrate. Okay, so what exactly are you wrestling with? Well, we know part of the answer to that, don't we? You've been very upset lately because Dan, in common with almost every other boy of his age who ever lived in the entire universe, has decided to experiment with the idea that he exists in his own right. What does that mean? It means that he's trying to move on to centre-stage of his own life, and *that* means that you – and me, if it comes to that – are relegated to new, equally important but purely supporting roles while he sorts himself out in the starring one. Like I said, that's upset you a lot.'

Yes, Violet, all the things you say about experimenting and existing and centre-stages and supporting roles are very, very true, but you haven't actually understood because you're not down here inside me. He was my little, big, growing friend, Violet. He was the only person I've held in my heart like a poor man holds a diamond given to him by a God who's actually there. He was the only toy I never broke or damaged. He was the one project to which I gave everything, without trying to cheat or cut corners. He was the best thing I've done. He was the hope that I might not be hopeless. He was the only mirror I ever wanted to look into. Down here in the dark, Violet, there's a lot of wailing and crying and agony going on. The pain, Violet, it's like a pneumatic drill thundering away inside my head. It doesn't let anything else happen. Excuse the jumble of mixed metaphors, Violet, but it's like the bloody Arctic – endless night, and I'm sick with fear that there aren't going to be any more mornings. Not real mornings where everything's all right after all, and the sun shines like in a picture book, and absolutely anything could happen, and you laugh at the things that frightened you when it was dark and we're all happy ever after. Violet, Violet, Violet, do you really not understand? Won't you come down here into the dark with me and hold me and look after me, just until the morning comes ...

'That has upset me a bit, yes.'

'A bit?'

'Oui, un morceau.'

Silence. Dilated nostrils. A determination to persevere just in case it should turn out to be worth it.

'Shall I go on?'

'I like your hair.'

Silence. Incredulous little shake of the head. Last chance, no doubt.

'Just now, for the first time since we've been together, you cried. Only a little bit. You packed it all back in the box straight away – as soon as that tiny fragment escaped, in fact. But it was there, Paul. I saw it. Something about this business with Greg and whatever it is he's got himself into has really got under your skin, hasn't it? It actually made you weep in front of me. Paul . . . '

I had renewed my china examination, but something in the quality of the ensuing pause made me look up. Violet's eyes were filled with an unusual softness now, her voice gentler than ever.

'Paul, please believe me – I *want* you to share your feelings with me. I know you think I don't understand and don't really want to support you, but have you ever faced the fact that you never actually tell me how you're feeling? What I mean is – have you realized that I get shut out from the part of you that cries? You know what's going on inside you, but I don't. How can I? I was pleased just now when you . . . when you got upset. No, that's not true. I wasn't just pleased. Paul, I felt a little twinge of excitement. We've lived in our own worlds for such a long time now. I've been so lonely. If you only knew how much I want us to be close . . . '

Her eyes begged me. I could see her waiting for me just out there on the outside. But though I shook the bars and kicked at the walls and shouted and screamed with all my might, I couldn't get out.

The thing is, Violet, that when Greg brought that man to the pub and said he'd got converted, and messed up our Friday evening – well, that wasn't fair, was it? I mean, that's our time – Greg's and mine. Our place. And he belongs to me. Greg belongs to me, not to a man called Steve who's all calm and nice and Christian. I mean – if I've got to lose Danny, surely I don't have to lose Greg as well, do I? Violet, I haven't got many people, you see. I can't go on losing them because in the end there won't be anyone left. That's why I cried. You'll stay with me, won't you, Violet? You won't let anyone take you away, will you? I couldn't bear that. Apart from Curly I'd be on my own, and I'll probably lose her as well, one day. Hold me. Please, hold me . . .

I heard my voice starting to speak, but I couldn't stop it.

'Ah, well, the reason for my tears is quite simple. I'm suffering from an illness that the doctors have only just properly classified. It's called P.P.M.T.T. which stands for Pre-pre-menstrual-tension-tension. It's a married man's thing occurring for about a week in every month, and it's invariably followed by another condition known as Post-pre-menstrual-tension-tension. The symptoms commonly include a quite uncontrollable desire to imbibe alcohol, and a tendency to burst into tears for no reason at all. I'm afraid that at these times we men are hopelessly at the mercy of our wives' hormones.'

There was no softness in my wife's eyes now, just distance, deep, deep disappointment and a strangely flavoured fear that chilled my heart.

'I'm going to go and see to Curly,' she said, and she went.

'I love your eyes,' I said, too quietly for her to hear.

Saturday lasted for about a decade. The day after drinking too much usually does. One is dismally aware that the chance of recovering enough physical or mental energy to actually enjoy anything more demanding than television is very slim indeed. Added to this general slump was the realization that any irritation on my part would be construed (with complete accuracy, of course) as a symptom of my recent alcoholic extravagance, and condemned accordingly. I went to bed early that night and fell fast asleep almost immediately.

Waking early on Sunday morning, I found my mind full of thoughts about Greg. Later today, I conjectured, he'd be getting up and dressing as smartly as he could (given the rather cowboyish nature of his wardrobe), then setting out with this new excitement of his to whichever church old smoothy Steve was part of. My whole body twitched involuntarily with embarrassment as I imagined my old friend and drinking partner explaining publicly how his heathen friend had reacted so negatively to the news of his conversion. Oh, God! They'll probably pray for me, I thought. Someone will ask the Lord to break through the barriers of doubt and resistance, and all that garbage. Sickening!

I turned my head to one side expecting to see Violet's head on the pillow and the dark shape of her body silhouetted beside me, but she wasn't there. For one wild moment I was full of breathless panic. She'd gone! Violet had finally had enough and left me in the middle of the night, taking Dan and Curly with her. I was on my own and I didn't even know where my family were. A moment's calmer reflection suggested that incest among the Waltons was marginally more likely than my wife doing something so disruptive and potentially harmful to the children. Violet's appearance at this point with a mug of tea (it was the nice, flowery mug) seemed to confirm this view. But why had she brought me tea this early in the morning? It was unlikely to be a gesture of affection.

'I've already been up for ages, worrying my head off,' said Violet, placing the mug down on the table beside my bed, 'so I don't see why you shouldn't wake up now. You and I have got some very serious thinking to do, and I suggest you get started on it right now. I can't carry on like this, and I don't intend to. Something's got to happen, so you'd better start asking yourself what it'll be. I'm going back downstairs.'

The cold, unyielding, mechanical quality in Violet's voice made my heart sink like a stone. I reached a hand out towards my tea, but drew it back as a wave of unhappiness passed through me. What on earth could I do about being me? I couldn't just decide to be a different kind of person, could I? Or was that silly and self-indulgent? Perhaps what was really required was for me to make a much greater effort to set aside my own stupid Pavlovian emotional responses and think about what others needed from me. Could I grit my teeth and tough it out? The trouble with doing that, as I knew full well, was that eventually I was bound to run out of motivation and no longer be able to resist the temptation to advertise my selfless heroism. And if that revelation didn't provoke enthusiastic and prolonged applause I just *knew* that I would descend into sludgy self-pity, and things would probably be worse than before. Perhaps counselling would help ...

I'm not sure how I managed to drop off to sleep again at about that point in my thinking, but I do know that I drifted into a very vivid and disturbing dream.

In my dream I found myself back in the pub, except that it wasn't just the pub any more – it was also my home, the place where I lived. I was there on my own in the private bar, feverishly polishing tables and windowsills and chair-backs in preparation for an impending visit. I desperately wanted to avoid being there when this mysterious visitor arrived, because, although I had no idea what his name was, I could picture his face in my mind, and I knew that he was the embodiment of evil. However, I also knew with absolute certainty, as one does in dreams, that if I were to leave before thoroughly cleaning every corner of my house, something dark and terrible would happen to me anyway.

In the manner of nightmares, I repeatedly reached a point where I thought I had finished my task, only to notice with a sudden thrill of horror that a corner or a table-top or a shelf had been missed in my frantic attempt to get the work done. At last, just as I heard the sound of car tyres crunching on the gravel outside, I reckoned that the whole place was done. Almost sobbing with urgency I rushed to the back door and had actually gripped the handle and was about to turn it and leave, when my heart seemed to stop. I'd missed something. Right in the middle of the room, between me and the front door, stood a small table, smeared, stained – obviously not cleaned. How could I have missed it? As the handle of the front door turned and the door itself began slowly to open, I rushed forward, frantically wiped the surface of the table with the cloth that was still in my hand, and threw myself in the direction of the back door, passing through and slamming it behind me just as a shadowy figure appeared at the other end of the bar.

The next part of the dream was like one of those adventure films where somebody tries to shake off a 'tail'. I found myself climbing in and out of taxis, ducking into department stores and leaving through side doors, even lying on top of a moving train at one point, and finally rowing a small boat across a vast, silent lake towards a tiny island sitting in a low cloud of mist. Abruptly,

I was on the island, and, rather improbably I suppose, walking towards a little tree-surrounded pub whose twinkling lights and general homeliness seemed to offer safety and comfort. Inside, sitting at a table in the furthest corner, I found, to my great joy, Greg smiling and beckoning just as he'd always done in the past before he got religious.

I moved towards him, filled with relief and pleasure, but even as I neared the table and was about to sit down, a dreadful foreboding swept over me. It was too late – I was already seated. Looking up, I watched Greg's face change before my eyes, the friendly smile twisting itself into one of vicious triumph. A silent scream filled my head as I realized that I had not avoided my visitor after all.

I really believed that I woke from this nightmare with an audible scream, but when Violet came into the room a few seconds later she didn't look as if she'd heard anything like that.

'You haven't touched your tea,' she said, and then suspiciously, 'you haven't been back to sleep, have you?'

I held my hand out in her direction.

'Violet – please, could you just hold on to me for a moment? I had the most awful nightmare a moment ago. I . . . I can't quite believe it wasn't real just at the minute.'

Despite the tremors that were still rocking my consciousness, it was lovely to see the look of compassion in my wife's eyes as she sat on the edge of the bed and took my hand.

'What sort of nightmare?'

'Oh, about someone coming to get me, and Greg in a sort of pub, and – oh, I don't want to think about it.' I grabbed a passing impulse and hung on to it before it could escape. 'Violet, I do love you very much, you know.'

Violet's eyes brightened a little for a moment, then she sighed and shook her head very slightly. It was only about the third time I'd said it since we got married.

'Do you?' she said, in a small, not very hopeful voice. 'Do you really love me?'

'I'm going to get up now,' I told her, 'and I'm going to go down to the river for a walk, and when I come back – I'll tell you what I've decided to do.'

We were both silent for a short time. Violet gently disengaged her hand and stood up slowly. 'I'll go and start the dinner,' she said, 'and I'll see you later.'

I didn't walk to the river in the end. It occurred to me as I went out of the door that there would probably be quite a lot of people down there, and just at the moment I wasn't interested in seeing anybody else. The tiniest little glimmer of hope was shining somewhere on the edge of my inner vision and I wanted a chance to look at it properly – to see if it would lead me anywhere. I had told Violet that I loved her. I had actually told Violet that I loved her! I had seen, if only momentarily, her eyes fill with something that wasn't exasperation, and she had held my hand and almost been – she'd almost been something that she used to be a lot. She had almost been a little bit happy.

I drove up to the top of Vokes Hill, left the car on the rough old parking space by the road, and walked slowly out towards the edge of the valley, humming very quietly to myself. There was a little spur of soft turf just where the level began to drop. It was one of my favourite places – always had been. I sat there and stared across the valley, hoping that some inspiration would hit me or fill me or do something to me.

What actually happened was that I suddenly began to cry again. I couldn't help it. This time it poured out like one of those geysers that spout hot water. I was so glad there was nobody else about because this wasn't a gentle, beautiful little weep, it was a release – I assumed – of years of holding everything in and back inside the part of me that felt things and didn't know how to express them. A small detached part of myself listened with amazement to the whooping, sobbing, desperate noises that I was making, noises that I'd never made before as far as I could remember.

Then the crying died down a bit, but only a bit, and I started to speak to someone. I hadn't a clue who I thought was listening, but I certainly seemed to want to communicate with him or her.

'The thing is,' I said, in between sobs and whoops, 'that I can't stand Dan being all grown-up and not liking me so much and looking at me as if he thinks I'm an idiot. Y'see, he always really looked up to me and he really – you know – really wanted to please me because I was his dad and we always did everything together and now we don't. And what's going to happen if little Curly suddenly gets all stroppy when she's a big girl – I can't, I just can't! And I want Violet to be happy, but I'm no good at saying the things that she ... the things that she wants me to say, although I did just now and I wish, I really wish that I could be what she wants, but I'm just not ... '

My emotions gradually came under control as I released all these swirling thoughts. Finally, I was just producing little sniffing noises, with an occasional shudder. I wiped my nose with a fragment of tissue excavated from an inside pocket and buried the result under a little tombstone of turf. Then I picked a tall grass stalk with a brown bobbly bit on top, and began to address it in quiet, serious tones.

'Now,' I said, 'we come to the subject of Greg. You' – I jabbed my finger accusingly at the grass stalk – 'have somehow managed to ensnare him into your *thing,* whatever your thing is, just when I am most in need of the kind of exclusive attention that, in the past, I've tended to find a trifle annoying. You bring this Steve person along with Greg to *my* pub for reasons best known to yourself, and force me to listen to him being tactful and generous and – uugh!' I made being-sick noises. The grass stalk waved gently and serenely. It seemed to have no shame.

The next five minutes takes some explaining, or rather, it would do, if it could be explained. It was as though some other fairly long chunk of dialogue had been going on underneath all the crying and my haranguing of the local vegetation. Suddenly I wasn't talking to that grass stalk any more, in fact I threw it to one side and looked out over the valley as I spoke.

'What's going to happen if I give in and go with you? What am I going to have to say and do? Who am I going to have to tell? Which branch of the living dead will I be publicly identifying with? What will Violet say? What will Greg say next week when he suddenly announces that he's made a mistake and he wants to be a Jehovah's Witness instead, and I'm all committed to the thing that he's just left? Will we still go down the pub?' Pause. 'What *will* Violet say?'

As I asked that last question for the second time, I saw Violet's face again, full of hope as it had fleetingly appeared that morning, and I knew – don't ask me how, but I did – that her tears and her hope and a lot of the sadness she'd been feeling were – well – inhabited by the person I was talking to up on top of this hill. I know that sounds absurd, but there was a solid reality in this new piece of knowledge that was simply unavoidable. I shook my head, embarrassed suddenly by the proximity of my own thoughts. What was going on? Was I talking to God? Was he talking to me?

I became aware, as I sat there, that there was something different about me – about the way I felt to myself, I mean. For some minutes I simply couldn't pin it down, but then it dawned on me what it was. Just for a few minutes I had actually felt more or less at peace.

Peace?

I'd almost forgotten what peace meant. I'd got used to living with a constant layer of tension. In bed at night I often had to relax the muscles of my neck by an effort of will before I was able to truly rest my head and get to sleep. For a little while the springs inside me had been released and allowed to move back into the shape they were intended to be. It was a strange, almost tipsy feeling. Very pleasant – very pleasant indeed.

I drove back down the hill in a dream, humming to myself as I had done earlier. I had no idea what I was going to say to Violet, and there was no plan of action in my mind at all. It didn't seem to matter somehow. I wondered if everything would revert to normal as soon as I got back home.

'Don't let it,' I implored the grass stalk substitute as I pulled into the front drive and stopped the car.

Violet and I were oddly shy of each other in the period leading up to lunch. It was rather nice in a way – a bit like we used
to be when we were courting. Both children were out for the day,
thank goodness. Neither of us wanted to spoil the moment by
bringing up the thorny subject of 'what I was going to do'. Violet did in the end, though. I knew she would. Despite this little
lull she was desperate for something to change, and I still felt a
fear deep inside me at the thought that she might stop loving me
and move away into herself forever.

'What have you decided to do?'

That's what she said just as I picked up my glass of traditional
lemonade, and I still had no answer prepared for her. What *was*
I going to do? Silently I asked myself the question again. What
am I going to do? What am I . . . ?

'I'd like to invite Greg and his friend Steve round to eat with
us one night soon.'

She looked steadily at me for a moment, then spoke quietly
but with a firm challenge in her voice. 'What about the day after
tomorrow?'

I swallowed. 'The day after tomorrow would be fine.'

'All right, then.'

'I love you, Violet.'

Four times in one lifetime! I could hardly believe it. Nor could
she.

'I love you too, but, Paul, if something doesn't change . . . '

I reached across. 'Have a tissue. Leave the washing up and
come for a walk up on the hill with me. Indulge my lunacy.
There's a grass stalk I want you to meet.'

The Final Boundary

It was mostly dreams now. Sleeping dreams, waking dreams, he drifted from one to the other knowing that time was short and there was no good reason for dredging up the physical energy needed to return to what he used to call the real world. Too old, too sick, too tired, and there were no sons, daughters or close friends to cluster round the hospital bed demanding that he notice them. Someone fed him, someone washed him, other things happened, but they didn't really happen to him. They happened to the worn-out body lying on the bed, the body that would soon be surplus to requirements. A jolly good thing too, in his opinion. It couldn't come soon enough. A couple more dreams and then he would step into a completely different kind of reality, and his friend would be there to smile, and take his hand, and show him the way. He looked forward to that. He wanted it more than anything now – he really did.

One shadow only. One small but stubborn sadness was lodged immovably in a corner of his mind, and he couldn't even quite identify it. Something to do with – not failing exactly – but not succeeding enough, or in the right way perhaps. It was, he thought vaguely, rather like when you haven't quite finished a biscuit or a sandwich, and you've forgotten where you put it down. Your mouth knows there was one more bite to come, and you feel disappointed. It was a bit like that, only more so – something to do with the tone or quality of his life, an anger not released, a love not expressed, a final word not said, an exhilaration not felt – something in his life . . .

It hadn't been a bad life, actually. Not eventful, but by no means unpleasant, and running through it all like two beautiful singing silver wires, his twin loves – cricket and Jesus. He heard a dry, wheezing little laugh coming from his own chest as he mouthed the words: 'Cricket – Jesus.' Folks would think he was barmy putting those two words together like that. But they did belong side by side, because that was where his soul had been for most of his life. In that game and that person. More in one than the other? No, it wasn't like that. Souls weren't like that. Jesus wasn't like that. He'd have made a jolly good cricketer, Jesus would. Leg spinner probably. Dead fair, but really crafty. Curl the ball all round your legs until, say, the fifth ball of his second over, then you'd jump out and go for a bad pitched one and it would break the other way and you'd be bowled, or stumped maybe. Opening bat he'd have been. Starting steady and firm and ending up dancing down the pitch to slam the ball to the boundary over and over again. Captain of course – he'd have to be captain. Useful to have Jesus around at the tea interval too, if it looked as if the cucumber sandwiches weren't going to go round. Yes, he'd have made a fine cricketer . . .

A lot of his dreams were about cricket now. Two sorts. Some about things he'd really done, matches he'd really played in, and others about things he wished he'd done, triumphs he knew he had never really been capable of. One or two bad memories.

School – that was one of the real memories, and especially that day he'd gone down to the second eleven nets by invitation for the first time, feeling shy and nervous and clumsy as he took off his striped school blazer and laid it with the others by the two long cricket bags. He recalled wishing that the new cricket trousers he'd been sent by his mother weren't quite so beautifully creased and shinily white. He'd noticed how Bovington, the second's wicket keeper, glanced at him for an instant and smiled very slightly to himself as he turned back to bowl at the man in the net. Then old Raddish, the sports master, the one they all called 'Salad', had tossed one of the worn practice balls over to him and said in a loud voice, 'Come on then, Crocker, send one down. Let's see what you're made of!' He'd flushed, and only just caught the ball. He wanted to tell everyone that he was a batsman and not a bowler, but that wasn't the sort of thing you said in the nets. Everyone had a bowl in the nets, whatever they were best or worst at. His muscles had felt stiff and unco-ordinated as he stepped up to the single stump to send a slow one down to Evert-Brown, who was hitting everything with his usual elegant competence. And the worst had happened, the bally, blush-making worst! He'd let go of the ball before he should have done, sending it soaring up into the air and right over the top of the net, causing Evert-Brown to shield his eyes with his hand and gaze at the arcing sphere in mock astonishment as though it was a shooting star.

'Is it counted as a wide if it goes into orbit, Mr Raddish?' Bovington had called delightedly. 'Watch you don't burn your hands when you pick it up, Crocker. It'll be red hot after re-entry, you know.'

Bovington had been quickly extinguished by Salad, who was a lot kinder than he was wise, but the burning cheeks seemed to go on for ever, their heat matched only by his determination not to make a fool of himself when it came to the batting. And he hadn't made a fool of himself – not in the slightest. It had been a magical, utterly satisfying fifteen minutes. Whether the delivery was slow or fast, simple or tricky, the ball invariably arrived like a firm, friendly, rosy fruit, quivering and revolving in its eagerness to be struck with sweet and sensual rightness by the very centre of his bat. After only a few minutes with the pads on, he'd heard Evert-Brown say, 'He's got all the shots, sir.' And Salad had replied, 'Whacks 'em too, eh?' Even Bovington was impressed. He wandered round to the side of the net and stood watching for a minute or two, hands in his pockets, head on one side.

'Where'd you get your coaching?' he'd asked in the pause when the balls had to be collected from the sides of the net and sent back to the bowler's end.

He'd thought with a special, warm pleasure about the patient persistence of the quiet man at home.

'My dad. He taught me. We had a net in the garden.'

'Did a good job,' said Bovington. 'You're a fine bat.'

Heaven! One sort of heaven anyway, but, oddly enough, he'd never quite managed to get back into that particular kind of heaven again. Except, of course, in those other pretending dreams. He'd done amazing things in those. Double centuries against the Australians at Lords, match-winning boundaries against the West Indies, great performances that received tumultuous applause from thousands of admiring spectators. But in real life, although he became a fixture in the second eleven, and later in the first team, he'd never quite achieved the abandonment of that knock he'd enjoyed so much on his first visit to the second eleven net. It was the same in the local team he had joined after leaving school. He was nearly always good for double figures at least, and he frequently scored twenty or more. A few times he'd even reached the half century. Heaven within heaven! But it had only been a few times. Most of the time he had been a solid, reliable, unexciting batsman, contributing usefully and popular with the rest of the team, except for – that match. How well he remembered that nightmare of a match when they played away against a team called the Bottlers, who had a picturesque little pitch just over the county border in Kent. It must have been the first fixture they'd had with them. By golly, that match had been a nightmare too! He stirred uneasily in his bed at the memory.

Chap called Kendall was captain at the time. Rory Kendall. Nice chap, and a good captain. He'd won the toss and put the home side in to bat. It was a good toss to win, and there was no doubt that Kendall had made the right decision. There were huge grey clouds lumping around overhead, but they were on the move. By the time the Bottlers' last wicket went down for just over the hundred, the sun was out, and everything was set for the visitors to make the runs and claim the victory. Things didn't quite go according to plan though. The first three men, including Kendall who was a really skilful player, were all out before the score reached double figures. Kendall was run out after responding to a lunatic call from the other end, the lunatic was caught fairly miraculously when a full-blooded drive was held inches above the ground by a man fielding close to the bat, and the other was clean bowled by a ball that rose and straightened in an almost unplayable way. He remembered the captain's words in front of the pavilion as the third wicket went down: 'Take your time, Crocks old man. There's nothing out there to worry you too much. Hundred and three to win. We'll do it.'

The other thing he recalled was how he'd thought tentatively as he walked out to join Danny Whatsisname in the centre, that this could be it. This could just be his chance to do something sensational, something mildly – well – heroic. If he could stick there long enough to get some runs together, then a little flourish at the end – a bit of a hit! And at first it had looked as though that was exactly how it was going to work out. He played, very, very carefully until he was ready to open up a little, scoring in singles with the occasional two. The bowling presented no great problems. It was all pretty orthodox stuff. Nothing faster than slow-medium pace and the ball wasn't doing very much. The only thing that disturbed him was the way in which he was running out of partners at the other end. A combination of bad luck and carelessness sent one after another tramping dolefully or angrily back to the pavilion, leaving him to play with increased caution for fear that his wicket would go down as well, and that then the rot would really set in with a vengeance.

One fellow scored well. Walter Barnett. Not renowned for any technical skill with the bat, but nevertheless very strong, and very effective if he stayed long enough to get his eye in. He certainly got his eye in this time. Twenty off one over, twelve off another, and eight off a third, all scored in sixes and fours, dispatched with little elegance but enormous power to the rather short boundaries at the edge of the little rural ground. That was a great little innings, but nobody else matched it. By the time the ninth wicket went down, Crocker had scored twenty-nine runs, and the next highest score, by the number five, Percy Vidler, was eleven (apart from Walter's thirty of course). If the home team kept their over-rate up, there would be two overs to play remaining and ten runs needed for a win. The number eleven batsman was a tall, thin, fair-haired lad called Watkins, clearly petrified by the position he found himself in, and quite useless with a bat when he was relaxed, let alone now when the tension of the moment was causing him to twitch visibly. Still, it should be all right as long as Watkins could be kept at the non-strikers' end.

'Hang on to the bowling, Crocks. It's up to you now.'

That's what Kendall had shouted from the pavilion. Up to him! He could still feel the pungent mixture of excitement and fear that had gripped his stomach as the first ball of the over before last pitched at driving length in front of him, and he was able to lean forward and stroke it smoothly back past the bowler for an easy two runs. Another two off the fourth ball, and from the sixth, a neat little steer through the slips which could have been another two if the single hadn't been needed for obvious strategic reasons. It was a good feeling. The runs were coming and he was getting them.

So there he'd been, A.J. Crocker, poised to accomplish what he'd dreamed of accomplishing so many times. Five runs to get from six balls against reasonably easy bowling, and he'd have won the match for his team, earned the applause of his friends, and deserved the congratulations of his captain. No Edwardian writer of public-school stories could have dreamed up a more dramatic scenario. 'Crocker of the lower fifth' was about to snatch victory from the jaws of whatever it was they always snatched it from in the books, for the sake of the jolly old school, and his chums in the lower fifth, and the head, who was a dashed good sort. What a lot of nonsense, but it honestly had felt a bit like that. Marvellous! The soft green grass of the outfield, the weighted plummy redness of the ball, the cool uniformed whiteness of the players, the wooden solidity of the bat in his hand, a sky that was now blue and clear of cloud, the merest hint of a breeze, and the opportunity to shine. What more could he ever ask for on this earth? As the bowler turned to begin his run for the first ball of the final over, he heard Kendall call out again.

'Let it go, Crocks! Let it go!'

Yes, that was exactly what he'd needed to do. Let it go! Only five runs. No problem . . .

He didn't add a single run to the score in that last over. His toes curled even now as it came back to him, ball by ball. A great gloomy shadow of caution and fear had seemed to settle over him like a blanket as the first delivery looped its obvious way towards him. It was a gift of a ball – more like a beach ball than a cricket ball, made for crashing away to leg for four runs. That would have left only one run to get. He played a meticulous forward defensive stroke, killing the ball dead in front of his bat. Absolutely safe. Absolutely useless. Everything that should have been firm in him had turned to water. It was as though he was being reminded in the very centre of his will that permission to hit out and succeed had been withdrawn a long time ago. The second ball had been dead straight and a good length. He played defensively again. This time it was justified, but he knew that he'd have played the same shot if the ball had been suspended motionless in front of his bat with a little label attached to it saying 'hit me'. The third ball was like the first. This time he simply took a small step forwards, raised his bat, and let it pass quietly by outside the leg stump. Quaveringly sensitive, his ears detected a barely audible groan coming from the direction of the spectators grouped in front of the pavilion. 'Crocker of the lower fifth' was letting his chums down. Rory Kendall's voice, tense with frustration, had rung out across the ground once more.

'For goodness' sake hit it, Crocker!'

But he couldn't hit it. He couldn't let go. He couldn't find permission to drive his intention down from his eyes, through his body, through his arm, through his bat, through the ball, to the boundary and beyond. All the different parts of him withdrew from co-operative effort, so that the only automatic action left in him was the one he practised most. He blocked and blocked and blocked, and the game was lost.

Oh, the silence on his return to the others, the general air of puzzled dejection, the way in which Kendall had just shaken his head slowly from side to side as if unable to grasp the fact that something which had seemed to be already won could have been handed back with such scant resistance.

It was soon all right of course. They were a good crowd of chaps and, after all, he had scored thirty-four runs when all was said and done. He'd tried to explain to Kendall later on how he'd felt during that last over, but although Rory said it was all right, and not to worry about it, and it might happen to anyone, it was obvious that the captain was far too healthily straightforward and uncomplicated to understand what had really happened. Yes, it had been all right in the end, but he never quite had that kind of chance again. It was a shame he hadn't done better. A real shame.

Funny how those two memories were the ones that came back most now. That great knock in the nets as a lad, and much later, his failure against the Bottlers. Not that that failure had coloured all his cricketing memories. Goodness gracious, no! On the contrary. He'd always loved being one of a crowd of fellows; really enjoyed belonging. The warm familiarness of home matches, the bustle of travel to away fixtures, the matches themselves, offering the ever-new opportunity to do well, if not brilliantly, and the time in the pub afterwards drinking just a little too much as the big enamel jug full of frothing draught bitter was passed round the increasingly mellow company. It had all been grand. Grand times, grand chaps, a grand game ...

And Jesus? Well, now that he thought about it, his friendship with Jesus had become more and more private as the years went by, more and more something that turned into a badly wrapped parcel as soon as you tried to tie it up with words. Maybe that was wrong, but it was a fact.

It hadn't always been like that, of course. He'd first met Jesus in a church where everybody talked about it all the time. He'd been the same. It was so exciting, so explosively invigorating to discover a love that had been directed to him personally since before the beginning of time, so thrilling to feel that he'd hit on the truth that underpinned the whole of creation – of existence. He'd felt a burning need to pass on to others the shining wonder of his encounter with the living God. Everywhere he went, his Bible went with him. Everyone he spoke to was likely to hear something about his faith, even in the course of very brief conversations. People in cafés, on trains, standing at bus-stops, at work or on holiday, they all got a little evangelical blast.

That wheezing chuckle rocked his slight frame once more. All those poor people having to put up with that young religious fanatic with the big black Bible and the shiny eyes. Anyone who had seen him coming the second time round must have given him a very wide berth indeed. He'd been far too pushy and crude. He knew that now. And yet – there was a strange sweet sadness in the memory of those days, something about the freshness and naïvety of his attitude to the whole business of expressing his faith, that he wished he could have hung on to a bit more as the years went by. Not that he'd altogether stopped telling people what he believed. He'd never actually done that, but he had learned not to shove it down people's throats. He'd come to realize that everyone needs space and respect and gentleness, and that only God ever did any real changing in anyone's life. Nevertheless, he knew deep inside himself that he'd never taken the trouble, or found the courage, to develop a language and an approach that would really convey the depth and importance of the love he felt for Jesus. Not in ordinary situations – not naturally.

Jesus. Strange really how, for him, Jesus had become something separate from religion and church and formulas and that sort of thing. And the reason for that, he was sure, was that when all those things had become meaningless to him for a while, Jesus had still been around, a stubborn friend who let abuse and rejection ride right over him when the dark times came – and there had been very dark times once or twice. What was it they quoted Karl Marx as saying: 'I am not a Marxist?'

If Jesus came back today, would he be tempted to say, 'I am not a Christian?' Was that an irreverent thought? He didn't know. Didn't care much either. It certainly didn't matter any more what any other human being on earth felt about what he thought or didn't think, believed or didn't believe. All that was left for him out of the world's great religious jumble sale was Jesus, living now, with him and waiting for him, sometimes on the cross and sometimes off it, depending on whether he was being made to suffer or not. And it wouldn't be long now before he met him in a completely new way and all the things that hadn't made sense before would be explained. All would be well. He was ready. Well – almost ready.

Why had he never talked to his cricketing friends about Jesus? What was it that had stopped him from openly mixing the two most important things in his life? Because he hadn't mixed them at all, in all the time that he'd played. A little over thirty years as a member of the team, and another twenty as a non-playing associate of the club. Naturally, he'd always done his best to be helpful and generous and all the other things that were important, but that wasn't the whole point, and he knew it. Why had he never shared the other great passion of his life with people he met once or twice a week – every week in the summer – for years and years and years?

Perhaps he'd believed that his total enjoyment of cricket was actually very fragile. Was it that he feared an alienation, a separation from the ordinariness of the activity that he relished? Had it, in fact, been a worry that he wouldn't be able to belong to it a hundred per cent any more if he once revealed that something else and unearthly burned in him?

What a lot of nonsense he was thinking! Did it really matter? No point in getting all worked up and troubled about it now. Better to just go on dreaming and wait quietly for the end. Even if he hadn't got it dead right, even if he had fallen short in one or two areas, it was too late to do anything about it now, and he knew he'd be forgiven for all the rotten things he'd done, and the caring things he hadn't. You could trust God for that as long as you had Jesus beside you. It was just that ... well, it was a pity he couldn't have rooted out that little shadow before he went. Rooted it out, seen what it was, and got rid of it. He sighed a little as he felt his body and mind slipping from consciousness to sleep.

He dreamed about Kendall that night. Kendall, long dead in reality, but young and straight and fit in the dream, just as he'd looked forty years ago. There was no question that it was him, despite the fact that he seemed to be a very long way away. His hands were cupped around his mouth, and he was shouting something. No matter how much effort he put into these shouts, though, it just wasn't possible to make out what he was saying because there was another and much greater noise that completely drowned out his voice. On investigation the sound turned out to be the roar of a deep and swiftly flowing river, dangerously split and thrown up into spray by angry black rocks. Kendall was standing on the far bank of the river, legs apart, head up, calling and calling for all he was worth. It wasn't quite the same as the way he had called out from the pavilion on the day of the Bottlers match – much more intense, more urgent. He was asking – pleading – for Crocker to do something for him. Then, the noise of the river must have decreased, or Kendall must have started to shout even more loudly, because one or two words began to filter through to the listener's ears: 'Please, Crocks ... over here ... please!'

There was no mistaking Kendall's message now. He was asking him to come across that dreadful river for some reason. Well, imploring rather than asking. Fearfully he peered down into the racing, leaping, tumultuous grey waters and felt the same paralysis of mind and body that had allowed the opposing team to achieve an effortless win on that pretty little cricket ground all those years ago. He knew that nothing would make him jump down into that terrible current.

Standing limply on his bank of the river, he looked up again and saw that Rory Kendall had given up shouting. He was just standing quietly now, hands in his pockets, gazing up at the sky as if waiting for something. He couldn't have been heard any more in any case. The noise of the rushing waters had suddenly become deafening. Strangely, too, it was becoming more and more difficult even to see the slim figure in the distance because, although on this side of the river the sun was shining and the air was bright, over where Kendall was, night was falling.

For once it was a relief to wake up, to be able to remind himself that it had just been a dream – that there was no fast-flowing river, that Kendall had passed on a long time ago, and that he hadn't really failed him again, except in a meaningless nightmare. But his peace was gone. Unaccountably, the little shadow had grown like a cancer and was darkening his spirit at a time when he should simply have been looking forward to meeting Jesus. Jesus? Where was Jesus? For the first time for a long time he had no sense of his friend being present. Dimly he became aware that someone was wiping his eyes and his cheeks. Far away in the distance he heard a woman speak: 'Poor old chap. He's been crying in his sleep. Won't be long now.'

He tried hard to make the right kind of waking dreams come; he'd been able to do that quite easily up to now, but he didn't seem to have the same kind of control any more. Memories, pleasant and unpleasant, ran into each other like spilled colours, swirling confusedly around his tired brain, preventing him from following a broad and peaceful pathway to death. But underneath all the confusion, from a small clear space in his mind, a voice – his voice – spoke the same prayer again and again with passionate urgency: 'One more chance! Please give me one more chance ...' And then – the confusion stopped abruptly, and the last dream of all came.

It was one of those dreams where colours and sounds and smells were vivid and real, as though he was wide awake, but in the wrong place. He found himself standing at the edge of the most beautifully serene lake, broad and still, surrounded on three sides by thick, lush woodland, while in the distance heavily elegant hills stepped gently up into mountainhood. The air was still and sweet beneath a sky of subtle, water-colour blue. Birds were singing. A slight breeze moved his hair. It was perfect cricketing weather, and looking down he realized that, appropriately enough, he was dressed not only in white shirt, trousers and boots, but also in a pair of batting pads. Nor was that all, for lying beside his feet on the bank was something that looked very much like a favourite old bat of his, the one that had split during a match played on his fortieth birthday, much to the amusement of his team mates. He picked it up and stroked the yellow wood gently with the tips of his fingers. There was no doubt about it. It was his bat, miraculously restored, as good as ever, well oiled and ready for action. It was like meeting an old friend. His own body seemed to be pretty well restored as well. Not, perhaps, to the first flush of youth, but certainly to the sort of lazy fitness he'd enjoyed in his mid-thirties.

He swung the bat briskly through the air a couple of times. Presumably all this gear meant there was a match on. Great stuff! But where was the pitch? Turning round and away from the water he saw, directly in front of him, a perfectly shaped, dead-flat rectangle of closely mown grass, like a little lawn in the midst of the undergrowth. Set in the centre of this ten-yard-by-five-yard area was a set of cricket stumps, complete with a pair of bails; and newly painted on the grass in front of the wicket, on the side furthest from the lake, were the white lines that marked the batting and 'popping' creases. A strange sort of cricket pitch with only one set of stumps, no fielders, no bowler and no umpires, but in his dream it all seemed quite natural. This was where he was to bat. He would simply take guard and wait. Someone would bowl to him eventually. Yes, it all seemed quite natural, and how wonderful to have the chance of a final knock.

As he took up his position at the crease, flexing his shoulders and patting the ground with the end of his bat in the old familiar way, he wondered what kind of attack he would be facing. Looking up, he could see nothing but low thick undergrowth stretching away into the distance, with the odd tree dotted here and there. Then, far, far away in the pale blue sky above the horizon, a tiny speck appeared, so small that it was hardly visible. Shading his eyes with his left hand, he stared intently at the distant object. It was very gradually increasing in size. Although still minute, the thing, whatever it was, was travelling in his direction at tremendous speed, and he knew with absolute certainty that this was the ordained target for his bat. This was the thing he was supposed to hit, and it was coming closer by the second.

'Hit out, Crocker! Give it all you've got!'

The voice came from his left. Snatching a glance in that direction, he saw that its owner was sitting on a grassy slope, his posture that of a typical cricket watcher – one leg outstretched, the other bent, and the top half of his body leaning its weight back on elbows and forearms, the very picture of keen relaxation. He had never seen the man before, but he knew who it was.

Switching his attention back to the task in hand, he found that the approaching target had acquired shape and colour. Whatever else it might be, it certainly was not a cricket ball. The shape was too shiftingly irregular for that and the colours were not right – blue, red and white, with a suggestion of yellow as well. It looked like nothing so much as a brightly coloured scarf or a wide ribbon curled loosely into the rough shape of a ball, forming and twisting and reforming as it hurtled towards him. It was also much, much bigger than a cricket ball. The speed and distance had been deceptive.

It was a snake – a huge, serpent-like creature with an evil flattened head, a tapering, pointed tail, and a horrible fleshy weightiness about the centre part of its body. It was close enough now for him to be able to see two little eyes glinting from a head that stayed quite still as the rest of the body rolled and coiled through the air. In seconds it would be upon him, heavy, vicious, enveloping, and able to be defeated only by one sound blow with the incongruously slight length of willow that at present rested quietly in his gloved hands. It was the chance he'd prayed for. Just one good hit . . .

'Let go, Crocks! Let it go!'

Dread seized him as the voice rang out once more. He was going to fail again. Cold fear drained down through his body, seeming to deepen his shadow on the close-cropped grass. It was going to happen all over again. He would make some feeble defensive gesture, there would be groans of disappointment, and the game, or battle, or victory, would be lost – irretrievably lost.

'Do it for *me*, Crocker!'

A strange illusion – that the words came arcing through the air, to enter, not through his ears, but straight into his chest, into his heart, warming and strengthening every part of him in a way he had never experienced before. Not before time either. With a furious hissing noise and an unspeakably nauseating stench, the creature filled his vision and was within hitting range. With a little stab of pure joy he raised his bat and dealt a thunderously perfect blow straight to the underside of the malevolently thrusting head. The follow-through was flawless. Despite its great weight, the serpent's body seemed to fly from the bat, sailing through the air in the direction from which it had come, its mouth emitting a loud scream of frustration which faded and died as the flailing blue and red carcass disappeared into the distance.

Filled with a thrilling ecstasy he dropped his bat and filled his lungs with sweet, clean air. A narrow path led away through the undergrowth to his left. He followed it to where it opened out onto the hillside, then stopped and looked up. The man was on his feet now, and even from a distance it was obvious that he was smiling. He took a step forwards and held out his hand . . .

'Mr Crocker's gone.'
'Poor old chap. Best really, eh?'
'Yes, you're right. Went happy though. Look at that smile . . .'

Ghosts

The Story of a Reunion

Adrian Plass

The strangest things happen when friends are reunited after twenty years apart. When together last, the friends were members of the same youth group and – on the whole – had life to look forward to. Now middle-aged, some are still optimistic but others are worn-out and weary. One has lost his faith, and another is struggling to reconcile the promises of his Christian beliefs with the recent death of his wife.

When reunited for a weekend away, the friends find themselves in Headly Manor, reputed to be one of the most haunted houses in England. What does it mean to stay in a haunted house? Strangely warm beds on cold days, objects unaccountably moving from room to room, and little girls in old-fashioned clothes seen walking across the lawn? Or something more subtle, but potentially much more frightening?

This engaging story blends Adrian Plass's rich style of humour with his knack for addressing the deep issues we all face, such as faith, grief, love, fear – and most crippling of all afflictions, the fear of fear.

Hardcover: 0-551-03109-3